MARY ELLEN BUTE: PIONEER ANIMATOR

In memory of Cecile Starr

Cover photograph:
Mary Ellen Bute working on an animated film ca. 1937, photo by Ted Nemeth Sr.,
courtesy KSB Collection of MEB, Yale Collection of American Literature, Beinecke Rare Book
and Manuscript Library.

MARY ELLEN BUTE:
PIONEER ANIMATOR

Kit Smyth Basquin, PhD

British Library Cataloguing in Publication Data

Mary Ellen Bute:
Pioneer Animator

A catalogue entry for this book is available from the British Library

ISBN: 0 86196 744 5 (Paperback)
ISBN: 0 86196 969 2 (ebook-MOBI)
ISBN: 0 86196 970 8 (ebook-EPUB)
ISBN: 0 86196 971 5 (ebook-EPDF)

Published by
John Libbey Publishing Ltd, 205 Crescent Road, New Barnet, Herts EN4 8SB,
United Kingdom   e-mail: john.libbey@orange.fr; web site: www.johnlibbey.com

Distributed Worldwide by
Indiana University Press, Herman B Wells Library—350, 1320 E. 10th St.,
Bloomington, IN 47405, USA. www.iupress.indiana.edu

Text © Kit Smyth Basquin
Photographs are copyright Kit Smyth Basquin, Center for Visual Music, Yale Film Study
Center, and the respective rightsholders.

Printed and bound in China by 1010 Printing.

Contents

Prologue

My Art Mother

Mary Ellen Bute, just over five feet tall, wearing a brocaded cocktail dress with large red and gold flowers, slit to her knee, blasted through the reception door at the York Club in Manhattan, November, 1973. Her chin length red hair fluffed, teased, and colored disguised her sixty-seven years, as did her energetic march in spike heels. "Darling!" She hugged me and then shook hands with others in the receiving line, including my sister, who was being honored belatedly for her wedding in England. Mary Ellen Bute reserved a kiss for my mother, Virginia Gibbs Smyth, whom she had known since childhood. They had grown up a few blocks apart in Houston, Texas. Coincidentally, Bute had been born two days before my mother in 1906. They celebrated birthdays together.

Although Bute and my mother lived in different New York worlds, they visited on the telephone. I always knew Bute was on the line because my mother would laugh loudly, talk for a long time, and revert back to her Texas accent. In the receiving line Bute gushed, "Virginia, Darling!"

Later, across the room, I could hear Bute's musical laugh, her response to anyone's jokes, even if they weren't particularly funny. She made her listener feel special. Perhaps she hoped to connect with someone who would invest in her current film, Thornton Wilder's *Skin of Our Teeth*. She had met Thornton Wilder years before through his sister, the actress and writer Isabel Wilder, a classmate of Bute's in the Department of Drama at Yale University in 1925. In 1965 Bute became friends with Thornton Wilder at the Cannes Film Festival, where she was awarded a prize for her direction of a first feature film, *Passages from James Joyce's Finnegans Wake*. After seeing Bute's creative interpretation of James Joyce's distilled time, from the cave dwellers to the present, incorporated into a story of death and rebirth, Wilder believed that Bute was the only person who could translate his Pulitzer Prize winning play *Skin of Our Teeth* into film. Like Joyce's book, Wilder's play employed archetypical characters throughout time. He gave Mary Ellen Bute the film rights.

Mary Ellen Bute was my "Art Mother". She believed in my creativity. In 1971, when I was writing press releases at the Indianapolis Museum of Art, having just acquired an MA in art history from Indiana University, and thinking of applying for the assistant director's job, which had opened up, Bute called me long distance to say, "Don't do it". This was before cell phones, when long distance calls were expensive, especially for an economically strapped filmmaker trying to raise money for a film. No doubt she had been talking to my mother. Bute felt that writing was creative, but that administration was a cop out, a squander of creative talent. I opened an art gallery instead. She approved.

In 1980, Bute called me in Milwaukee, where my husband and I were living with our three young children. She expressed great interest in my life and in what I was doing. Her film *Passages from James Joyce's Finnegans Wake* was going to be screened in the area. She asked me if I would write a press release for it and mail it out the next day to the local art critic to help with attendance. Showings of *Finnegans Wake* raised money for her current film on Walt Whitman, *Out of the Cradle Endlessly Rocking*. She had abandoned *Skin of Our Teeth* in 1975 after Thornton Wilder, her major donor, died. Of course I agreed to write the publicity, but I had to get up at 4 am the next day to do it, before my youngest son demanded breakfast at 6 am.

In Bute's last few years, when she was trying to raise money for her film on Whitman, she became so desperate for funds that she pushed hard and could come across as artificial. Her son Ted Jr. noted:

> Mary Ellen's optimism was not a mask. She grew up when women were supposed to be jolly and warm, positive … She found it useful. She found that she could charm people … gradually she turned the volume up and up and got more and more … she sustained it until it did seem like a mask toward the end. Perhaps it was a mask. When she put it on, it worked less well than when it was a logical extension.[1]

I visited Bute at Cabrini Hospital when I was in New York in early October, 1983. My mother had told me that Bute would like to see me. I brought her two pieces of cake, thinking we could have a party in her room, but she was too sick to eat. Later that day she called me at my mother's apartment and said she and her nurse "loved the cake, laced with rum!". She probably ate one bite. She died there October 17, 1983, a few weeks before her 77th birthday.

Reference

1. Theodore J. Nemeth Jr. transcript of taped responses for author 11/8/1988, KSB Collection of MEB, YCAL.

Chapter 1

Early Education:
The Lavender in the Shadows

Importance of Filmmaker

A short, bubbly red-haired debutante from Texas, steel magnolia Mary Ellen Bute (1906–1983), a painter, escaped to the male world of filmmaking in New York in the early 1930s. With her future husband, a talented camera man, Ted Nemeth, she was one of the first people in the USA to create abstract animated shorts, a new art form; one of the first filmmakers in the USA to incorporate electronic imagery into her films, forerunner of digital cinema; and one of few pioneer animators to screen her shorts at movie palaces, educating a large audience to the possibilities of film as art. Her film *Tarantella* was selected in 2010 to be in the National Film Registry of the Library of Congress.

With her keen eye and ear for talent, Bute cast Christopher Walken, at age fourteen, as the boy in her film *The Boy Who Saw Through*. He later became a famous character actor in Hollywood. Norman McLaren, who animated Bute's *Spook Sport*, created an animation unit for the National Film Board of Canada and later won an Academy Award, among many honors. Bute employed McLaren's partner, Guy Glover, as script writer for *The Boy Who Saw Through*. Glover became a producer for the National Film Board of Canada and was nominated for four Academy Awards. Ted Nemeth, Bute's cinematographer, was nominated for two Academy Awards. Composer Elliot Kaplan created original music for Bute's *Finnegans Wake*. A young man in his thirties, he had already earned two degrees from Yale and a Fulbright Scholarship. He would go on to an illustrious career composing scores for film, ballet, and television, including *The Twilight Zone*, *Fantasy Island*, and *Ironside*.

Bute was the first person to interpret a work by James Joyce for the screen, enabling a broad public to visualize the excitement of Joyce's words. She won a Cannes Film Festival Prize for her live action feature, *Passages from James Joyce's Finnegans Wake* in 1965. MOMA honored her with a Cineprobe in 1983, their series presenting the work of independent and experimental filmmakers.

Fig. 1. Clare Robinson as Queen, Jesse Jones as King, 1903 of Notsuoh Ball, Houston, *Houston Post*, courtesy Kit Smyth Basquin Collection of Mary Ellen Bute, Yale Collection of American Literature, Beinecke Rare Book and Manuscript Library.

Bute's persuasive powers helped her achieve performances no one else could have obtained. She inspired filmmakers and influenced animators such as Norman McLaren who, like Bute, incorporated educational text at the beginning of his films. This dynamic, driven woman, a role model for experimental filmmakers, both men and women, turned personal challenges into spring boards for success.

At the 11th Annual International Film Festival of New Cinema, Montreal, Canada, November 1982, Mary Ellen Bute, or M. E. as her family and close friends called her, was selected as one of the twenty-five most exciting independent filmmakers working. She said: "I started as a painter and I painted on a ranch".[1]

Houston, Texas 1906–1923

Mary Ellen Bute, born November 21, 1906, was the oldest of six children of a society couple, Clare Robinson Bute and Dr. James House Bute, a cousin of Col. Edward M. House, advisor to President Woodrow Wilson. Dr. Bute had graduated from Columbia Physicians and Surgeons in New York City with his neighbor, Dr. James Philip Gibbs, father of Virginia Gibbs (Smyth), Bute's life-long friend.[2] Dr. Bute was a pediatrician, but in 1916, he gave up medicine because he blamed himself for losing a case.[3] What he said publicly, however, was that he was tired of spoiled children.[4] Dr. Bute, who had inherited money from his father, who founded the

Fig. 2. Dr. James House Bute as a young man,
ca. 1910,

Bute Paint Company in Houston, also earned money from oil leases and other investments.[5] Dr. Bute had had TB before he was married, a disease that later affected his two oldest daughters, Mary Ellen and Maud.[6] His youngest daughter, Lois, said that she thought the source of the disease was on Dr. Bute's ranch.[7] The cattle on the ranch or the unpasteurized milk from the cows could have spread TB.

Clare Robinson Bute, Mary Ellen Bute's mother, had attended boarding school in England.[8] She had been the queen of the society ball in Houston, Notsuoh (Houston spelled backward) in 1903, before her marriage. The king of the ball that year with her was Jesse Jones who had his own lumber business and later would become a major builder in Houston and the U. S. Secretary of Commerce under Franklin Delano Roosevelt. Clare was socially prominent.

Mary Ellen Bute's brother Jim, a year younger, contracted polio at the age of five and lived in leg braces for much of his life. She was closest to Jim not only in age but emotionally. She named one of her sons after him, as well as after her father. Her next brother, John (I) died in infancy. Her sister Maud died in her twenties of tuberculosis. Her younger sister, Lois (Mrs. Randon Porter), not as strikingly beautiful as Mary Ellen, was an artist called "talented". Needless to say jealousy dictated Lois' feelings for her oldest sister. John (II), ten years younger than Mary Ellen, would take over the family paint business.[9]

At first the family lived in an apartment at Butler Flats in downtown Houston, where Dr. Bute had an office.[10]

Houston around 1906 was a small city of under 100,000 people. Cotton and commerce were the main businesses until oil was discovered at Spindletop in 1901, at Humble in 1905, and at Goose Creek in 1906, putting Houston at the center of new oil and oilfield equipment development. In 1912 Rice Institute, later called Rice University, opened, modeled on Princeton. In 1913 the Houston Symphony started. In 1914, the new 25-foot deep Houston Ship Channel allowed the entrance of deep-water vessels, crucial for international commerce. Houston would become the largest city in Texas and the fourth largest city in the United States.

Dr. Bute and Clare would spend weekends on his ranch, twenty-five miles from Houston in Lake City on the highway to Galveston, a commercial port. They left the children with Clare's parents who lived in a five-bedroom house with a stable at 2316 Fannin Street in downtown Houston. Clare would ride sidesaddle at the ranch, not the typical image of a rancher. Dr. Bute hired help to care for the animals and the ranch itself. The single story house there had one bedroom with beds only for Dr. Bute and Clare, but the children visited during the day.[11]

Bute Escape

When Jim Bute contracted polio in 1912, the family moved into Clare's parents' home, a few blocks from the Gibbs home at 3618 Fannin. This area is now midtown Houston, blocks from Interstate 45.[12] Mary Ellen Bute was six years old. The Robinson home accommodated the grandparents; parents; children; Clare's unmarried sister "Dolly" Robinson (Mrs. Geiston King); Sylvia Norsworthy (Harrison), the step-daughter of Clare's married sister Agnes Robinson Norsworthy, but called "cousin"; a live-in Scandinavian masseuse to massage Jim's legs daily; and a housekeeper. The Robinson house had screened sleeping porches, no doubt fully utilized.[13] Later, after Mary Ellen Bute moved away but came back to visit, her youngest sister, Lois, obviously envious and feeling neglected, complained: "When she came home, 'Sis is home' – big to do. Everyone else was forgotten".[14] John Bute, Mary Ellen Bute's youngest brother, said, "She would visit for five or six months. We had to fix up a room for her".[15] Rooms in the Robinson-Bute house were at a premium. Mary Ellen Bute, not fully appreciated at home, was called not by her name, but "Sis". As a visiting relative, she was treated as a guest and given a bedroom, so she did not need to share the sleeping porch with her siblings, but no one in the family recognized her originality as a pioneering filmmaker, a new field unfamiliar to them.

Mr. C. W. Robinson, Mary Ellen Bute's grandfather, was of British descent. He was President of Markham Rice Milling Co. in Markham, Texas. Mary Ellen Pittet Robinson, Bute's grandmother, after whom she was named, was Scottish. She was called "Granny" and became Mary Ellen Bute's first protector and role model. Granny was smart, literary, and devoted to her first granddaughter.[16] Granny would read to all of the children, filling a literary gap in the family, according to Bute's brother John:

> Granny read to us after supper, Dickens. She loved poetry, Shakespeare, old English murder stories...Granny took care of us when Mom and Dad were at the Ranch … . Our father was an outdoor man, not musical or a reader. Mom was not literary, not in a book club. No one was musical.[17]

"Cousin" Sylvia Norsworthy (Harrison), who lived in the Robinson-Bute home, expressed her love for Mary Ellen Bute and confirmed Bute's attachment to her grandmother:

> She [Mary Ellen Bute] was the most wonderful cousin. Unique. I loved her … Most effervescent, enthusiastic, cheerful, optimistic … Every man who came to call on her fell in love with her … She talked a lot about Granny … She didn't talk about her brothers and sisters … Granny was a great reader … Granny was brilliant … .[18]

Bute's vivacity and optimism were cherished by friends and colleagues throughout her life. Clearly Granny Robinson gave her support that no one else in the family could offer and was an important force in her break from home. Typical of expectations in well-to-do American families at the time, and in fact for decades to come, young women were expected to choose marriage as a career. This was not Mary Ellen Bute's goal.

Clare Bute was preoccupied with having babies, running the household, and caring for sick children, especially Jim. She had little time for Mary Ellen. Dr. Bute stayed on his cattle ranch most of the time. As Mary Ellen Bute's younger sister Lois Bute (Porter) said, "Nothing was encouraged".[19] Mary Ellen Bute also was estranged at school. Sylvia Norsworthy (Harrison) observed that Bute was not popular with the other students. "She was unusual, with different ambitions and expectations".[20] Understandably she thought of escape.

The Robinson house in Houston in 1906 had a pony with a cart.[21] Movie Theaters were public places and required the children to have a chaperone.[22] Bute said that her grandfather Robinson, who loved films,

Fig. 3. Mary Ellen Bute and her mother, Clare Robinson Bute, ca. 1907, courtesy KSB Collection of MEB, YCAL.

sometimes took her to movies such as "Perils of Pauline", 1914.[23] Later she commented:

> Films always seemed so commercial … they were so prosperous from the beginning that I thought they weren't an art form. Now I think they are the greatest art form of all ages, and especially animation, where you can do anything that you can imagine with superimpositions.[24]

Bute performed dramas on the stair landings of the Robinson house at the age of eleven or twelve.[25]Fifth and sixth grades were at the Allen School, a public school, where Virginia Gibbs (Smyth) and Mary Ellen Bute were joined by James Stewart Morcom, who would later become Art Director at Radio City Music Hall in New York, and Elizabeth

Fig. 4. Sarah Elizabeth Gibbs, Mary McAshan Gibbs, and Virginia Sandford Gibbs (Smyth), ca 1913, photograph in personal collection of Kit Smyth Basquin.

Sherwood, who, with Jim Morcom, went on to high school with Bute.[26] Elizabeth Sherwood said about Bute:

> She was always artistic. She and I both studied with Mrs. Cherry. M.E. saw the lavender in the shadows. She was not much of a student, but artistically ran circles around us … She was not intellectual.[27]

Despite Bute's accomplishments, however, she was not academic. She struggled with writing and had no interest in theory.

The public school art teacher, Emma Richardson Cherry, also gave private lessons and was known for her portraits and especially for her flower paintings. She had studied at the Art Institute of Chicago and Art

Students League in New York, where she had worked with William Merritt Chase and with Henry McCarter, who also taught at the Pennsylvania Academy of Fine Arts.[28] In addition she had studied at the Académie Julian in Paris and traveled to Paris several times to paint, with the support of her husband, abandoning her domestic responsibilities for weeks and sometimes months. She was aware of avant-garde art in Paris, including the Impressionists and Paul Cezanne. She was considered one of the first professional women artists in Houston.

In 1900 Mrs. Cherry had co-founded the Houston Public School Art League. This group dedicated land for an art museum in Houston in 1917. (In 1924 the first building of the museum opened, then called the Museum of Fine Arts.) Mrs. Cherry's trained eye enabled her to identify artistic ability. Her independence and devotion to art provided a role model for Bute. Mrs. Cherry became Bute's next major champion. She knew the family through the Bute Paint Company established by Mary Ellen Bute's grandfather. Mrs. Cherry bought her art supplies and frames there. The store also had a room with prints for framing. (This later developed into a contemporary regional art gallery.)

Bute won an honorable mention for one of her paintings in the spring, 1923, in a county fair in Austin, Texas. At that time she was painting ranch animals in the realistic style of Rosa Bonheur. Mrs. Cherry recognized Bute's talent and helped her get a Scholarship to the Pennsylvania Academy of Fine Arts.

Mary Ellen Bute entered the Pennsylvania Academy of Fine Arts at age sixteen. She turned seventeen, two months later, in November, 1923. Her parents thought she was too young to leave home, but Granny convinced them to let her go East to school.[29]

Philadelphia, PA 1923–1924

Mary Ellen Bute lived in Philadelphia with a teacher, Miss Macklin, known to the family.[30] To earn money for board, Bute read to an older woman.[31] At the Pennsylvania Academy of Fine Arts, Bute studied painting composition with Henry McCarter, Mrs. Cherry's former teacher at the Art Students League in New York. Bute said later:

> Henry McCarter, a distinguished painter and a member of the faculty at the Academy, had a wide list of friends, some of whom had an 'eye' for Modern Art and had picked up extraordinary canvases at the sensational 1913 Armory Show in New York.
>
> Mr. McCarter invited me, along with a few other students, to tea with one of these avant garde collectors – the Speisers. Maurice Speiser was an attorney. On the walls of Mr. and Mrs. Speiser's large, handsome living room were canvases of painters I had read, or heard about briefly – mostly in a derogatory way. One

canvas was especially interesting – a large, non-objective Kandinsky. It had enormous presence! Mrs. Speiser graciously suggested that if I wanted to return to study it, she would be happy to have me do so. I went back several times.[32]

Bute was particularly attracted to the energy of Kandinsky's abstract work. She related Kandinsky's canvases to time continuity, like music or dance. She said later:

I was invited back to study Kandinsky. It seemed to me that those beautiful abstractions were similar to a musical and if they were developed in time continuity they would become more interesting than just on a canvas, where if you went to see the climax before you solved the theme and development, you could, just by closing an eye and looking.[33]

Lois Bute Porter, who painted floral watercolors herself, commented "She [Mary Ellen Bute] did sketches in watercolor, there was always motion in her paintings, some geometric, some architectural. She played with colors on top of each other, experimental, playing, feeling, finding out".[34]

Bute said:

This one instructor [Henry McCarter] opened the whole door to what was happening in France, of which we had almost no inkling at all except in New York with the Armory Show [1913] … When I saw the first Picassos with their great deviation from African art, and the Klees and Leger and Braque, and when I came to New York and saw, after being indoctrinated by these artists about the possibilities of abstract form in art, and when I was exposed to all this art, some of which was only shown in one private gallery, the Paul Rosen Gallery, it was a complete shock … the inspiration was indescribable. It was an enormous change from anything we had ever seen … and I was determined to learn everything I could about the French painters, and Cubism etc. … I had already begun to wish for movement within painting … we had much freedom as individuals at the Pennsylvania Academy to try to produce movement without the painting really moving … .[35]

Bute found most painting too static. She said:

At the Pennsylvania Academy of Fine Arts … everyone was concerned about Cubism, Impressionism, and other styles that derived from the desire to obtain the illusion of movement on canvas.

It was particularly while I listened to music that I felt an overwhelming urge to translate my reactions and ideas into a visual form that would have the ordered sequence of music. I worked toward simulating this continuity in my paintings. Painting was not flexible enough and too confined within a frame.[36]

Bute further described her experience as a painter at the Pennsylvania Academy of Fine Arts:

Philadelphia was exhilarating. The young Leopold Stokowski had just taken over The Philadelphia Orchestra and was building toward his brilliant presentations of very modern composers Igor Stravinsky, Scriabin, and the like. The Forum had prominent speakers, and the faculty at the Academy of Fine

Arts were outstanding. They were very helpful. They would buy my Saturday morning sketch class work and were encouraging. I loved to paint and had been invited to attend Julien's Atelier the following year [Académie Julian, a private art school in Paris, France] – there was no question about my being anything but a painter.[37]

Leopold Stokowski conducted the Philadelphia Orchestra at this time (1912–1938). Bute would meet him in 1934 and show him her first abstract animated film *Rhythm in Light*, before he appeared in Disney's abstract film *Fantasia* in 1939. In 1950, she filmed Stokowski on camera conducting Bach's "Sheep May Safely Graze", from the Birthday Cantata, in one of her shorts, *Pastorale*.

New York 1924–1925

Leaving the Pennsylvania Academy of Fine Arts after one year, Bute attended the Inter-Theater Arts School, at 42 Commerce St., in Greenwich Village, New York. Lois Bute Porter said about her sister:

Granny adored her – someone who got up and did something. Sis didn't stay home and raise kids. Granny fought my father about letting her go to New York. Granny believed in New York … Sis had more nerve and guts – born independent – First minute she was going to get the hell out."[38]

Lois Porter added: "When she left Pennsylvania, she starved in New York. She was so poor she only had one can of tuna fish a day to eat. She cared. Hell bound. I asked her to live with me. She wouldn't leave New York for love or money. She wanted to do her work … She [Mary Ellen] worked like a dog and wanted me to paint more, but I had three children [later] and stopped … ."[39]

In 1925 a Houston magazine, *Women's Viewpoint*, reported that several other Houston students were at the Inter-Theatre Arts School and an administrator was from Austin, Texas. Writing about Bute the magazine said:

Mary Ellen Bute is one of the young women whose aim is to design scenery and costumes for the professional theatre and she is considered to have remarkable talent. At a recent performance given in the Cherry Lane Playhouse [New York], Miss Bute designed the settings for Synge's *Riders to the Sea* and designed and executed a very remarkable African background for a Voodoo dance, which created much comment. The dancer performed on top of a tom-tom which was lighted from underneath with a red light – to the beating of another tom-tom. She is the daughter of Dr. and Mrs. James House Bute of Houston. Just after she completed her first year's training at the Inter-Theatre Art School she was made designer for Alys Bentley's and Michio How's School of Dances.[40]

At the Inter-Theater Arts School, Bute made costumes, helped with set designs, and assisted Joseph Mullen with lighting. She said that she exhibited a set design for a Voodoo dance that the Theatre Guild, a theatrical society that produced plays on Broadway, saw in a theater exhibition in Cincinnati and bought in the spring of 1925.[41] This purchase gave Bute the professional requirement for entrance into the Department of Drama, Yale University.

References

1. Mary Ellen Bute, transcript of interview with filmmaker Peter Wintonick and Derek Lamb, 1982, Montreal, Canada, during 11th Annual International Festival of New Cinema, for Peter Wintonick, Cinergy Films Inc., Montreal, 1983, Kit Smyth Basquin Collection of Mary Ellen Bute, Yale Collection of American Literature, Beinecke Rare Book and Manuscript Library.

2. Virginia Gibbs Smyth, life-long friend of Mary Ellen Bute, transcript of interview with author, at Mrs. Smyth's apartment in New York 8/11/1984, KSB Collection of MEB, YCAL.

3. Elizabeth Sherwood, who attended high school with Mary Ellen Bute in Houston, transcript of telephone interview with author 5/18/1987, KSB Collection of MEB, YCAL.

4. John Bute, youngest brother of Mary Ellen Bute, transcript of interview with author at his home in Houston, 10/19/1995, KSB Collection of MEB, YCAL.

5. Lois Bute Porter, youngest sister of Mary Ellen Bute and artist, transcript of telephone interview with author, June, 1984, KSB Collection of MEB, YCAL.

6. Lois Bute Porter, transcript of telephone interview with author, June, 1984, KSB Collection of MEB, YCAL.

7. Lois Bute Porter, transcript of telephone interview with author June, 1984, KSB Collection of MEB, YCAL.

8. Elizabeth Sherewood, transcript of telephone interview with author, 5/18/1987, KSB Collection of MEB, YCAL.

9. John Bute, transcript of interview with author at his home in Houston, 6/20/1984, KSB Collection of MEB, YCAL.

10. John Bute, transcript of interview with author at his home in Houston, 10/19/1995, KSB Collection of MEB, YCAL.

11. John Bute transcript of interview with author at his home in Houston, 10/19/1995, KSB Collection of MEB, YCAL.

12. John Bute said that his mother Clare, who much later moved to an apartment hotel called The Warwick, asked that her home be torn down because the neighborhood had changed, interview with author 6/20/1984, KSB Collection of MEB, YCAL.

13. Virginia Gibbs Smyth, transcript of interview with author, at Mrs. Smyth's apartment in New York 8/11/1984, KSB Collection of MEB, YCAL.

14. Lois Bute Porter, transcript of telephone interview with author, June, 1984, KSB Collection of MEB, YCAL.

15. John Bute, transcript of telephone interview with author, August, 1984, KSB Collection of MEB, YCAL.

16. Lois Bute Porter transcript of telephone interview with author, June, 1984, KSB Collection of MEB, YCAL.

17. John Bute, transcript of interview with author at his home in Houston, 6/20/1984, KSB Collection of MEB, YCAL.

18. Sylvia Norsworthy Harrison, transcript of interview with author at her home in Houston, June 1984, KSB Collection of MEB, YCAL.

19. Lois Bute Porter, transcript of telephone interview with author June, 1984, KSB Collection of MEB, YCAL.

20. Sylvia Norsworthy Harrison, transcript of interview with author at her home in Houston, June 1984, KSB Collection of MEB, YCAL.

21. Elizabeth Sherwood, transcript of telephone interview with author, June, 1984, KSB Collection of MEB, YCAL.

22. Lois Bute Porter, transcript of telephone interview with author, June, 1984, KSB Collection of MEB, YCAL.

23. Mary Ellen Bute, transcript of interviewed by Peter Wintonick and Derek Lamb in Montreal, November, 1982, during 11th Annual International Festival of New Cinema, for Peter Wintonick, Cinergy Films Inc., Montreal, 1983, KSB Collection of MEB, YCAL.

24. Mary Ellen Bute, transcript of interview by Peter Wintonick and Derek Lamb, Montreal, November, 1982, during 11th Annual International Festival of New Cinema, for Peter Wintonick, Cinergy Films Inc., Montreal, 1983, KSB Collection of MEB, YCAL.

25. Elizabeth Sherwood, transcript of telephone interview with author 5/8/1987, KSB Collection of MEB, YCAL.

26. Virginia Gibbs Smyth, transcript of interview with author, at Mrs. Smyth's apartment in New York, 8/11/1984, KSB Collection of MEB, YCAL.

27. Elizabeth Sherwood, transcript of telephone interview with author 5/18/1987, KSB Collection of MEB, YCAL.

28. Lucy Runnels Wright, Art Page Editor, "A Woman Extraordinary: Mrs. E. Richardson Cherry". *Texas Outlook Magazine*, May 1937, KSB Collection of MEB, YCAL.

29. Lois Bute Porter transcript of telephone interview with author June, 1984, KSB Collection of MEB, YCAL.

30. Virginia Gibbs Smyth transcript of interview with author at Mrs. Smyth's apartment in New York, 8/11/1984, KSB Collection of MEB, YCAL.

31. Lois Bute Porter transcript of telephone interview with author June, 1984, KSB Collection of MEB, YCAL.

32. Mary Ellen Bute, undated typescript of application for New York Federation of the Arts Grant, ca. 1978, KSB Collection of MEB, YCAL.

33. Mary Ellen Bute, transcript of interview with Peter Wintonick and Derek Lamb, Montreal, November, 1982, during 11th Annual International Festival of New Cinema, for Peter Wintonick, Cinergy Films Inc., Montreal, 1983, KSB Collection of MEB, YCAL.

34. Lois Bute Porter transcript of telephone interview with author, June, 1984, KSB Collection of MEB, YCAL.

35. Mary Ellen Bute, transcript of interview with Ramona Javitz, Picture Curator of the New York Public Library and friend of Mary Ellen, May 4, 1976, from tape given to the author by Ted Nemeth Sr., KSB Collection of MEB, YCAL.

36. Mary Ellen Bute, "Abstronics: An Experimental Filmmaker Photographs the Aesthetic of the Oscillograph", *Films in Review* 5, no. 6 (June–July 1954), KSB Collection of MEB, YCAL.

37. Mary Ellen Bute, typescript of undated application for New York Foundation for the Arts Grant, ca.1978, KSB Collection of MEB, YCAL.

38. Lois Bute Porter transcript of telephone interview with author, June, 1984, KSB Collection of MEB, YCAL.

39. Lois Bute Porter, transcript of telephone Interview with author, June 1984, KSB Collection of MEB, YCAL.

40. *Women's Viewpoint: Magazine Serving Humanity, Edited and Published by Women*, Nov. 25, 1925, Vol. III no 7, pp. 38–39, KSB Collection of MEB, YCAL.

41. Mary Ellen Bute, typed copy of application for Guggenheim Grant, 1932, KSB Collection of MEB, YCAL.

Chapter 2

Yale 1925–1926, Floating University 1926–1927, Houston Debut 1927–1928, New York 1929–1930

The Department of Drama in the School of Fine Arts, at Yale University trained Mary Ellen Bute in the stage lighting and technology crucial for her manipulation of light, shadow, and abstract forms, the basis for her future films. Yale also gave Bute an impressive academic credential that compensated for her lack of a high school

Fig. 1. Mary Ellen Bute in Houston ca. 1927, photo by Keystone Portrait, Houston, courtesy of Kit Smyth Basquin Collection of Mary Ellen Bute, Yale Collection of American Literature, Beinecke Rare Book and Manuscript Library.

Fig. 2. Isabel, Thornton, Isabella, and Janet Wilder in Surrey, England, celebrating the international success of *The Bridge of San Luis Rey*, 1928. Courtesy of the Wilder Family LLC and the Yale Collection of American Literature, Beinecke Rare Book and Manuscript Library.

diploma. In addition, it increased her confidence and introduced her to classmate Isabel Wilder, Thornton Wilder's sister, who became a life-long friend, and paved the way for her later acquisition of film rights to Thornton Wilder's play, *Skin of Our Teeth*.

Bute and Isabel Wilder were among the ten women in a class of sixty-eight students in the Department of Drama in 1925. The program was a three-year professional course that led to a certificate, but not a degree.

The Department of Drama was established by a gift from a wealthy Yale graduate, Edward S. Harkness, BA Yale 1897, in 1924, and opened the following year.[1] A major philanthropist in the early twentieth century, thanks to inherited money from investments in oil, Mr. Harkness focused on colleges and schools, art museums, and hospitals. This author, and Bute's first son were born at Harkness Pavilion at Columbia-Presbyterian Medical Center, named after Mr. Harkness' father. Edward Harkness recruited George Pierce Baker, the renowned teacher of playwriting, from Harvard, to become the Chairman of the Department of Drama.[2] Eugene O'Neill had been one of his students at Harvard. According to Isabel Wilder, Mr. Harkness first offered to build the drama school at Harvard, but they rejected his gift, so he turned to Yale.[3] Entrance into the Department of Drama was open to men and women of 16 years and older. It required: "a statement giving age, previous education, and an outline of previous work, amateur or professional, in any of the arts of the theater, producing, lighting, scenic or other design, acting, playwriting".[4] The annual tuition fee was $200.00. There were no dormitory accommodations but the school provided a list of furnished rooms in private houses, some with board as well. The Yale cafeteria was for upperclassmen and men students only.[5]

Bute submitted drawings for stage sets that she had made in a theater class in New York, including one sold to the Theatre Guild or to the Shuberts, owners of many theatres in New York. Her stories differed on the actual purchaser. Bute later said:

> After Studying at the Pennsylvania Academy of Fine Arts, I went to New York and learned stage lighting at the Inter-Theatre Arts School in Greenwich Village. There were always Texas connections, and others who introduced me to the next step in my quest. When I created a stage set for the dancer, Jacques Cartier, the Shuberts bought if for *The First Little Show*. That meant I had theater credentials necessary for acceptance in George Pierce Baker's drama workshop at Yale in 1925.[6]

At Yale, George Pierce Baker was Professor of the History and the Technique of Drama, Director of the University Theater, and Chairman of the Department of Drama. According to Isabel Wilder, he was a professional and he expected his students to get paid for free-lance work done: "He saw the need for stage design, costume design, carpentry, lighting … the practical, physical aspects of theater to support playwrights".[7]

A 750-seat theater at Yale was completed in February, 1926. Isabel Wilder said that of the sixty-eight students in the program, forty-seven of them were studying playwriting. She added that three years later, only five of the original class finished the three-year certificate course, including her, and these five were only interested in playwriting. One faculty member came from Carnegie Tech in Pittsburgh to teach costume design. Some female students studied this. Donald Oenslager, a graduate of Harvard, who lived in New York City and commuted to New Haven, taught set design. Later he won Tony Awards for his set designs on Broadway. Sandy McCandless, who was just a few years older than his Yale students, with a B.A. from Harvard School of Architecture, instructed lighting.[8] Isabel Wilder commented: "He treated us like equals, with enthusiasm, passion, intense focus. In the beginning, acting was not taught, because it was considered unnecessary as there were several professional schools in New York City teaching it, including Academy of Dramatic Art. However, later acting was added.[9]

Bute took three subjects her first and second terms at Yale, Lighting, Producing, and History of Stage Design, which became Practice and Theory of Stage Design the second term.[10] The 1925–1926 Yale catalogue described her classes as follows:

> 12A History of Stage Design – History of the physical features of the stage from its origin to the present day, emphasizing the great periods of drama – Greek, Roman, Medieval, Renaissance, and Eighteenth Century. The following subjects will be studied: employment of machines, engines, and mechanical devices for "effects" in theatrical entertainment … construction in model form of typical theaters of each period: development of the Masque, Pageant, Court Festival, Ballet, Opera, and Marionettes … Consult Mr. Baker.

> 13B Practice and Theory of Stage Design – The following subjects will be studied with a view to developing a thorough understanding of elementary problems of design (tone, relations, composition, perspective, etc.) as applied to stage decoration: general composition grouping, planes etc. as represented in the visual arts … the "New Movement" in the theater – the theory and work of Appia, Craig, Reinhardt, Jones, etc.; theoretical and abstract discussions on the treatment of modern theatrical performances … Consult Mr. Baker.[11]

> 14 A and B Stage Lighting – this elementary course will take up the theory and application of stage lighting. Every student is expected to spend a certain number of hours each term in actual work on the stage, or in the rehearsal room. Although the theory of light, optics, and electricity will be specially covered in the course, a preliminary study in general physics is strongly advised … Consult Mr. Baker.

> 30 A and B Producing – Fundamental principles: relation of producer to the play, author, actors, and to the complementary works in settings, costumes, and light; groupings, movement emphasis, speed, rhythm, discipline, organization; simple, practical problems leading to charge of production in the rehearsal room … Consult Mr. Baker.[12]

Isabel Wilder observed that Bute was young, good looking, independent, and outspoken, not typical of the girls in the East. She was also more informal. She stood out. Isabel Wilder, who grew to love Bute, thought that "her loud laugh in college was ostentatious...conspicuous, too much so. She was a pioneer. She had a freedom, pushiness, and was not afraid to get up and ask. She had a good nature and breeziness. Most people responded and were fascinated."[13] Isabel Wilder remembered that at a dance on campus once, during a rigorous Charleston number, Bute's breasts showed above her neckline. The chaperone at the dance was horrified and asked her to leave … Isabel Wilder continued:

> Mary Ellen was so alive and generous, but she put some people off because she was very frank … I didn't know Mary Ellen well then, because I lived at home and took care of my father who had strokes, and I worked in New York on Saturdays … In the 1940s, Mary Ellen looked me up at a School of Drama

reunion, when she was interested in Thornton Wilder's plays. I got to know her when she worked on *Skin of Our Teeth* … .[14]

Isabel added: "M.E. had a passion, a calling to find a way of combining music with light and drama. The Yale program offered something to her. It was important."[15]

Isabel Wilder was a writer and actress in her own right. She later published three novels: *Mother and Four* (1933), *Hearts Be Still* (1934), and *Let Winter Go* (1937). In 1924 she worked in New York as an assistant to literary agent Elizabeth Oñativia. After enrolling at Yale in 1925, Isabel commuted to New York on Saturdays for her job, while living at home in New Haven to take care of her loving but demanding farther, Dr. Amos Parker Wilder, PhD, a former diplomat, teacher, and journalist who still lectured occasionally but had suffered strokes. Thornton Wilder taught French at Lawrenceville. Their older brother Amos studied to be a preacher at the Yale Divinity School. Their sister Charlotte was an editor at *Youth's Companion* in Boston while completing a master's degree at Radcliffe. Their youngest sister Janet, a teenager, still lived at home in New Haven with their parents. All of the family members were literary, a very different background from Mary Ellen. Thornton Wilder would publish his first novel *The Cabala* in 1926. His next novel the following year, *The Bridge of San Luis Rey*, which won a Pulitzer Prize, supported the Wilder family and brought fame to the author.[16]

When The History of Stage Design turned into a theory course the second semester, Bute took an incomplete in it. As her son Ted Jr. said, "Mary Ellen did not care about theory. She was all about the practical."[17] She did her best work in the lighting course with Sandy McCandless, which Isabel Wilder said she raved about, but her grades gradually slipped over the second semester, suggesting that she was not interested in academic writing and deadlines.[18] She was listed under "Producing and Stage Force", with Isabel Wilder and fourteen other students, in the program for "The Patriarch", produced by the Department of Drama, February 10 and 11, 1926. In 1926, she was denied re-admittance to Yale. Bute was proud of studying at Yale. It was a jumping off point.[19] She never mentioned not being re-admitted and was probably happy to move on. She had gotten what she wanted.

Next Bute took a job teaching drama and dance on a chartered ship called the Floating University, traveling around the world for a year, 1926–1927. The Floating University was launched by New York University under the auspices of International University Cruise, Inc. to foster in co-educational students an interest in foreign affairs and to develop international goodwill.[20] The S. S. Ryndam was owned by the Holland America Line.

The brochure for the trip described the vessel: "The steamer has unusually spacious decks, two swimming pools, outdoor gymnasium and apparatus, library of several thousand volumes, classrooms, study-halls, pianos, hospital and dental offices, laundry, and barber shop.[21]" It was "Open to students (men) of all American Colleges and Universities".[22] However, a limited number of pre-college students were enrolled. In addition, "a limited number of mature men and women will be enrolled as advanced students in research or in conference courses".[23]

Communication with parents was by radio message to dispatch offices and then by telegram. $2500.00 included tuition and trips ashore, passports, visas, gratuities, and laundry.[24] This trip was a huge luxury for Bute, who could not have afforded to pay for it, and an outstanding opportunity for wide-ranging experience, invaluable for the artist. *The Ryndam* returned from London to Hoboken in May, 1927. It had traveled to cities including Constantinople, Havana, Honolulu, Haifa (Palestine), Suez, Venice, Lisbon, Hamburg, Copenhagen, Yokohama, Hong Kong, and London.[25]

According to Virginia Gibbs (Smyth), the Floating University thought that M. E. Bute from Yale was a man. They offered the job to Mr. M. E. Bute. Bute accepted the job but said that she was a woman. The Floating University replied that they only wanted a man for the job. Bute wrote back and told them about the shadow plays she was going to demonstrate and teach in Thailand. She was again turned down, but indefatigable and confident, she kept responding with new information about the theatrical programs she planned for the visit to each country. Eventually she got the job.[26] She saved her acceptance letter.

Bute said about her job on the Floating University, on the S.S. Ryndam, which started its trip around the world September 18, 1926 from Hoboken, NJ:

> The ship was the *Ryndam* with 450 young men and 50 young women and a staff of 60. The director told me a Columbia University professor already had the job I wanted. I didn't 'hear' him. My father got me a secretary and I began working on drama pages for the *Ryndam*. Every few days I mailed some pages to the director, including plans for a collapsible stage set based on lead pipes. Six weeks before the sailing date, the man originally hired, cancelled and I got the job.[27]

Later, Lillian Shiff, a writer interested in film, commented on Bute's travel in her interview with her:

> It was clearly a major experience in her life with stored impressions and ideas for a future career. As the ship went through the Panama Canal, students presented a pageant about the original inhabitants of North and South America. Eight months later, the group – some of them with diplomas earned en route –

arrived in Hoboken. They had visited 33 countries, studied traditional academic subjects, prepared dramatic entertainments for foreign guests, hosted foreign students and lecturers and explored museums and galleries, theaters and countryside from Tokyo to London.[28]

There was a student orchestra on board. Bute saved some of her lecture notes and also poems and cards from her male admirers on the trip.[29] She continued to be popular, especially with men. Several cousins and acquaintances of Virginia Gibbs (Smyth) from Houston traveled on the ship. Mrs. Smyth heard that Kelly Eikel from Houston danced the Charleston with the King of Siam.[30] James Stewart Morcom, head of scenic design at Radio City Music Hall in New York, wrote after Mary Ellen's death: "Mary Ellen was quite a gal! ... I realize even more how unique she was – one of the people you will never forget. I would love to have watched her captivate the King of Siam on the round the world college cruise. I'm sure she is sitting at the Captain's table wherever she is right now!"[31]

The next year, 1927–1928, Bute, building on her theater experience on the *Ryndam* and Yale training, took a part time job with the Little Theater in Houston as assistant director. She painted scenery and supervised lighting. Clark Gable was acting there that year.[32] In addition, Bute made her Houston debut that season. She was not interested in being a full-time debutante for the winter and attending three social functions a day. Bute's family was socially prominent and Allegro, the most distinguished debutant organization at the time would have accepted her if she had agreed to the regime. Instead, her family gave her a private dinner dance at her grandmother's home. She saved the clipping from The *Houston Post-Dispatch*, November 23, 1927, which described her debut as follows:

> At a charming tea Tuesday afternoon, Mrs. C. W. Robinson and Mrs. James House Bute received their friends in honor of Miss Mary Ellen Bute. The debutantes of the winter received with them, and assisting through the home were friends of the hostesses and the honoree.
>
> Autumn shades were combined in decorations with a profusion of beautiful flowers everywhere. Handsome bronze and gold chrysanthemums filled Marie Antoinette baskets in the hall and on the stair posts. In the library where the receiving party stood red roses were used.
>
> Two tables were arranged for the tea service. The one in the living room was in dainty pastel shades with a centerpiece of butterfly roses and lavender tapers. The other in the dining room was decorated with yellow Pernet roses, sweetheart roses and lavender candles.
>
> Following the receiving hours, the young people of the house party were joined by a number of young men for a buffet supper and there was music for those who cared to dance.[33]

Bute attended evening parties and continued to work at the Little Theater.[34] Her good friend from high school in Houston, Elizabeth Sherwood, said that Bute was not like the Houston social butterflies. She was not interested in bridge and tennis at the country club. She was insecure, outspoken, and had a loud, nervous laugh. People made fun of her. "Her interests were so different. She acted artificial to fit ... As a friend, I loved her dearly."[35]

From the time Bute finished her debut season in Houston in June, 1928, and completed her work with the Houston Little Theater, probably in the summer of 1928, until September, 1929, is an undocumented year. She frequently mentioned studying at the Sorbonne, but the school would not confirm that, so her studies were probably more like a course in French culture for foreigners, taught in English. Bute did not speak French. She probably took the course in the summer of 1928. In an application for a Guggenheim grant, Bute mentioned studying lighting in Germany, but this could not be documented.[36] As both filmmaker Lewis Jacobs and film historian William Moritz said that Bute had not seen experimental films before she started making them in 1932, it is unlikely that she spent much time in Europe in 1928–1929 or she would have stumbled across experimental films in Paris or in Germany.

A more likely scenario for the year 1928–1929 is that she was sick. Bute never talked about her health, as her younger brother John said, "She was very private. Everything was always fine."[37] However her younger sister Lois said:

> Mary Ellen had TB for a year in New York. She had been heavy and then lost a lot of weight and discovered – [her illness]. The family paid the hospital bills. Granny visited on her way to Boston to see Aunt Dolly King.[38]

Bute's son Jim said that TB weakened Mary Ellen's heart valves.[39] He also mentioned that her brother John resented being sent away to boarding school, probably for high school, to give up his room to his oldest sister who was sick.[40] John would have been in high school around 1928–1929. Possibly Bute had contracted TB from the cattle or from the unpasteurized milk on her father's ranch while she was in Texas for her debut and for her theatre work.

In the fall of 1929, Bute, well again, was Maid of Honor at the launch of the USS Houston in Newport News, Virginia. The force behind naming the ship "Houston" was William A. Bernreider, a handsome Texan who was an officer in the Navy Reserve six years older than Bute. In 1929, he worked for the Mayor of Houston, but was secretary of the Cruiser "Houston" Committee. He would become a life-long friend of Bute. He said "She was one of the finest women I've ever met. Great, gracious, beautiful lady. I had the highest respect for her. I treated her like a sister." Then he added with realism, "She used people to get whatever the hell she wanted!"[41] He later sold real estate in Houston. Bute gave a party at the Bute/Robinson home on Fannin Street in Houston for him and his wife when they were married in 1939.[42] During World War II, he was on active duty on the staff of five admirals, including Admiral Byrd.

Also, in the fall of 1929, Bute worked in New York for Thomas Wilfred, inventor of the Clavilux, a color organ manipulating colored lights with a keyboard. In a draft of her application for work, she said, at about age twenty-three:

My Dear Mr. Wilfred,

I am extremely interested in all phases of the theater but especially in the lighting and settings ... I hope to be a producer who uses the theater with all of its facilities developed and organized as an instrument to help solve ... problems. The Clavilux, as well as being a stunning thing in itself, is bound to have a large influence in drama ... I am extremely anxious to work with it ... [43]

As Lillian Schiff reported after an interview with Bute:

"For a time Bute worked with Thomas Wilfred, perfecter of the Clavilux – Museum of Modern Art habitués will remember its long running performance in a little downstairs room – a light organ which could be played to create amorphous, moving colors on a screen, but the instrument could not give her the kind of control she was seeking.[44]

Even in Bute's early work, she expressed her need for total artistic control, a problem for her later when she was shooting live action films and needed to work with a team of people. The stock market crashed in November of 1929 starting the Great Depression. Jobs were scarce, but in 1930, Bute was hired as Director of Visual Arts at Gerald Warburg Studios in New York, where she first became involved with film.

In the five years since entering Yale, Mary Ellen Bute had transformed herself into a confident, driven professional, already skilled in lighting and stage design. Through the manipulation of light, she moved closer and closer to filmmaking.

References

1   The Department of Drama became a separate professional school in 1955, Yale School of Drama.

2.   Isabel Wilder, Thornton Wilder's sister and Mary Ellen Bute's classmate at Yale in 1925, and life-long friend, transcript of telephone interview with author 7/28/1984, Kit Smyth Basquin Collection of Mary Ellen Bute, Yale Collection of American Literature, Beinecke Rare Book and Manuscript Library.

3.   Isabel Wilder, transcript of telephone interview with author 7/28/1984, KSB Collection of MEB, YCAL.

4.   School of the Fine Arts of Yale University, Department of Drama, Preliminary Announcement 1925–1926, Supplement to the *Bulletin* of Yale University, New Haven, KSB Collection of MEB, YCAL.

5.   School of the Fine Arts of Yale University, Department of Drama, Preliminary Announcement 1925–1926, Supplement to the *Bulletin* of Yale University, New Haven, 1924, pp. 2–4, KSB Collection of MEB, YCAL.

6.   Lillian Schiff, free-lance editor and writer with a special interest in film, interview with Mary Ellen Bute July, 1983, *Film Library Quarterly* 17, Nos. 2–4, 1984, pp. 53–61, KSB Collection of MEB, YCAL.

7.   Isabel Wilder, transcript of telephone interview with author 7/28/1984, KSB Collection of MEB, YCAL.

8.   Isabel Wilder, transcript of telephone interview with author 7/28/1984, KSB Collection of MEB, YCAL.

9.   Isabel Wilder, transcript of telephone interview with author 7/28/1984, KSB Collection of MEB, YCAL.

10.   Mary Ellen Bute, transcript at Yale 1925–1926, KSB Collection of MEB, YCAL.

11.   Adolph Appia 1862–1928 Swiss architect, theorist, and stage lighter famous for using three-dimensional sets enhanced by light and shadows; Edward Henry Craig 1872–1966 English actor, director, and scenic designer, the illegitimate child of actress Ellen Terry, known for using neutral, mobile screens as staging devices and lighting from above, including colored lights; Max Reinhardt 1873–1943 Austrian born American stage and film actor and director who used powerful staging techniques harmonized with music and choreography; Robert Edmond "Bobby" Jones 1887–1954 American scenic, lighting, and costume designer who integrated realistic scenic elements into the storytelling combined with bold color and simple, yet dramatic lighting.

12.   School of the Fine Arts of Yale University, Department of Drama, Preliminary Announcement 1925—1926, Supplement to the *Bulletin* of Yale University, New Haven, KSB Collection of MEB, YCAL.

13.   Isabel Wilder, transcript of telephone interview with author 7/28/1984, KSB Collection of MEB, YCAL.

14.   Isabel Wilder, transcript of telephone interview with author 7/28/1984, KSB Collection of MEB, YCAL.

15.   Isabel Wilder, transcript of telephone interview with author 7/28/1984, KSB Collection of MEB, YCAL.

16.   Penelope Niven, *Thornton Wilder: A Life*, 2012 (New York: Harper Perennial, 2013) 234–235.

17.   Theodore J. Nemeth, Jr., transcript of taped response to questions from author 11/8/1988, KSB Collection of MEB, YCAL.

18.   Mary Ellen Bute transcript, Yale Department of Drama, 1925–1926, KSB Collection of MEB, YCAL.

19.   Marilyn Ripp, friend of Mary Ellen Bute from Parkside Residence in the 1970s, transcript of telephone interview with author 6/26/1984, KSB Collection of MEB, YCAL.

20.   Letter to Mary Ellen Bute from University Cruise, Inc., ca. 1926, KSB Collection of MEB, YCAL.

21.   New York University, College Cruise Around the World Eight Months, October 2, 1926 – June 1, 1927, brochure, KSB Collection of MEB, YCAL.

22.   New York University, College Cruise Around the World Eight Months, October 2, 1926 – June 1, 1927, brochure, KSB Collection of MEB, YCAL.

23.   New York University, College Cruise Around the World Eight Months, October 2, 1926 – June 1, 1927, brochure, KSB Collection of MEB, YCAL.

24.   New York University, College Cruise Around the World Eight Months, October 2, 1926 – June 1, 1927, brochure, KSB Collection of MEB, YCAL.

25.   New York University, College Cruise Around the World Eight Months, October 2, 1926 – June 1, 1927, brochure, KSB Collection of MEB, YCAL.

26. Virginia Gibbs Smyth, transcript of interview with author 8/11/1984, at Mrs. Smyth's apartment in New York, KSB Collection of MEB, YCAL.

27. Lillian Schiff, interview with Mary Ellen Bute July, 1983, *Film Library Quarterly* 17, Nos. 2–4, 1984, pp. 53–61, KSB Collection of MEB, YCAL.

28. Lillian Schiff, interview with Mary Ellen Bute July, 1983, *Film Library Quarterly* 17, Nos. 2–4, 1984, pp. 53–61, KSB Collection of MEB, YCAL.

29. Mary Ellen Bute's greeting cards and lecture notes from Floating University, 1927, KSB Collection of MEB, YCAL. Note: These materials saved by Mary Ellen, were given to the author by Ted Nemeth Sr. after his wife's death, in 1984.

30. Virginia Gibbs Smyth transcript of interview with author 8/11/1984, at Mrs. Smyth's apartment in New York, KSB Collection of MEB, YCAL.

31. James Stewart Morcom, Houston classmate of Mary Ellen Bute and later Art Director at Radio City Music Hall in New York, letter to author 9/30/1984, KSB Collection of MEB, YCAL.

32. Virginia Gibbs Smyth, transcript of interview with author 8/11/1984, at Mrs. Smyth's apartment in New York, KSB Collection of MEB, YCAL.

33. "Miss Bute Honored at Party", *Houston Post-Dispatch*, November 23, 1927, KSB Collection of MEB, YCAL.

34. Virginia Gibbs Smyth, transcript of interview with author 8/11/1984, at Mrs. Smyth's apartment in New York, KSB Collection of MEB, YCAL.

35. Elizabeth Sherwood transcript of telephone interview with author 5/18/1987, KSB Collection of MEB, YCAL.

36. Mary Ellen Bute, typescript of application for Guggenheim application, 1932, KSB Collection of MEB, YCAL.

37. John Bute, transcript of interview with author at his home in Houston, 6/20/1984, KSB Collection of MEB, YCAL.

38. Lois Bute Porter, transcript of telephone interview with author 8/14/1984, KSB Collection of MEB, YCAL.

39. James House Bute Nemeth, Mary Ellen's younger son, transcript of telephone interview with author 7/8/1984, KSB Collection of MEB, YCAL.

40. James House Bute Nemeth, interview with author at his home in Hampton Bays, LI, NY, 8/9/1984, KSB Collection of MEB, YCAL.

41. William Bernreider, escort during Mary Ellen's debut year in Houston and life-long friend, transcript of telephone interview with author 9/10/1984, KSB Collection of MEB, YCAL.

42. William Bernreider, transcript of telephone interview with author 2/17/1986, KSB Collection of MEB, YCAL.

43. Mary Ellen Bute, undated fragment of letter draft to Thomas Wilfred, inventor of the Clavilux, ca. 1929, in KSB Collection of MEB, YCAL.

44. Lillian Schiff, interview with Mary Ellen Bute July, 1983, *Film Library Quarterly* 17, nos. 2–4 (1984), pp. 53–61, KSB Collection of MEB, YCAL.

Chapter 3

Abstract Animation (1934–1953)

Mary Ellen Bute's background as a painter, influenced her visual choices for her films. The avant-garde films of the 1920s and 1930s in Europe relate to paintings, music, poetry, and dance of the period and provide context for Bute's pioneer, animated short films first created in 1934, although she had not seen these European films before starting her own. Fernand Léger's "Ballet Mécanique", 1924, in France, demonstrates the influence of Picasso and Braque's Cubism and of the industrial machinery of the time.[1] Some of Oskar Fischinger's films from the 1930s in Germany and the US, which Bute did not see until after creating three abstract films of her own, reflect Wassily Kandinsky's burst of abstract geometric forms, as do Bute's films. Bute said many times that painting influenced filmmakers, including herself.[2] Her first exposure to Kandinsky's abstract explosions of colors and forms seen in the Speiser Collection in Philadelphia in 1923 opened a new world of form, color, and movement to her. She wanted even more movement in her visual art. Film offered movement in time continuity.

Fischinger had early training in drawing and watercolor at school and later looked at and read about contemporary paintings, particularly those by Kandinsky and Klee.[3] He earned a diploma in engineering, so he could fabricate his own filmmaking equipment. He also had early training as a violinist. He loved music.[4]

Photographs of Bute's early paintings from about this time reflect the influence of Cezanne, Seurat, Matisse, Toulouse-Lautrec, Degas, and Picasso. A depiction of a man with part of his face obliterated, nicknamed by Bute's family "One-eyed Pete", displays the flat surfaces and organic colors of Cezanne and the fragmented space of Picasso and Braque's Analytical Cubism.

See Colour Plate 1.
Mary Ellen Bute, *One-Eyed Pete*, ca. 1928, oil on canvas, collection of Tom Harrison, photo by Tom Harrison, courtesy Kit Smyth Basquin Collection of Mary Ellen Bute, Yale Collection of American Literature, Beinecke Rare Book and Manuscript Library.

Bute's untitled painting with a female performer entering stage center, recalls Georges Seurat's *The Circus*, 1891, with a woman riding into a ring on a white horse. However, Bute's painting displays swirling brush strokes like elongated banners that suggest motion, unlike Seurat's Neo-Impressionist Pointillist dots. Some of Bute's curved forms are similar to those of Matisse or Toulouse-Lautrec. The jutting bass reminds the viewer of Degas.

See Colour Plate 2.
Mary Ellen Bute, *Untitled*, oil on canvas, ca. 1928, Collection of Tom Harrison, photo by Tom Harrison, courtesy KSB Collection of MEB, YCAL.

These works show Bute's increased awareness of the art world and her developing artistic sophistication. She had moved a long way from painting realistic Texas cattle.

Duchamp's Cubistic "Nude Descending a Staircase" had entranced Bute since seeing it in *Literary Digest*, February19, 1921, at her father's ranch.[5] Considered the most shocking image in the New York Armory Show of 1913, it was widely reproduced for years. It simulated stop-motion, a technique used for filmmaking. Although ridiculed in cartoons and in conservative reviews, it called attention to Cubism which had been developed about 1909 by Picasso and Braque. This style transformed the depiction of space in Western art from one-point perspective, constructed to simulate realism since the Renaissance, to a flat space that called attention to the process of making art. Cubism gave rise to the idea of art for art sake, art as an object itself, not as a recreation of a view outside the frame. This concept launched Modernism in the 20th century.

See Colour Plate 3.
Marcel Duchamp, *Nude Descending a Staircase, No. 2*, 1912, oil on canvas, Philadelphia Museum of Art, The Louise and Walter Arensberg Collection, 1950 @Artists Rights Society (ARS) New York/Estate of Marcel Duchamp.

Experimental art films were not available to Bute until she moved back to New York in 1929, and were difficult to find, screened in alternative spaces, usually up several flights of stairs. Although the Museum of Modern Art opened in 1929, showcasing European modernist painters and sculptors, including Picasso and Matisse, MOMA's Film Library did not start until 1935, after Bute had released her first abstract, animated film, *Rhythm in Light*, in 1934. Film historians Lewis Jacobs and William Moritz both noted that Bute had not seen experimental films before she started making them.[6] She created original work from experimentation, drive, and determination, assisted by the skilled cameraman Ted Nemeth. These were the early days of sound films, only launched in 1927 by the *Jazz Singer*, produced by Warner Brothers. Nemeth often had to improvise equipment that he and Bute could not afford during the Depression of the 1930s.

In 1930 Mary Ellen Bute became director of Visual Arts at the Gerald Warburg Studios in New York. Filmmaker Lewis Jacobs said she probably made up her title.[7] Warburg, a cellist and a wealthy man interested in art, apparently not affected by the Depression, supported young Russian mathematician and composer Joseph Schillinger, who had been his teacher.

Schillinger had composed music for Leon Theremin and Theremin's instrument that was at the forefront of electronic music. To operate the Theremin, hands moved around metal antennas that controlled an oscillator that produced electric sounds and manipulated light. Joseph Schillinger headed Warburg's experimental studio, to apply math theory to stage design, painting, music, and film.[8] Schillinger developed a system of music composition based on mathematics, using mathematical variations as a tool to suggest harmonic relations and visual layouts. He believed that art forms could be created with scientific rigor.[9] George Gershwin, Glenn Miller, Benny Goodman and other famous musicians and composers studied with Schillinger.

After Bute met Leon Theremin, he sent her to Schillinger to learn more about math and musical composition. From the beginning and throughout Bute's life, she made an effort to adopt new technology and thinking that would serve her needs. Following Schillinger's method, she created graph patterns from mathematical inversions, expansions, and duplications of paired numbers. She used these as a springboard for her visual patterns transforming geometric forms into moving compositions of change. Squares on the graph represented visual space, synchronized with tones, indicating the amount of visual time needed for a sound. Although Bute started developing her visual patterns based on Schillinger's system, she clearly layered spontaneous emotional gestures, sometimes created by waves of heavy cream floating in coffee, behind her carefully controlled geometric patterns.

Bute, pursuing the latest information in electronics, entered Leon Theremin's studio December,1931.[10] She said:

> Theremin was one of those unique physicists, electrical people ... I went to hear him and told him how I wanted to do with color and form what he was doing with sound. You know he did it all through electrical magnetic field and one wand controlled the pitch and the other the volume so we started to work.[11]

Later, Ted Nemeth Sr. said, "M. E. met Theremin through a group doing music ... Theremin gave M. E. the idea of what she wanted to do, visualizing music".[12] Lillian Schiff reported: "Bute worked with Leon Theremin, inventor of an electronic musical instrument, later used by avant-garde composers Edgard Varese and Henry Cowell, and others".[13]

Bute helped Theremin with his paper for the New York Musicological Society January 31, 1932, "The Development of Light as Art Material and

Possible Synchronization with Sound", according to her typescript, although later the organization printed a slightly different title in their report of the evening, "The Perimeters of Light and Sound and Their Possible Synchronization".[14] Theremin connected an optical device to one of his electronic instruments.[15] Bute commented in an interview later, that his paper concerned "the use of electronics for drawing ... but we couldn't continue with the experiments for lack of money".[16]

The paper for the Musicological Society that Bute presented with Leon Theremin in 1932 said:

> My subject this evening is The Art Form of Light. This is not a new subject, it is concerned with an art which has had as logical development as other arts, perhaps slowly but naturally and progressively.

> This art is an elaboration of the phenomena of color as an aesthetic experience per se, free from musical or literary associations. Here color is not in *static* balance with static space relations. The plastic arts, although making use of the sensation of sight, address not the *eye* but the intellect ... .[17]

Basically, Bute commented that for Theremin and for herself, color was pure, abstract, free from literary associations like the other plastic arts, such as sculpture, that appealed to the intellect, rather than just to the senses.

Later, Bute said about her work with Theremin:

> Theremin and I immersed a tiny mirror in a small tub of oil, connected by a fine wire which was led through an oscillator to a type of joy stick control. Manipulating this joystick was like having a responsive drawings pencil or paint brush that flowed light and was entirely under the control of the person at the joy stick.

> Mrs. Lucie Rosen, who owned the townhouse Theremin's studio occupied, was an accomplished musician. She would come by to practice on the new electronic instruments. The sheer beauty of the sound thrilled her. She would exclaim: "What a lovely sound!" I felt that way but this little point of living light – it seemed so responsive and intelligent. It seemed to follow what you had in mind rather than the manipulation of the oscillator.

> The result on the screen was pristine and pure light. Theremin connected this with one of the electronic instruments – so that the sound modified and controlled the light. The musicologists were delighted.[18]

Later Lucie Rosen and her husband Walter Rosen would establish the Caramoor Center for Music and the Arts in Katonah, New York. In their main house, they exhibited a Theremin musical instrument.

Bute continued working with Theremin and starting her first film:

> The work continued at a great clip. The atmosphere in the studio was increasingly creative and free flowing. This "flowing with it" spirit stood me in good stead when soon after that, Theremin was suddenly and unexpectedly claimed by Mother Russia. I had to shelve this idea of interrelating and

inter-composing kinetic visual material and aural material which had motivated me since the afternoon of 1923 [when she saw Kandinsky's painting in Philadelphia, and related it in her mind to music and dance].

Bute applied for a Guggenheim Grant in 1932 to study "A new kinetic art form, the art of light", in support of Theremin's work.[19] Typically in her formal writing she was grandiose and not particularly convincing. In some instances in the application she quoted educator and philosopher John Dewey, who had brought Schillinger to this country in 1928.[20] She concluded her Gugenheim Grant application with:

My ultimate purpose as a student being to aid in the development of this new art form [light controlled through electricity] born of our civilization and which is destined to aid in the intellectual and emotional coming of age of our culture.[21]

Her son Ted Jr. later explained her difficulty with writing, "When she couldn't deal with people face to face, a great number of her tools and confidence went away".[22]

In 1932, Bute painted rhythmic images based on Joseph Schillinger's mathematical principles for *Synchromy*, (1932) an abstract film (never completed) with music composed by him, and with camerawork by Lewis Jacobs, filmmaker, writer, and teacher. This was Bute's first hands-on experience with filmmaking. Lewis Jacobs said:

I shot film based on what Schillinger composed. Schillinger was interested in movies but not set up for them. He wanted to apply his theories to film – he taught musical composition at Columbia."[23]

Synchromy illustrated the principles of rhythm in motion. Lewis Jacobs continued:

"Schillinger was interested in set design, multiple images, and the ability to use only a few actors with lights and mirrors ... and models. As Schillinger became interested in film, Bute did too ... At that time she had not seen art films ... She knew about Maya Deren later ... Schillinger had composed music for Leon Theremin. Theremin developed something that looked like a typewriter. You pressed the keys and got a sound ... Theremin's instrument was not a color organ. It was a sound thing ... Ed Warburg gave Schillinger $25 a week and expenses.[24]

Looking back, Jacobs added about Bute, "She was very good ... She was less rigid than Fischinger and [used] more sensuous light and color".[25]

Later, in 1976, Bute, commented on Schillinger and on silent films of the 1920s and early 1930's:

In Schillinger I found someone who had worked out a system by which mathematically you could compose music. Mathematically you could make paintings (Marvelous!) and meanwhile, there were several people there working on electronic music and the control of sound with their hands [Theremin] ... This whole thing seemed to me the opening of the world I wanted to enter, but enter by working towards translating it into some really moving form. I did not want to go into anything that was still. Of course I was a movie buff, but at that time it was Chaplin or Griffith … We didn't have museums of film. That came decades later. We didn't have libraries of film. We had one or two arty movie places where you went and saw silent pictures and you were very timid about admitting that these American comedies were really art in any way … much of our theater was spontaneous from the point of view of heckling with an audience, inventing jokes, while audiences would call things back, having stooges in the theater yell things out … Broadway and its theater had not developed in the use of imaginative backgrounds that would enhance the life of the play. It took some time before we had sets by – I mean the whole Gordon Gray, Donald Oenslager [who had taught at Yale] influence for example barely touched the Broadway legitimate theater … .

When it came to movies, when it came to film, film was something the children saw on Saturday and that we would see on weekends and we loved, and they were silent, but it wasn't art … The theater was theater, and that was a performing art, but the movies, well they were popular people stuff. So it took many decades before film entered museums, and then that became a problem, because they decided that some films were art and some films weren't art. And of course that has changed from one year to the next … I mean Charlie Chaplin couldn't put his toe in … [wasn't considered an artist]

You have this shock when books came out. The first few books that came out on film as art form were considered extremely snobbish and just so off beat … Some of the finest early films were shown on the top floors of old rundown buildings where they'd have private showings of early French films, Cocteau etc. and you paid fifty cents to go up six flights of stairs to see those shows with a guy playing piano … in other words, it was a very mysterious thing. It was in the Village, Greenwich Village … It wasn't until very recently that the Library of Congress accepted films as copyrighted material and began to restore them … .

And now my part of all of this, I was plodding away studying all sorts of what must seem esoteric side lines. … Theremin … oscilloscope … . I decided to absorb everything possible that would give me a means for the production of visual forms, whether they were abstract or not … and I searched for the color aspects of it and the black and white aspects of it, but most thoroughly I was searching for anything that would catch motion and be able to control it into a design whole. I wasn't thinking of art. I wasn't thinking of documentation. I wasn't thinking of experimentation... I had a non-commercial aim … .[26]

Years later Bute's friend Marilyn Ripp, said that Mary Ellen had a romance with Theremin and that she felt that he was taken to Russia as a captive because of his mathematics.[27] Bute was always attracted to men, enjoyed flirting, and could be engaging. Her former classmate from high school James Stewart Morcom described her: "Flashing eyes and teeth. She came on like gangbusters!"[28] She was petite, about five feet tall, but energetic. In 1932 Theremin, young, handsome, and charming, was already smitten with the Russian violinist Clara Reisenberg (Rockmore), who played the Theremin in New York.[29] Also he was married to Klara Pavlovna Constantinova, however she now worked in the medical field in New Jersey, and was separated from Theremin for the most part. They would divorce in 1934. Nevertheless, Bute made an impression on Theremin. In 1967, after he had been found in the Soviet Union at the Moscow Conservatory of Music by chief music critic for The New York Times, Harold Schonberg, after almost thirty years of social and political oblivion, Theremin wrote to Schillinger's widow and asked about Bute.[30]

Lewis Jacobs commented "Theremin, a pioneer electronics man, was kidnapped by the Russians in the 30s. The Russians wanted his knowledge. No one was working in electronics at that time. He had already made an eye that opened and closed doors."[31] Albert Glinsky in his book *Theremin: Ether Music and Espionage* clarified that Theremin was not really kidnapped in 1938. Theremin planned his return to the Soviet Union as a ship passenger, but his plans had to be kept secret during the buildup for World War II when trans-Atlantic passage was canceled for passengers. Even Theremin's second wife, Lavinia Williams, an African-American dancer who spoke six languages, had not been informed of his plans to return to Russia.[32] Theremin was a secret espionage agent for the Soviet government. He left the U.S as a member of the crew with a counterfeit passport on a cargo ship to the Soviet Union. He owed taxes in the United States and had debts connected with the production of his instruments. He wanted to go home, although he did not realize how changed his country had become. He had expected to send for his wife later. However, because of his espionage work and contacts with foreign governments, he was suspected by the Soviets and thrown into a prison camp for eight years. People in the USA thought he had died.

Bute's early black and white films, starting in 1934, employ the sleek, modern type of Art Deco and the shadows and ambiguities of Surrealism, suggesting mystery and inner life. She photographed three-dimensional moving objects, such as models of staircases, simplified gothic arches, and paper flowers, synchronized to music. Sparklers, crackling cellophane, and duplicating mirrors enlivened her imagery. The movements of the objects synchronized to music place a positive spin on the forms.

Bute said about the film world in the 1930s and 1940s:

> Into the 1940s, the filmmaking that could be considered non-commercial were those made by oil companies and the U. S. Government, and Air Force … and the British and Canadian Film Boards, which we must salute … they were like balloons … they were able to make local, ethnic films and films that were non-commercial … the films that were made by the oil companies … I think those films were breaking ground for documentaries and the educational films … I wanted to keep things beautiful with the sound and the image coordinated. I experimented with that … the oscilloscope was fun.[33]

> It was terrible trying to find money to do this. I just felt I must seek methods by which I could produce motion on film that would have beauty ... It wasn't until I had completed a series of abstract films ... the whole field of filmmaking had burgeoned and there were Italians and French ... I don't believe there's a filmmaker alive who hasn't been sustained by his knowledge of art ... painting and sculpture...Eisenstein with his government film *Potemkin* ... he honors the filmmakers of Hollywood in what he learned from them. He took that and added a daring spirit of action with figures ... films were so exciting in their attempt to do something that had not been done before ... camera angles and the use of actors ... and amusing inanimate objects ... all these things were being done here and they influenced everyone from Fellini on ... .[34]

Bute also said:

> But imagining visual accompaniment to already composed music continued to be a real source of enjoyment. I liked "Anitra's Dance" and made sketches as I listened to it. Melville Webber and others had completed *The Fall of the House of Usher*. I 'invited him to see my sketches for "Anitra's Dance". He volunteered to help.

> I had done a 16mm experiment with Joseph Schillinger and Lewis Jacobs in a Bolex with a stop-frame device. But "Anitra's Dance" was to be a 35mm production suitable for theatrical distribution. We had a preliminary camera sheet and were about ready to get started when Webber, one of the producers of the film, turned to me and said, "Miss Bute, you know I'm not a cameraman".

> I hurried down to Paul Guffanti's laboratory at Ninth Ave., where I had an appointment with a cameraman who had been suggested. Unfortunately, he stood me up a couple of times. That day he was late and hadn't phoned. In breezed Ted Nemeth and another cameraman. It seems they were aware of why I was there. They went into an adjoining room and flipped a coin. Ted Nemeth came out and announced with zest he had access to some great equipment – a 35mm camera etc. He whisked me away to see it. I took him up to talk to Webber.

> Ted Nemeth, an ace cameraman, had also worked on trailers for National Screen and is a genius at setting up flip devices and panning boards – It was a perfect combination. I quickly approached two of my friends, young men who had the best jobs among my friends in our crowd. They were complimented to get this on film. "Rhythm in Light" was quickly completed.[35]

Nemeth first studied cinematography at the New York Institute of Photography, which taught commercial still photography and one motion picture course, the only one in the city. He then worked as a portrait photographer at Bachrach, the best in the business, but he felt there was no money in still photography. His next job was at National Screen Announcement, at a motion picture studio in Flushing where he used a lot of different cameras, including Pathé and Bell and Howell. He filmed in open sets with bed sheets over the top of his cameras, which were hand cranked. He would slow the camera down so that the film would last longer. Less than sixteen frames per second. [36]

Lewis Jacobs commented:

At National Screen Announcement, Inc., we made three-minute films using ideas of the new pictures, like coming attractions ... We couldn't get movie scenes. A company had a monopoly on them. We had to create scenes out of drawings and photographs ... We worked in the Motion Picture Building on 9th Avenue, between 44th and 45th Streets. I was in charge of production and writing. Ted was my camera man ... He was a great technician ... Ted had equipment and know how, not creativity. He was an astute technician. [Later] Mary Ellen supplied the creativity ... Ted was a master of animation and special effects."[37]

Nemeth was tall, six foot one, with dark hair and Hungarian good looks, later inherited by his two sons. Five years younger than Bute, he was born in 1911 in Cambridge, MA, of Hungarian parents. He had five brothers. His mother supported the family with a tailor shop, while continuing to cook and clean for her boys.[38] His family moved to a farm in New York State, then to Bridgeport, CT, and finally to Queens.

Nemeth, talking about his work at National Screen Announcement said that the lab developed film with "rack and tank". They wound film onto a wooden frame and then transferred it from the racks onto a drum. They developed 200 feet at a time. The film was washed in three baths in the dark room. They used red dye on one side and blue tone, red and pink on the other. This was before there were optical printers (except three crude ones). He explained:

Fade-ins and fade-outs were created by chemicals. You'd dip the film into a solution and slowly pull it out. You'd dissolve the emulsion. Then you'd lift the whole sequence out in a 100-foot section, tinting and toning the positive. You had to splice the scenes, hundreds of splices for dialogue titles and credits. You had a script. The titles were tinted separately. In a Griffith film, the fire scene was done in red.

We shot the outside scenes on Long Island. The crew worked for Beaumont Company in Flushing. Then the film went to Consolidated Laboratories in Long Island City to the printing room with duplex printers. There were five machines in a row. We moved the negative from one machine to the next. We made 300 prints in a night for MGM Newsreels. We changed the printing light at the end of a loop, while the machine was running. As stock ran out, we added stock to the machine while it was running. If we missed, we'd misprint ten prints, because we couldn't keep up. The printing machine was a duplex printer, a step printer. It did frame by frame printing ... registration was done by the night crew ... The negatives were a mess by the time the crews got through. Five crews worked on ten machines each. Every week there was a whole new show...editing was done. It was hectic. It was the late 1920s at National Screen Announcement. Universal News was the trademark. With no optical printers, the film required eight exposures, running through the camera eight times ... Universal connected with different newspapers in the city ... we superimposed effects. Smoke coming out of an airplane was another exposure. We used a model plane and Bell and Howell cameras, one frame at a time. We used a stop-motion motor.[39]

Nemeth, reflecting on meeting Mary Ellen, said:

> When Mary Ellen entered the New York Film Service Laboratories, I and another man saw Mary Ellen enter, and flipped a coin to see who would take the dynamic red head out for a date. I won. When Mary Ellen asked for Mr. Dangsburg, the cameraman she was looking for, I told her that he was out! I said, 'Let's get out of here and talk.' I was walking out with Dangsburg's client![40]

At another time he commented: "I built myself up to pursue her. I formed Ted Nemeth Studios ten minutes before I met M. E.".[41]

Nemeth left New York Film Service Laboratories on Ninth Avenue after he met Bute and formed first Ted Nemeth Studios, a production company for commercial films, and then, in a partnership with Bute, Expanding Cinema, a production company for art films. Soon she and Ted left the Hotel des Artistes and moved into a carriage house behind a Chinese laundry at 9th Avenue and 46th Street, near 630 Ninth Avenue. The rent was $75 a month in 1934. (In 1984 it was $400.) There was a sculptor downstairs, Rutherford Boyd, who would supply models for Bute's later film, *Parabola*. Nemeth said:

> "Mary Ellen had made a crude 8mm film with Lewis Jacobs, *Synchromy*. He was an artist ... by the time I met Mary Ellen, I had a lot of experience."[42]

Ted then described the optical printer that he made for Mary Ellen:

> Belle and Howell had a fading device, which opened and shut automatically. It dissolved and faded. You didn't have to do it chemically. I could calibrate the shutter speed and determine how many frames for a fade. I used the camera as an optical printer ... From the 30s–60s, effects were cut in, as opposed to doing the effects through the scene. We used dupes. Dupes were bad at that time. Printers could do dissolves later ... The guy Mary Ellen was supposed to see had built an animation stand. It didn't work ... I rebuilt it.[43]

Nemeth also characterized Bute working:

> She worked quickly. She knew what she wanted. She sketched. ... She invited me to see her sketches. Crude, but they gave me an idea. Friends told her to borrow money to make a film. One of the co-signers, and therefore producers, was Melville Webber. Mary Ellen thought he was a cameraman. He had worked on *The Fall of the House of Usher*. But he wasn't a cameraman, but he was helpful ... Jim Hart in New York also signed the note. He was Liz Dillingham Hart's husband. Mary Ellen grew up with Liz Dillingham in Houston.[44]

On December 27, 1932, Radio City Music Hall opened. It would play an important role in the screening of Bute's abstract films and would enable her short films to reach a huge audience, unusual for experimental filmmakers in the United States. Bute believed that her shorts would entertain the general public and were not limited in appeal to specialized art-oriented audiences. She was criticized for this. Film critic, historian, and teacher Cecile Starr, who later distributed Bute's shorts and her live action films, said:

Fig. 1. Mary Ellen Bute and Ted Nemeth Sr. ca. 1934, photo by Ted Nemeth Studios, courtesy KSB Collection of MEB, YCAL.

She didn't attend the New York Film Council meetings once a month. She was outside always, because of her 35mm work for commercial theaters. Documentary films were the center of New York filmmaking. People were not interested in *Anitra's Dance* [*Rhythm in Light*]. Mary Ellen was not taken seriously among film people or museum people … I didn't know Mary Ellen very well. She was always considered a strange person. I didn't see her as a working person. She was too cheerful. The rest of the film world were quiet or big drinkers.[45]

Money was an ongoing challenge for experimental filmmakers, not only during the Depression, but afterward. Their work was not commercial,

Fig. 2. Mary Ellen Bute and Ted Nemeth with camera 1934, photo by Ted Nemeth Studios, courtesy KSB Collection of MEB, YCAL.

although Bute was able to rent most of her films to commercial theaters for projection, to cover her costs. Places like Radio City Music Hall would pay Bute every time they showed one of her shorts with their features. However, exhibiting work in commercial houses separated Bute from the avant-garde filmmakers in New York, who shunned anything adding a commercial taint to their art. Partly because of this, she was not fully recognized for her pioneering work in cinema. Women filmmakers had more difficulty then men raising money, because women directors at that time were not taken seriously, except in rare cases, such as Leni Riefenstahl in Germany in the 1930s and Dorothy Arzner in Hollywood. Maya Deren didn't become known until 1945. At the First International Festival of Women's Films in New York City in 1972, the difficulty of getting funded was a topic of concern, and still is.

Film editor Thelma Schoonmaker, who briefly edited Butes *Passages from James Joyce's Finnegans Wake,* said: "Bute was not part of the avant-garde in New York … Her films were treated as commercial releases. Ted was commercial. She had press releases, showed in commercial houses."[46]

But animation historian William Moritz saw this introduction of experimental films to vast audiences as enterprising for Bute at the time.[47] Bute discussing the distribution of her short films theatrically said:

Fig. 3. Still from *Rhythm in Light* (1934), directed by Mary Ellen Bute,
©Center for Visual Music, Los Angeles.

MGM offered me $3,000 for one of my early ones, but I made $3,000 in just one booking at the Trans-Lux with *Lili* (1953). My films are totally abstract, so though that subject had played Radio City, it went so well with the feature that Trans-Lux booked it as a first run. It's just like music. You can see it over and over.[48]

Dates for Bute's films vary, depending on whether they reflect the production or the release of the film. The earlier production dates are used here because they tie in with Bute's chronology as a filmmaker. Release dates are often difficult to determine.

In 1934 Ted Nemeth filmed and Mary Ellen Bute directed the five-minute black and white abstract animated short, *Rhythm in Light*. It was co-produced by Mary Ellen Bute, Theodore J. Nemeth, and Melville Webber. It starts with explanatory words in stylized type: "A pioneer effort in a new art form … An artist's impression of what goes on in the mind when listening to music." Then stylized spirals, rings, curves, sparkles, cones, and dots, move, sometimes in soft focus, superimposed over cloud-like forms, syncopated to the music of "Anitra's Dance", from Edvard Grieg's *Peer Gynt Suite*.

Reflective images ripple across the screen. Dots float in space like stars in a universe. The film is a study in moving super-impositions.

Ted Nemeth's brother Ernest taught Bute to use the 35mm camera, said writer Lillian Schiff. "She became quite independent as a cameraperson as well as an image designer and painter."[49] *Rhythm in* Light was screened at Radio City Music Hall, an unheard of first-run commercial venue for an experimental film, shown with the feature film "Becky Sharp", 1935. Radio City Music Hall would continue to present films with stage shows until 1979. Over twenty-five years after its premier, *Rhythm in Light* was shown in Boston at the Exeter Theater with the feature "Last Year at Marienbad",1961, reflecting the longevity of interest in Bute's experimental films in mainstream theatres. Bute said about *Rhythm in Light*:

> It was mostly three-dimensional animation. Pyramids, and ping pong balls, and all interrelated by light patterns – and I wasn't happy unless it all entered and exited exactly as I had planned.[50]

From the beginning, Bute insisted on complete control of her film images, possible with animation, but impossible with live action shots, as she would find out later.

Ted Nemeth described their filming process for *Rhythm in Light*:

> We started to shoot in her room at Hotel des Artistes. I brought big professional cables in from the hall...I built an animation stand horizontally, with runners down the room ... Webber got us going with special effects ... we repeated images and used refracted glass ... We edited as we went along. The ratio [sound to image] was close. We had it broken down carefully. 35mm ... 10–15 foot table, runners three feet wide. Revolving drum ... all these things we built to fit on the table. We could zoom (with dolly). We could flip at same time. ... We developed it at the lab where we met. The sound track was done before. We analyzed the track and shot to it. We broke it down by eye. Optical sound track. With a Moviola, we projected it. We could see where the beats were, and the number of frames. We worked it out ... multiple exposures by putting the film back in the camera. We tried different devices and multiple passes. We made exposure tests. Sent them to the lab. Spot lights, concentrated spots. The table moved. The camera was stationery. The lights moved with the table. Two months for our first film. The cable was in the hall for two months! They didn't throw us out. Hazardous. We sent *Rhythm in Light* to the lab in 1934. The final editing was done on the Moviola. We checked it out. We went to the MGM Screening Room, 10th floor, 670 Ninth Avenue ... There were no inter-negatives until the 1960s.[51]

Always pinched for money, Bute and Nemeth fabricated equipment that they could not afford to buy and created effects from whatever they had at hand, such as mirrors, a colander, heavy cream floating in coffee, a turn table, and also sculptures and drawings. Later animation historian William Moritz said in an interview that Bute's simple approach to filmmaking influenced renowned Canadian filmmaker Norman McLaren.[52] McLaren, like Bute, also used introductory educational texts and simple, available materials for making his films. He was particularly well known for drawing directly on the film, eliminating the need for a camera, which in the beginning, he could not afford.

Lillian Schiff, in an interview with Mary Ellen Bute, wrote of the link between Bute's film and her personality:

> She seriously observed, she'd always been a joyous person. It's incredible. Anyone in this generation who is lucky enough to see the lively, happiness-making first film, *Rhythm in Light*, and others that followed in the 30s, 40s and 50s, will understand that an upbeat person had transferred her feelings to the dancing ping pong balls, crumpled cellophane, sparklers, and patches of light, all rhythmically moving against a painted background.[53]

Nemeth said that Bute took *Rhythm in Light* to Philadelphia for a private screening for [conductor] Stowkowski. Bute described the incident in an interview:

> Leopold Stokowski wanted to see the first film I did, *Rhythm in Light*, so I took it to Philadelphia to screen it for him. The projectionist ran it first to check it out and he said "This is great. You should take it by the Radio City Music Hall." And I did. They said, "Well, we like it, but we're not sure about the ladies from New Jersey". And I said "Well won't you keep it and insert it in a show and let me know?" In a few days, I called them and they said to come in, and they would book it. I didn't talk about money at all but what they gave me practically paid for all the costs of the film. You see they were trained by Disney, and Disney always got very good prices. So I've a lot to be grateful to Disney for … They put it in with a feature they thought would run for a long time. And they still play my films whenever I do any … The people at Radio City have always been nice; they'd give you the names of other theater managers around the country and you'd send your print out, write them a letter and say it was used at Radio City, and it just worked out.[54]

Ted Nemeth added:

> The next theater to run *Rhythm in Light* was a Herman Weinberg Theater in Baltimore, then the Trans-Lux on Madison Avenue, New York. They made a deal to screen it. They started with numerous trailers a half hour before the film... "Rhythm and Light" was considered startling![55]

Mary Ellen Bute appreciated Ted Nemeth's skill with the camera. She said later "I learned from an excellent cinematographer. Ted was great."[56]

Rhythm in Light is in the Anthology Film Archives, MOMA, the New York Public Library for the Performing Arts, UW-Milwaukee, and in the Cecile Starr Collection at the Center for Visual Music, Los Angeles. It is on the Anthology Film Archives DVD set, *Unseen Cinema*.

Their next film, *Synchromy # 2*, 1935, 35mm, was 5 minutes, black and white, part of the Seeing Sound series. Produced by Ted Nemeth and Mary Ellen Bute through their production company for art films, Expanding Cinema. Mary Ellen Bute directed it. At the beginning, words

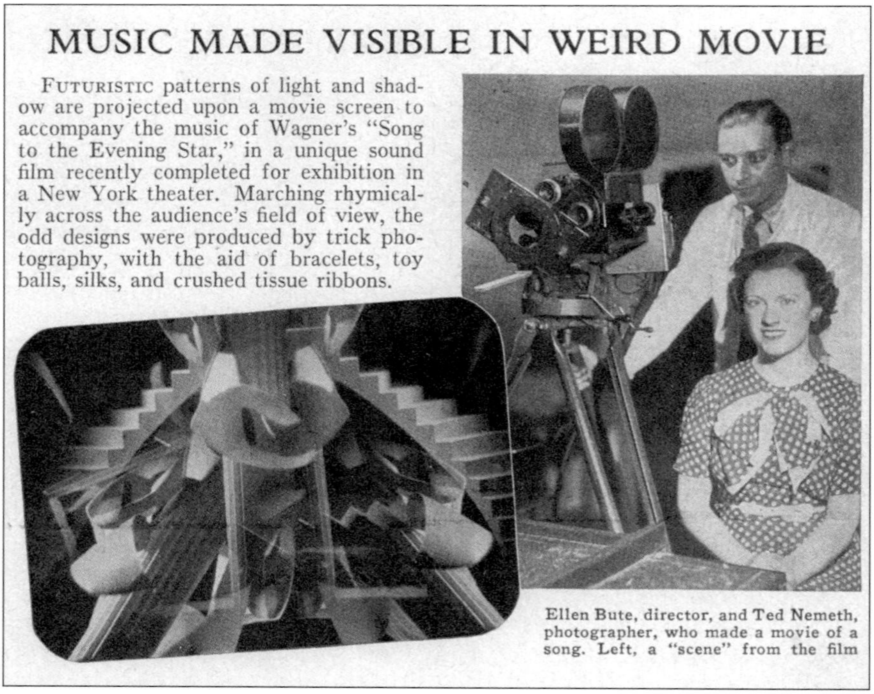

MUSIC MADE VISIBLE IN WEIRD MOVIE

FUTURISTIC patterns of light and shadow are projected upon a movie screen to accompany the music of Wagner's "Song to the Evening Star," in a unique sound film recently completed for exhibition in a New York theater. Marching rhymically across the audience's field of view, the odd designs were produced by trick photography, with the aid of bracelets, toy balls, silks, and crushed tissue ribbons.

Ellen Bute, director, and Ted Nemeth, photographer, who made a movie of a song. Left, a "scene" from the film

Fig. 4. Mary Ellen Bute and Ted Nemeth, "Synchromy No. 2", 1935 in *Modern Mechanix Yesterday's Tomorrow Today*, Nov. 1936, courtesy KSB Collection of MEB,

explain Seeing Sound. This abstract film pairs abstract images and a star and Tannhaüser's flowering rod, a lily, and gothic arches to Wagner's "O Evening Star" from Tannhaüser, sung by Reinald Werrenrath. Other images moving to the music are stacked discs, stairs, lilies, open circular forms, crosses, poles, and stars, shadows, and plaster heads with classical features. Cloud forms move in the background. This film was shown at Radio City Music Hall in 1938 with the feature "Mary of Scotland", starring Katharine Hepburn.

By 1935, Bute and Nemeth had a regular studio behind a Chinese laundry, in the area which later became Lincoln Center.[57] For *Synchromy # 2* he and Bute used models of a staircase and plaster forms that were in the sculpture studio below their apartment. Nemeth said that sound was new to film and even a Moviola was a new piece of equipment. They had fun making the films and wanted to bring them to the masses.[58] *Synchromy # 2* was distributed by Commonwealth Picture Corporation, until Cecile Starr took over distribution in the late 1970s.

Nemeth related that Disney was printing "Steamboat Willy" near his studio. [This film was produced originally in 1928, so his title is probably incorrect.] "He had a big staff. Disney was so particular. He'd throw a whole print out. I'd collect it. The film deteriorated quickly."[59] In an interview, Nemeth compared his and Bute's filming process and Disney's:

> From *Mickey Mouse* to a serious expression of music in terms of light is not a great transition for a cameraman. The difference ... is that Disney photographs flat cartoon surfaces, while we have to take shots of three-dimensional models set up on a little stage the size of a platter. For the single reel of one of our Expanding Cinemas, I have to take 7,000 separate, yet closely related photographs."[60]

In the same interview, Bute said about *Synchromy # 2*:

> We are trying to express music in terms of light ... It's not a new idea – goes back to Aristotle's idea of poetic motion in the "Poetics", and was fore-shadowed by the modern Thermin instrument and the Clavilux ... My interest in the relations between light and sound rhythms began when I was a child on my father's ranch ... I read about abstractionist French art and Marcel Duchamp's "Nude Descending a Staircase" in the *Literary Digest* (February 19, 1921).[61]

Images in magazines and books inspired Bute, as did Modern work in museums and galleries in New York. Nemeth and Bute came up with a system for sound tracks by plotting them on graph paper, influenced by Joseph Schillinger's mathematical system of music composition:

> We had graph paper around the room three times! We looked at the sound through the Moviola, then transferred the highs and lows to graph paper. We used a different color pencil for each instrument ... It took months. M. E. did the art work herself.[62]

The voice recording was added to *Synchromy # 2*, Wagner's song, "Evening Star".[63] To create the trigonometric order of the images, Bute worked with the editorial board of *Scripta Mathematica*, scholarly journal of Yeshiva College in New York, where Bute had taken a class in mathematics. The professors worked out equations for the scale of the model and tempo of the images, which Bute arranged and Nemeth photographed.[64] Bute added:

> The Yeshiva mathematicians, who inspire us, eventually aim to construct music from the equation in a sequence of pictures, not pictures from already-written music.[65]

About this time, 1936, critic Jesse Zunser quoted Bute's explanation of her mathematical system:

> A mathematical system serves as a basis for our particular work in the inter-composition of these visual and aural materials in time continuity. We take the relationship of two or more numbers for instance 7:2, 3:4, 9:5:1 – factor them around their axes, raise to powers, permutate, divide, multiply, subtract, and invert, until we have a composition of the desired length in numbers.

Then we realize this composition in the materials we have selected to employ. We use the composition of numbers to determine the length width, and depth of the photographic field and everything in it, this numerical composition determines the length, speed, and duration of a zoom, a travel back with the camera the curve and angle at which the camera approaches a subject etc. It determines the shape, size, color, and luminosity of the subject – how, when and in what relationship to other elements of the composition it develops and moves.[66]

Synchromy # 2 is on Anthology Film Archives' DVD set, *Unseen Cinema*, 2005. It is in the collection of Anthology Film Archives, UW-Milwaukee, and the Center for Visual Music, Los Angeles.

Bute's next short film was still in black and white, *Dada*, 1936, 3 minutes. This film was produced for Universal Newsreel. It animates a collage of effects from previous Bute films. The Center for Visual Music in Los Angeles has this black and white film. Rings, bars, crinkled cellophane, stacking poles forming a ladder, match sticks, mirrors, rectangles, spirals, cubes and other geometric forms move through space, from side to side and back and forth. The movement slows enough to allow the viewer a chance to focus on the shapes. The idea of "a collage of earlier forms" is appropriate for the Dada artistic movement which often integrated collage with different media. The music was a waltz. Film critic Jesse Zunser for Cue said: "Animated with Dada humor to a waltz tune. Witty and delightful, it flashes off the screen too soon."[67]

Dada is in the collection of the Center for Visual Music in Los Angeles, Anthology Film Archives, The Yale Film Study Center, and UW-Milwaukee. It is in the Anthology Film Archives' DVD set, *Unseen Cinema*.

In 1936 Oskar Fischinger passed through New York on his way to California, where he was hired by Paramount. Ted Nemeth said that he and Bute met Fischinger at this time.[68] They already had seen his films.

Film historian William Moritz said: "After working with Lewis Jacobs, she [Mary Ellen Bute] did see films here and in Europe … She met Oskar Fischinger in New York and saw screenings of his films. She was thrilled and delighted. They were inspirational."[69]

Bute was excited to find someone else interested in creating abstract, animated shorts. Moritz said that Fischinger was Bute's closest contemporary. Fischinger's *An Optical Poem*, came out in 1938 in the United States. The Museum of Modern Art acquired this film later. Moritz added that in the late 1930s, you could see European films at the Museum of Modern Art and in film clubs, including Eisenstein's *Battleship Potemkin*, famous for its montage editing, and other silent films, and that Bute could have seen these.[70]

Fig. 5. Still from Oskar Fischinger, *Study no* 7, 1931,
© Center for Visual Music, Los Angeles.

Bute's color films seem more sensuous than Oskar Fischinger's, with softer imagery, and floating colors and lights. Bute often created backgrounds by filming heavy cream floating in coffee, seen through colored filters! Also, by contrast, Bute's geometric forms alternated with whimsical images created out of her imagination or with objects like sparklers, mirrors, and cellophane, which increased the texture of her films. Unlike Bute who learned as she went, often with no formal background, Fischinger had trained as a musician, draftsman and engineer. This education enabled him to modify his own equipment and exactly synchronize his images with the music. Both artists created abstract images moving to a musical beat, in a framework of time.

Bute said about Disney and Fischinger:

> I've always been enormously impressed with what Disney did. I think he's a fabulous genius. I mean there's nothing like Mickey Mouse. But I got a great bang out of Oscar Fischinger's first film that was shown here ... a delightful little thing. I'd done some films before then that were quite different, but then I realized that there were other people around the world as nutty as I. I used to entertain myself by visualizing sounds. The visual aspect of sound would occur to me without my realizing it, and so I started putting it on film really to entertain myself.[71]

Fig. 6. *Parabola*, 1937, film still, directed by Mary Ellen Bute, courtesy
Yale Film Study Center.

Later Bute wrote:

> One day, worn out by this hard concentration, I decided to just go to the movies
> and relax. I've forgotten what the feature was, but in those days, the early 1930s,
> it was probably full of songs and dances – but I don't remember because first
> came a short subject, a little animation by Fischinger set to a jazz song "I've
> Never Seen a Smile Like Yours". It was the simplest thing, drawn lines fluttering
> about in graceful swirls in perfect time to the music. Suddenly it all made sense
> for me. That was how to do it, not by mathematical theories, but rather an
> intuitive choreography.[72]

Lillian Schiff wrote in her interview with Mary Ellen Bute about her
influence from both Kandinsky and Fischinger:

> She did no cell animation, she said, and all the work was in 35mm. Early
> influence came from Kandinsky, himself an observer of relationships between
> color and music, whose paintings made her think of frozen music. She wanted
> to 'undo' the parts and make them move. Other ideas and impressions derived
> from the work of Oskar Fischinger, whose 'absolute films' using simple shapes
> such as squares, circles and triangles, were closely related to rhythms and
> emphases.[73]

Ted compared Mary Ellen's films to those of Oscar Fischinger:

> Oscar Fishinger's films don't come close ... His stuff takes forever. He made 25
> finished films before he came to US. Only made 5 once in USA. We met him
> before he left for California.[74]

Another black and white film followed, *Parabola*, 1937, 9 minutes, 35mm, directed by Mary Ellen Bute, produced by Expanding Cinema, assisted by William Nemeth, one of Ted's brothers, with music, "La Création du Monde", by the contemporary composer, Darius Milhaud. It is on Anthology Film Archives' DVD set, *Unseen Cinema*, 2005, and on Flicker Alley's 2017 CD, *Early Women Filmmakers: An International Anthology*. It is in the collection of the Yale Film Study Center, the New York Public Library for the Performing Arts, UW-Milwaukee, Anthology Film Archives, and the Center for Visual Music, Los Angeles.

The music is less well synchronized than in Bute's earlier films. Sometimes images flow across the screen while the music has a staccato jazz rhythm. Flower-like forms, Slinkys, and overlapping arches extend the space around the parabolic sculptures of Rutherford Boyd syncopated to changing rhythms. This film was never shown in a major theater, possibly because of conflict with Rutherford Boyd.[75]

Bute incorporated instructional words at the beginning of this film. She wanted to educate and reach the general public as well as to entertain. In *Parabola* Bute defined a parabola as "nature's poetry of motion, written with a single line". Also, on film, the dictionary defines a parabola as "a plane curve which is the path of a moving point that remains equally distant from a fixed point and from a fixed straight line".

Nemeth said:

> We also created *Parabola* in the carriage house studio. We used kaleidoscopes for it... We saw the parabolas in the studio below and we thought we could do something with them. We moved them. 10–15 pieces. We sliced a cone and used moving lights ... most of the film was stop motion. It was not shot frame to frame. We moved the cameras around.[76]

Not able to afford Technicolor film, Nemeth and Bute used color filters, superimposing their shots for their next film, *Escape*, 1937, (also called *Synchromy # 4*) 4 minutes, color, 35mm, directed by Mary Ellen Bute, produced by Mary Ellen Bute and Ted Nemeth. Nemeth's brother William Nemeth also assisted on the film. In this abstract narrative film, made from black and white drawings with colored filters, a yellow triangle, trapped behind horizontal bars, tries to escape to Bach's Toccata and Fugue in D minor. Later, in 1940, Walt Disney would use this music in *Fantasia*. In the end, the bars bend and merge with the triangle, which becomes bigger and in a stronger color, red instead of yellow. This film resonates with Bute's struggle to be a woman filmmaker in a man's field, and possibly alludes to her domestic challenges as well. The absorption of bars could be a metaphor for interior controls set in place by the filmmaker as a form of survival, or simply as the escape of the triangle from limitations and barriers. The increased size and intensified color of the triangle could be interpreted as Bute's growing strength and confidence as a filmmaker.

See Colour Plate 4.
Film still from *Escape*, 1937, (also called *Synchromy #4*), directed by Mary Ellen Bute.
©Center for Visual Music, Los Angeles.

Bute said about this film:

> I took well known musical compositions and added a visual interpretation as an auxiliary stimulus. In … *Escape*, I started with the skeleton of a dramatic idea – of the appearance of a grating imprisoning a triangle – of the triangle's struggle and escape – of the grating transforming into a triangle.[77]

In a talk, Bute described her filming process in *Escape*:

> In *Escape*, I had the idea of a triangle struggling to get from behind bars – which then merged into a triangle … from Bach's Toccata and Fugue in d Minor. The filming was done in the most advanced color of the day – which was a two-color process. It employed a magenta and cyan [blue] filter. It required shooting one frame with the magenta filter, changing filters, and shooting a second frame [with the cyan]. When the film was completed, these frames were superimposed optically.[78]

Nemeth expanded on the technical process of filming *Escape*:

> The set-up for *Escape* was flat, not three-dimensional. Color was just coming in … We used two separate films, a two-color dye process, Kinecolor. Technicolor, using three films, was too expensive … It required a special camera which we didn't have. We filmed it stop-motion, shooting alternate frames red, blue, red, blue. We shot it to see the action, then re-photographed it frame by frame, alternating red and blue. Step printing. Stop frame. Red filter, blue filter. It was printed from the two films superimposed. Tedious. Disney had an automatic camera. In Hollywood, we saw how they registered the film. They held the film in position, put dye on one film, next time the blue dye, third time multiple exposures.

> Our apartment was hard to clean or change your clothes in. Problem of dust. The dyes had vibrant colors … *Escape* was a two-color film … *Color Rhapsody* was created that way … for *Escape* we put together a multi-place camera, like the one Disney had used. Disney's multi-place system was $100,000. Ours was $50.00.[79]

> In the first part of *Escape*, the focus shifts, sometimes to us, sometimes outputting 6000 frames. Alternate framing. Amazing to do! We built our multi-plane camera on our animation stand. For *Escape*, we changed levels. Fun.[80]

Abstract film animator Norman McLaren, who would work with Bute on her next film, said in 1938 at a screening of *Escape*: "The best abstract film I've seen!"[81] Lilian Schiff noted the humorous qualities "which she

Fig. 7. Mary Ellen Bute working on an animated
film circa 1937, photo by Ted Nemeth Sr.,
courtesy KSB Collection of MEB, YCAL.

[Mary Ellen Bute] probably could not avoid in view of her effervescent
personality and wide interests in literature and theater".[82] Film critic for
Cue, Jesse Zunser said when the film came out:

> A dramatic struggle between two geometric forms to Bach's "Toccata" from
> "Toccata and Fugue in D Minor". Here Miss Bute combines color and sound
> in a film of mood portrayal. ... its movement on the screen delicately accents
> the cascade of notes pouring from the strings in Bach's lovely Toccata.[83]

Escape was part of the opening exhibition of the Whitney Museum of
American art when they moved to a new building at the bottom of the
High Line in lower Manhattan in 2015. *Escape* is on the Anthology Film
Archives' DVD, *Unseen Cinema*, and in the collections of MOMA, the
Yale Film Study Center (in black and white only), the George Eastman
House, UW-Milwaukee, and the Center for Visual Music, Los Angeles.
In 1939, Nemeth and Bute moved their filmmaking studio to the United
Artists Building, 729 Seventh Avenue at 49th Street, with professional
studios and screening rooms.[84]

Spook Sport, 1939, was also a color film, 8 minutes, 35mm, produced and
directed by Mary Ellen Bute, animated by Norman McLaren, and a Ted

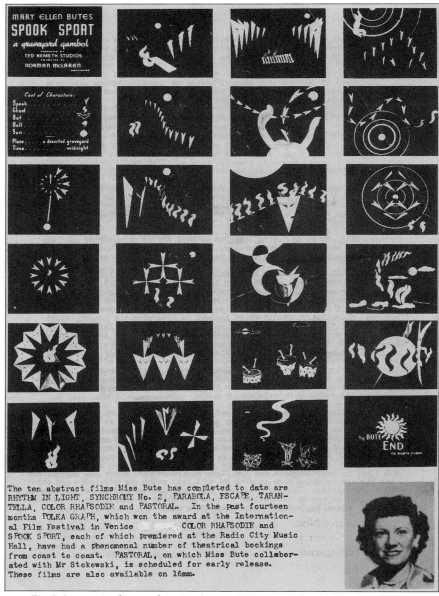

The ten abstract films Miss Bute has completed to date are RHYTHM IN LIGHT, SYNCHROMY No. 2, PARABOLA, ESCAPE, TARANTELLA, COLOR RHAPSODIE and PASTORAL. In the past fourteen months POLKA GRAPH, which won the award at the International Film Festival in Venice COLOR RHAPSODIE and SPOOK SPORT, each of which premiered at the Radio City Music Hall, have had a phenomenal number of theatrical bookings from coast to coast. PASTORAL, on which Miss Bute collaborated with Mr Stokowski, is scheduled for early release. These films are also available on 16mm.

Fig. 8. A synopsis of images from *Spook Sport*, 1939, courtesy KSB Collection of MEB, YCAL.

Nemeth Studios production. Introductory words say: "A Short Film Novelty … A Film Ballet". Bute conceived this film featuring a cast of symbolic images, including stylized spooks, ghosts, bats, a bell, a sun, a clock, and a stylized rooster which moves to Saint-Saens "Danse Macabre". At midnight, spooks and ghosts party, in a graveyard. Abstract forms play on bones like a xylophone. The outline of a rooster announces morning. Ghosts retire to their graves. A sun winks at the viewer! The film was animated and hand drawn frame by frame by Norman McLaren. It is on Anthology Film Archives' 2005 DVD set, *Unseen Cinema,* and on Flicker Alley's 2017 CD, *Early Women Filmmakers: An International Anthology.* It is in the collection of the National Film Board of Canada, Anthology Film Archives, MOMA, the Whitney Museum of American Art, the Yale film Study Center, the New York Public Library for the Performing arts, UW-Milwaukee, and in the Cecile Starr Collection at the Center for Visual Music, Los Angeles. It is also in the collection of the National Film Board of Canada.

Baroness Hilla Von Rebay, Curator of the Solomon R. Guggenheim Foundation, bought a 35 mm print of it in 1941.[85] Nemeth commented that Hilla Rebay was particular about non-objective films not having realistic elements, such as Bute's use of stairs and arches, and that was perhaps why the Baroness didn't buy Bute's other films.[86] *Spook Sport* was booked at Radio City Music Hall with the feature "Where's Charley", 1952, starring Ray Bolger. It ran for over two years at the Trans-Lux Theater in New York with the feature film "Lili", 1953.

Mary Ellen Bute said ca. 1940 about this film:

> I designed the film very much as one would the choreography of a ballet. Through a special process the bold figures which carry the line of the melody are painted directly on the film … The animator of this unusual work is a brilliant young Scotchman named Norman McLaren. Mr. McLaren is now doing this type of work for defense films for the Canadian Government.[87]

See Plate 5.
Spook Sport, 1939 animation by Norman McLaren, directed by Mary Ellen Bute, film still.
Courtesy Yale Film Study Center.

Bute also said about *Spook Sport:*

> With *Spook Sport* I had all of the key sketches on the wall of my apartment. When Scottish animator Norman McLaren first arrived in New York, with his British partner Guy Glover [poet and actor/producer]. McLaren offered to animate *Spook Sport* commenting that his work had been directly on film following the dictates of his stream of consciousness, and that he would enjoy this project of holding work to key drawings. I enjoyed his work, so that's *Spook Sport.*[88]

Nemeth said:

> This was a three-color separation: red, yellow, magenta. Will never be done again. Black ink on transparent film. Drawing. Used as pos or neg (white line). Need technique, charm, money, imagination. [89]

Norman McLaren and Guy Glover, his partner, were invited to join the National Film Board of Canada in 1941. McLaren created an animation unit for the NFB in 1943 and was head of Studio A, their first animation

Fig. 9. Mary Ellen Bute and Norman McLaren in Canada, 1982,
KSB Collection of MEB, YCAL.

studio. Bute hired him later to write the screenplay for her live action film, *The Boy Who Saw Through*. McLaren won an Academy Award for one of his films, and Guy Glover was nominated for four Academy Awards. Bute early recognized their talent, one of her outstanding abilities.

Mary Ellen Bute didn't marry Ted Nemeth for six years. She said in an interview:

> I wasn't against marriage at all, but I never thought of marrying and ... well, Houston would have been the ideal place to marry the boy ... you know, dozens of them, everything was so coeducational in the West ... But that wasn't a part of my picture. So I took about six years before I married him.[90]

A *New York Times* article Nov. 1, 1940 described a dinner in honor of the recently married Nemeths and printed the wedding date as October 15, 1940, which coincides with the marriage certificate.[91] Broadway producer Margo Lion, Bute's ex-daughter-in-law said, "She found Ted dashing and exotic. She was in conflict about her duties, responsibilities, and loyalties. She had a conservative Texas upbringing."[92] Bute's sister Lois said, "When Mary Ellen was first married, she said Ted was a dreamboat. She idealized people."[93] Bute's friend from her last years, Marilyn Ripp, also said "Mary Ellen was idealistic".[94]

Fig. 10. Ted Nemeth standing in his studio ca. 1940, photo by Ted Nemeth Studios, courtesy KSB Collection of MSB, YCAL.

Ted Nemeth continued to shoot commercial films, including English titles for foreign films, while working on Bute's experimental ones.[95] Probably he obtained these jobs through cinema owner and film critic Herman Weinberg who translated film titles into several languages, including German and French. Nemeth knew him from booking Bute's films in Weinberg's theaters. Nemeth also filmed commercials for Chiquita Banana, for soda companies, and produced training films for the military, hospitals, and special interest organizations. In addition, he supplied camera work for other directors.

In 1940 color plays an increasingly important role in Bute's films. Impressionism and Abstract Expressionism inspired her ambiguous, cloud-like, moving color backgrounds and colored forms. Geometric forms in the foreground recall Mondrian's grids, Picasso's Cubism with geometric shapes, Paul Klee's imaginative figures, Kandinsky's exploding compositions, and Rothko's soft edged, rectangular areas of color. Bute could have seen these at The Museum of Modern Art, started in 1929, but moved to 53rd Street in 1939, or in the Guggenheim Foundation's Museum of Non-Objective Painting which opened in 1939. Both of these museums screened avant-garde films that Bute could watch, including Fischinger films.

See Plate 6.
Film Still from *Tarantella* (1940), directed by Mary Ellen Bute,
© Center for Visual Music, Los Angeles.

Fig. 11. Mary Ellen Bute working on *Tarantella*
1940, photo by Ted Nemeth Sr., courtesy KSB
Collection of MEB, YCAL.

In *Tarantella*, 1940, 5 minutes, 35mm, color film, colored squares and bars of light dance in a pattern similar to Mondrian's abstract paintings. *Tarantella* was directed by Mary Ellen Bute and produced by Ted Nemeth Studios. It was part of their Seeing Sound series. According to Nemeth, Bute photographed most of it herself before her first child, Theodore J. Nemeth, Jr. was born July 1, 1941.[96] It opens with definitions of Tarantella as a swift moving dance and also a spider. Colored squares and bars of light dance in Mondrian like patterns to a staccato rhythm. Flame like forms, reused footage from *Spook Sport*, dance. Piano music for *Tarantella* was composed and played by Edwin Gerschefsky, a Yale graduate who had studied composition with Arthur Schillinger. He later headed the music departments at Converse College, NC, at the University of New Mexico, and at the University of Georgia. *Tarantella* premiered at the Paris Theater in New York and had theatrical bookings here and abroad. Bute said about this film:

> "*Tarantella* is the last of this group I did for seven years. I used the printing process we had used in *Spook Sport*. It required three complete negatives. One to make the magenta, one to mask the cyan, and a third to mask the yellow."[97]

Bute, writing an undated typescript, "Composition in Color and Sound", probably a slide lecture to a film group ca. 1940, used *Tarantella* as an example of the counterpoint between color and sound "in a way that the complete composition is equally dependent on both materials".[98]

She commented:

> Edwin Gerschefski, a brilliant young composer, and I developed it from a series of rhythms which we worked out arithmetically. Gerschefski translating the mathematical composition into a dance for the piano and I translated it into color and linear forms. In this case, neither of us adhered to the mathematical composition very strictly but rather used it as a springboard.[99]

In the above quote, Bute clarified, especially in later films like *Color Rhapsodie*, that while she started with mathematical formulas derived from Schillinger's system to create compositions and to synchronize sound and image, she moved on to her own spontaneous, creative impulses, reflecting her positive disposition, high energy, and imagination. Bute commented on her working process:

In the last two subjects [*Escape* and *Spook Sport*], as well as in *Tarantella*, I made a graph of the musical composition and interpreted it in color so that I had the suggestion of colors and their time duration before me as I designed the film.[100]

In connection with an undated "Composition in Color and Sound" program, ca. 1940, Bute showed slides of a graph of her plotting of the colors for *Tarantella*. She explained her process as follows:

> We see the twelve semi tones of the octave *arbitrarily* related to twelve colors of the spectrum. They are: C–Red Violet, C#–Red, D–Red Orange, D#–Orange, E–Yellow Orange, E# or F–Yellow, F#–Yellow Green, G–Green, A–Blue, A#–Blue Violet, B–Violet, and C again is red violet, an octave higher in luminosity. We use seven degrees of luminosity to correspond with the seven octaves on the piano – with a key at the extreme top for white in all colors and one at the bottom for black. Various degrees of saturation would be achieved by using complementary colors in time succession or simultaneously in identical areas of the visual field. Colors adjacent in the spectrum would give us a color harmony.
>
> We can obtain contrast by opposing color, degrees of illumination or saturation.
>
> The spatial forms would be the result of the succession and arrangement of the color Pantones, lines and dots on the screen. So in composition with mobile color we take the shortest time interval which will evoke a reaction; in motion pictures is it a single frame of film or 1/24th of a second, and use it as a unit of measurement in working out our rhythms. This is represented by one box on the graph which also represents the shortest note or time interval in the musical composition. The other units are arrived at through addition. In *Tarantella*, one box on the graph represents one eighth note … And so we go on through the graph of the complete composition.[101]

Tarantella was selected in 2010 to be in the National Film Registry by the Library of Congress. With twenty-four frames per second, it has about

7,000 cell animations. It was in the opening exhibition of the Whitney Museum of American Art's new building at the bottom of the High Line in lower Manhattan in 2015 and in the Whitney's collection, as well as in the collections of MOMA, the George Eastman House, UW-Milwaukee, Center for Visual Music, Los Angeles, and Anthology Film Archives. It is also on Anthology Film Archives DVD set, *Unseen Cinema*, 2005.

After 1941, there was a major change in Bute, in her work, in the art world, and in the world at large. Mary Ellen became a mother, no doubt fulfilling her family's expectations and bringing her much joy, but also conflicting with competing demands on her time and energy. Filmmaking won out. The United States joined World War II December 7, 1941, after Pearl Harbor was attacked. Women increasingly took jobs vacated by service men, from factory workers to lawyers in firms headed by men, expanding women's horizons and expectations. Peggy Guggenheim opened The Art of the Century Gallery in New York in 1942 featuring contemporary European artists like Surrealist Max Ernst, but also Jackson Pollock. Pollock's Surrealism evolved into Abstract Expressionism, reflecting his emotional state rather than the world outside.

Summarizing Bute's approach to visual composition, filmmaker and author Lewis Jacobs wrote about Bute and Nemeth's films:

> Their films … were composed upon mathematical formulae, depicting in ever changing lights and shadows, growing lines and forms, deepening colors, and tones, the tumbling, racing impressions evoked by the musical accompaniment.
>
> Their compositions were synchronized sound and image following a chromatic scale or in counterpoint.[102]

In Jacobs' book *The Rise of the American Film*, he compared Bute's films, including *Tarantella*, and Fischinger's:

> At first glance, the Bute-Nemeth pictures seemed like an echo of the former German pioneer, Oscar Fischinger, one of the first to experiment with the problems of abstract motion and sound. Actually, they were variations of Fischinger's method, but less rigid in their patterns and choices of objects, tactile in their forms; more sensuous in their use of light and color rhythms, more concerned with the problems of depth …
>
> The difference … between the Bute-Nemeth pictures and Fischinger's came largely from a difference in technique. Fischinger worked with two-dimensional animated drawings [Note: in "An Optical Poem" he worked with paper cutouts]; Bute and Nemeth used any three-dimensional substance at hand: Ping-Pong balls, paper cutouts, sculptured models, cellophane, rhinestones, buttons, all the odds and ends picked up at the five and ten cent store. Fischinger used flat lighting on flat surfaces. [Note: he actually worked with an animation stand] Bute and Nemeth employed ingenious lighting and camera effects by shooting through long-focus lenses, prisms, distorting mirrors, ice cubes, etc. Both utilized a schematic process of composition.

Fischinger worked out his own method. Bute and Nemeth used Schillinger's mathematical system of composition as the basis for the visual and aural continuities and their interrelationship.

Along with their strangely beautiful pictorial effects and their surprising rhythmic patterns, the Bute-Nemeth "visual symphonies" often included effective theatrical patterns such as comedy, suspense, pathos, and drama[for example in *Spook Sport* and *Escape*] in the action of the objects, which lifted the films above the usual abstract films and made them interesting experiments in a new experience.[103]

In an article for *Films in Review*, Bute described her abstract films, as "Absolute Films", a movement in Germany in the 1920s of which Fischinger was a part:

The Absolute Film is not a new subject … This art is the interrelation of light, form, movement, and sound – combined and projected to stimulate an aesthetic idea. It is unassociated with ideas of religion, literature, ethics or decoration. Here light, form, and sound are in dynamic balance with kinetic space relations.[104]

In an interview, Bute said:

To achieve strong emotional reactions, we must charge our perceptive sensual apparatus with greater and more intense exciters. In the field of art these stronger exciters are synchronized art forms.[105]

Bute reported to her friend Virginia Gibbs Smyth that Disney had offered her a job, but that she told him the only one she wanted was his![106] This may not be a reliable statement, but it is possible and it does sound like Bute who never wanted anyone to limit her creative choices, as Disney surely would have done. Disney, according to Ted Nemeth, had seen Bute's early films before he made *Fantasia* in 1940. Interestingly Disney hired Oskar Fischinger to work on that film, the abstract animator whose work was the most like Bute's. However, Fischinger did not fit into the studio system with multiple people contributing to the development of the film. Also Fischinger's English was not good enough to communicate well with the diverse staff. Although his ideas were influential, his actual animation was not used in the final film.

Ethel Mae Gullette, wife of Bute's good friend Bill Gulette, who ran a screening studio in New York, said that Bute was supposed to have lunch with Disney in late 1946 before her son Jim was born, but that she was too sick to go.[107] Again this is possible. Mrs. Smyth reported that Mary Ellen Bute had suffered at least one if not two miscarriages before Jim was born, so she would have been careful about her health at this time, if at no other. James House Bute Nemeth was born January 8, 1947, by Caesarian, a risky procedure in those days.

Polka Graph, 1947, 4½ minutes in color, 35mm, directed by Mary Ellen Bute, produced by Ted Nemeth Studios. It still adhered to Schillinger's mathematical system for constructing the composition and synchronizing sound and image. Moving graph lines, squares, diamonds, rectangles, and dots, as well as stylized stars polka to the music from the ballet suite "The Age of Gold" by Shostakovich. Graphs lines dance up as the music ascends. Bute wrote that *Polka Graph* "uses the graph pattern of the music as a springboard for the visual interpretation".[108] There is a sense of fun! It was shown at the first run Sutton Theater in New York with the feature film "The Man in the White Suit", 1951. Cecile Starr, film historian and critic, suggested to Bute that she send *Polka Graph* to the 1952 Venice Film Festival.[109] Bute traveled there to do a story for the *New York Times*. *Polka Graph* won a prize. *Polka Graph* also won the Festival of Contemporary Art award, University of Illinois, 1953. It was included in an all Shostakovich TV program for CBS, February, 1978.

See Plate 7.
Polka Graph (1947), directed by Mary Ellen Bute, film still courtesy of Yale Film Study Center.

In *Polka* Graph the synchronization of sound and image look exact. Bute introduced the film with a few words about "Seeing Sound". She asked the viewers to let their eyes and ears dance, as the colored triangles, bars, dots, squiggles and stars do in the film. Often a xylophone going up a scale can be heard synchronized with a rising colored graph line. Some images suggest the colored rectangles used by Mondrian in his abstract paintings.

Bute said about this film:

> By 1947 color film was greatly improved. However, to get color as the eye sees it, each color needed a different exposure. Technicolor got around this by exposing for the skin tones – and painting the trees, shrubbery, sets, props, costumes, so that the colors would be as compatible as possible. With independent abstract film it was a real question as to which end of the palette to favor ... .[110]

Later Bute commented on Schillinger's mathematical system that she used in *Polka Graph*:

> With numbers you could analyze what had been done and then by expanding or contracting or permutating you could get the most fabulous new material. I started out with it as an exercise and then did *Polka Graph* on that system of graph projection.[111]

Clarifying this process, Bute said:

> My animation was in the non-objective area. I tried to do it to sounds of music that appealed to me; they were developed either in direct line with the sound or in counterpoint to it. I worked for quite a while with the great musicologist, Joseph Schillinger, and he would make graphs of the music and put it through

all of its permutations – expand one element, contract the other. That's the sort of thing I did visually with sound.[112]

Ted Nemeth Sr. said, "M.E. liked *Polka Graph*, 1947, and *Color Rhapsodie*, 1948. She had been working with graph paper to analyze the sound."[113] After Jim Nemeth was born (January 8, 1947), Bute seemed to break loose from the restrictions of Schillinger's mathematical system and freely express her emotions through color and moving forms. The improvement of color film helped her transition, as did her exposure to Abstract Expressionism at New York museums and galleries.

Polka Graph is in the collection of Anthology Film Archives, MOMA, the New York Public Library for the Performing Arts, the Yale Film Study Center, UW-Milwaukee, and the Center for Visual Music, Los Angeles. It is on CVM's 2017 DVD *Visual Music 1947–1986*.

Bute's paintings at this time pushed way beyond the style and subjects of Rosa Bonheur's lively, realistic horses, one of her early influences. Her 1948 *Sketch # 1 for the Loved Ones* (a film short, never produced, after Evelyn Waugh) depicts a stylized black cat projecting out of a colored background with swirling lines and amorphous colored forms, some with a geometric pattern, on top of flat areas of color. The composition combines a surrealistic image of a menacing, black cat-like shadow with the flat color areas of Abstract Expressionism and the ebullient spirit and energy of Mary Ellen Bute.

See Plate 8.
Mary Ellen Bute, *Sketch # 1* for *The Loved Ones* (a film short after Evelyn Waugh, never produced) 1948, oil on canvas, 15 x 12 ¾ in., Collection of Matthew Nemeth, photo courtesy Kit Smyth Basquin.

Imagination, 1948, 3 min abstract film in color, 35mm, without titles, set to the music of "Imagination", was seen on NBC television by millions of people on the Steve Allen Show, for which it was created. Directed by Mary Ellen Bute, filmed by Ted Nemeth, characteristic of Bute's other films, abstract and geometric forms moved in syncopation to the popular song "Imagination". Clouds float across the background. Images in the foreground include flowers, squares, spirals and the crossed rods seen in Bute's 1935 film *Synchromy No. 2*. *Saturday Review* film critic Gilbert Seldes wrote about *Imagination*: " … surrealist film … unreal and delectable shapes floating about … the work of Mary Ellen Bute … a pioneer in this sort of thing whose talents should be more often used.[114] *Imagination* is in the collections of MOMA, UW-Milwaukee, and the Center for Visual Music, Los Angles.

Bute, in her last short subjects, especially *Color Rhapsodie*, 1948, was clearly influenced by Abstract Expressionism for her amorphous bursts of color, billowing clouds, and linear abstract forms. Peggy Guggenheim's gallery,

Art of the Century, exhibited surrealistic and abstract works by Jackson Pollock, Robert Motherwell, and Mark Rothko. *Color Rhapsodie* expressed Mary Ellen's joyous personality and energetic movement.

Color Rhapsodie, 1948, some think, was Bute's most beautiful short. Bute and Nemeth agreed on this. Her later shorts with the addition of the jittery imagery of the oscilloscope were technologically innovative, but less harmonious. The oscilloscope imagery, while energizing, distracted from the abstract backgrounds of color blocks and super-imposed linear constructions.

See Plate 9.
Color Rhapsodie (1948) directed by Mary Ellen Bute, courtesy of Yale Film Study Center.

Color Rhapsodie, 1948, 6 minutes in color, 35mm. As with some of Bute's films, she introduced it with instructions to the viewer about "seeing sound". Beautiful explosions of color in the foreground animate flowing color variations painted on glass with red cloud formations, to the music of *Hungarian Rhapsody # 2* by Franz Liszt. Soft focus reds, blues, greens, pinks and yellows float across the film frame like tinted clouds. These images were akin to Mark Rothko's rectangular blocks of amorphous color and Robert Motherwell's abstract expressionist canvases with minimal images and expanses of flat color. Colored lines spiral toward the viewer and at times away, creating a sense of three-dimensions. Shaped colors dance over checkerboards, synchronized to music. The tempos of the music and images speed up. Concentric circles move forward and back. At the time this film was released, thirty-nine feature film houses across the country were booking Bute's experimental short films.[115] This film premiered at Radio City Music Hall in 1951 and screened there for seven weeks. It also showed at the Criterion Theater in New York, with the feature film "Hans Christian Anderson", among many bookings. Jonas Mekas wrote for the *Soho Weekly News*, "I like the romantic flair of *Color Rhapsodie*, its visual density ... I think it is time to re-see and re-evaluate all of Bute's work in a new light".[116] Ted Sr. said: "*Color Rhapsodie* took a long time. Variety of effects. I liked it the best. And *Mood Contrasts*."[117] These films came alive as moving abstract paintings, which Bute created with light, fulfilling her ambition to synchronize light, color, and motion into an art form.

Ann Holmes, Fine Arts editor of the *Houston Chronicle* later captured the magic of Bute's *Color Rhapsodie*:

> The film urges the eyes to "see" the music in a swirling, shifting panorama of forms, and abstract color thoughts and visual rhythms ... there is nothing mechanical or accidental about the patterns which swim before your eyes on her films. Each movement, each color, each dissolving pattern was planned, carefully devised and impeccably timed with the music.[118]

Fig. 12. Kit Smyth (Basquin) and Teddy Nemeth ca. 1949 age 8 at Miss Harris's dance
class, New York City. Photo by Ted Nemeth Sr.,
courtesy KSB Collection of MEB, YCAL.

Film critic Howard Thompson of the *New York Times* in an interview
with Mary Ellen Bute, said that she used:

> Two large Mitchell, Hollywood-type cameras, three smaller Bell & Howell
> cameras and a separate animation camera for her 'flat art drawing.' Each "frame"
> is gauged to one second of camera speed, requiring three drawings in the case
> of multiple-color work … her experimental standby is an optical printer, a
> machine which she claims can do all but flip an egg.[119]

Bute said about her short experimental abstract films:

> I'm convinced that this new interest by the public is simply an adjustment to
> what was always there. The war, for one thing, made us aware of new horizons
> in all directions. For years I've studied, explored and experimented in art and
> music in schools all over the East. Now I'm simply combining music and the
> visual in my own way. And when the public responds, somehow you feel you
> have the right answer.[120]

Color Rhapsodie is in the collections of Anthology Film Archives, the Yale
Film Study Center, UW-Milwaukee, and the Center for Visual Music,
Los Angeles. It is on CVM's 2017 DVD *Visual Music 1947–1986*.

New Sensations in Sound, 1949, a 3-minute color, 35mm film, produced
for RCA TV. It contains a collage of effects from previous Bute films and
some new images. The sound track is a catchy jingle. It is in the collections
of MOMA, the George Eastman House, and the Center for Visual Music,
Los Angeles, Los Angeles.

Fig. 13. Mary Ellen Bute painting on glass for a
film background, ca. 1948, photo by Margery
Markley Courtesy KSB Collection of MEB,

In the late 1940s, Bute rented a house and spent some summers at
Candlewood, New York. Her mother, Clare Bute, came up from Texas
to babysit for the boys. There was also a housekeeper who cooked and
cleaned. Mary Ellen Bute would visit every second weekend and continue
to work on her films in the city.[121] One summer, she found Nemeth in
the arms of a young actress at a summer theater near where they rented
their house. She was furious![122] As Margo Lion said, "Ted ran around".
Marilyn Ripp commented, "Ted flaunted his women, but professionally
he couldn't be beat. That's why she [Mary Ellen] stayed ... Ted disillu-
sioned her ... She treated him badly."[123] However, Bute preferred to
smooth the surface socially, as she was trained to do by her conservative
Southern family. Jim Nemeth said later that his mother never cooked a
meal. First a housekeeper did the cooking and then when she left, Ted
Nemeth, Sr. cooked and bought the groceries.[124] Ted Nemeth, Sr. later
said "I was sorry that I couldn't treat Mary Ellen as an equal, but my
European upbringing wouldn't allow me to do that.[125]

Pastorale, 1950, 9 minutes, color, 35mm, directed by Mary Ellen Bute,
produced by Ted Nemeth in Musikolor. Ted Nemeth also was the
cinematographer. Music conductor Leopold Stokowski appears on film
dressed formally in white tie and tails. In soft focus he directs on camera
his own arrangement of "Sheep May Safely Graze", from Johann Se-
bastian Bach's Contata No. 208, also called *Birthday Cantata*, in honor of
Duke Christian who commissioned it for his birthday in 1713. Stokowski

turns to different parts of the orchestra off camera, actually just a sound recording. The sound recording is by Philips of the Resedentie Orchestra, Den Haag, Holland. Bute had met Stokowski years before when she had shown him her first film in 1934. Words in the beginning of *Pastorale* say that this is a "Visual Interpretation by Mary Ellen Bute". She knew Walt Disney's 1940 feature film *Fantasia* with Stokowski directing *Bach's Toccata and Fugue* in D minor on camera, music Bute had used in 1937 in *Escape*. Bute probably couldn't resist referencing Disney in her own work. Bute's short is more abstract and has softer imagery than Disney's feature, and in parts has more tightly synchronized music with images. Filmmaker Hilary Harris, who assisted on *Pastorale* said that he poured thick cream into an aquarium of coffee to create the undulating forms in the background of the film. Sparklers and other light effects were also used.[126] Disney's feature incorporates multiple whimsical characters throughout. Disney's animated characters distract from the emotional power of the music. Bute's abstract images reflect the notes and rhythms, a more effective interpretation of a Bach piece.

Ted Nemeth said that for *Fantasia*, Disney recorded the music first, then added the images. Bute's process was to shoot the images on paper and then break down the music bar by bar to synchronize with the visuals. Images were designed for each musical sequence and timed to cover the number of frames needed.[127]

See Plate 10.
Leopold Stokowski in Film still of *Pastorale* (ca. 1950), directed by Mary Ellen Bute,
courtesy Yale Film Study Center.

Bute's film *Pastorale* premiered at the Paris Theater in New York, with the feature "Seven Deadly Sins". Nemeth said: "I enjoyed Stokowski![128] Bute reportedly split her good profits with the conductor.[129] *Pastorale* was distributed widely by Harold Weiss. It is in the collections of the Yale Film Study Center, UW-Milwaukee, and the Center for Visual Music, Los Angeles.

At that time, Nemeth also was working as a cinematographer on another film *Mobilcolor*, 1952, 16mm film documenting Charles Dockum's Mobilcolor performance at the Guggenheim Museum that year. Charles Dockum, a Texan working in California, with an electrical engineering degree from Texas A & M, invented a large projection instrument that created moving colored light forms on a screen, controlled by an operator, essentially creating silent symphonies of light. He built many different Mobilcolor Projectors. The Solomon R. Guggenheim Foundation funded his experiments from about 1942–1952.

Dockum died in 1977. In about 1980, his wife Gretchen wanted to make a film about his work. Bute was to direct it. Ted Nemeth was to be the cinematographer, and Cecile Starr the script writer. Unfortunately, Mrs. Dockum died before the work could be completed. A rough cut exists in the Dockum collection at the Center for Visual Music, Los Angeles.

Hilla Rebay, called "Baroness" because of her family social status in her native Alsace, advised Solomon Guggenheim, leading him away from traditional art to contemporary non-objective work. She directed the Museum of Non-Objective Painting, which opened with temporary quarters on West 54th Street in May, 1939, and would later become the Guggenheim Museum. Rebay, a painter herself, who spoke German, French, and English, had many avant-garde artist friends in France and Germany, where she had grown up, who led her to the work of Kandinsky and others. She believed that non-objective art had a spiritual quality and differed from abstract art because it was not abstracted from Nature. She had acquired Bute's *Spook Sport* for the Museum, but was not interested in her other shorts with realistic references such as arches and flowers.

However, Hilla Rebay awarded several grants to abstract film animator Oskar Fischinger, who is sometimes compared to Bute. The Baroness could be charming and captivating, but also dogmatic and exasperating. Ted Nemeth described her as "difficult".[130] She believed that film was an art form of the future and wanted to establish a film center for non-objective films at the Guggenheim, which she discussed with Fischinger, who drew up plans for the center. When Solomon R. Guggenheim died in 1949, support for the film center was dropped.[131]

Abstronic in 1952 and *Mood Contrasts* in 1953 were Mary Ellen Bute's last abstract animated shorts, before she moved on to live-action films. At the age of forty-six, with the help of scientists, she finally found a tool for drawings with light, using an oscilloscope, a search that started when she was a teen-age painter at the Pennsylvania Academy of Fine Art, inspired by the abstract paintings of Kandinsky.

With these last two works, Bute had created fourteen short animated films synchronizing drawn images and sometimes moving models with music frame by frame according to Joseph Schillinger's mathematical system. However, she began to get tired of all the work involved with creating the thousands of drawings or paintings involved with producing an animated short. She said in an interview for the American Film Institute:

> When I worked with Schillinger I was also working with Leon Theremin on that marvelous Theremin wave machine. On the first five or six films I did, I would work day and night, do all of the art work and everything myself. Finally I decided it was too much work and maybe I would just relax and amuse myself

by letting these things go on in my mind. Than Ralph Potter who worked at Bell Telephone Labs asked to see my films when I said I was throwing in the sponge and I told him why. I also told him about my work with Theremin, how we had immersed little mirrors in tubes of oil and connected them with an oscillator and drawn with them. He said, 'That's nothing but a cathode ray oscilloscope. You buy one and I'll show you how to modify it.' So I did and I did electronically animated films which were much easier than frame-by-frame drawings.[132]

Film critic Cecile Starr said that she received a letter on Radio City Music Hall stationery in 1952 suggesting that she might be interested in seeing Mary Ellen Bute's film that was showing. On reflection, Starr thought that the letter was probably written by Bute. She could have gotten the stationery from her high school friend James Stuart Morcom, who was the Art Director at Radio City Music Hall. In 1952, Cecile wrote the following critique for *Saturday Review*:

> It is certainly noteworthy that a virtually unknown independent animator has had two of her "seeing sound" abstractions shown this year at the Radio City Music Hall, the largest motion picture theatre in the world. Mary Ellen Bute is an energetic painter from Texas who began making her hand-drawn films nearly twenty years ago with a short abstraction set to the strains of "Anitra's Dance". When wifely and motherly duties permitted, she concentrated on work (in her husband's commercial animation studio), and has come up with an impressive number of items. This year her "Spook Sport" and "Color Rhapsodie" were shown at the Music Hall, while a third film "Polka Graph" won mention at the Venice Film Festival. Granted that the familiar acceptability of the music (Lizst, Greig, etc.) is a good basis for audience and theatre approval, still this is no minor triumph for Miss Bute, her work, and the experimentalists who follow hopefully.[133]

The best summaries of Bute's creative and technical processes are by the filmmaker herself writing about "Abstronic" a title made up of the words for "abstractions" and "electronics", suggested to Bute by critic Albert Tomkins, Bute said:

> Of the ten films I made, two were not abstract: one, *Escape*, was based on a simple plot set against a musical background, and employed geometric figures for the action; the other was about the parabolic curve [*Parbola*]. The abstract films were made by the animation technique, that is, by use of countless drawings on paper. In this 'cartoon' technique, the spontaneity of the artist's concept and design becomes extremely attenuated.[134]

Bute went on to describe her work with Dr. Ralph Potter of Bell telephone Laboratories. She ended by saying:

> The resulting beauty and *movement* contain intimations of occurrences in the sub-atomic world that hitherto have been access to the human mind merely as mathematical possibilities.[135]

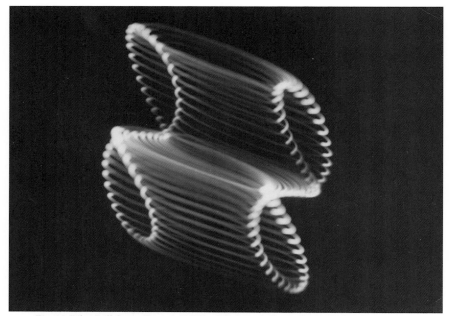

Fig. 14. Film Still from *Abstronic* (1952), showing oscilloscope image, directed by Mary Ellen Bute. Courtesy KSB Collection of MEB, YCAL.

In customary Bute formal writing style, she claimed grandiose feats for the possibilities of her research:

> I venture to predict that the forms and compositions artists can create on the oscilloscope, and organize and preserve on motion picture film, will not only give aesthetic pleasure to all kinds of men and women in all climes and times, but will help theoretical physicists and mathematicians to uncover more secrets of the inanimate world.[136]

Abstronic, 1952, 6 minutes, in color, 35mm, part of Seeing Sound Series, a Ted Nemeth Studios Production, directed by Mary Ellen Bute. Bute incorporated the use of an oscilloscope in *Abstronic*. Before that, in 1949, she had used the oscilloscope in her short film *New Sensations in Sound*, before Norman McLaren employed it for the National Film Board of Canada in 1951.

Opening words of *Abstronic* say, "Electronic Abstracts to Music". The colored background forms, like colored cream floating in coffee, are soft focus. The electronic images vibrate in the foreground. Background starry skies, targets, and spirals move toward the viewer and at times away. Behind the oscilloscope images, circles, spirals, squares, and lights dance to the music of Aaron Copland's "Hoe Down" and to "Ranch House Party" by Don Gillis, recalling Bute's Texas roots. Bute combined two films, one for each piece of music.

Bute said:

> The figures and forms in *Abstronic* have been hand colored. But I have been promised three-color electronic tubes. If these prove successful, the last animation technique I still employ can be eliminated.[137]

The *New York Herald Tribune* wrote:

> Free-wheeling patterns painted on neither canvas nor paper, but on the screen of an oscilloscope, an instrument which converts electric impulses into ever-moving visual patterns. The artist is Mary Ellen Bute, a long-time experimenter in musical-abstract films. While she juggled dials, recordings of work by Aaron Copland and Don Gillis were played on the oscilloscope. The result – fascinating, complex, rhythmic ribbons of light.[138]

Lillian Schiff described the images in detail:

> At the controls of her instrument, Bute created light forms: wheels within wheels, lively ghosts, combinations of curves, lariats, ovals, disks, parabolas. She moved the forms electronically in a series of whirlings, twirlings, vortexings, zoomings, pinweelings, splittings, somersaultings, all in counterpoint to backgrounds of endless roadways, a sunset, a diamond. As she directed the light forms onto the fluorescent screen of the cathode ray tube, their action was photographed.[139]

About this time, Fine Arts Editor, Ann Holmes of the *Houston Chronicle* said about Mary Ellen Bute's use of electronic imagery:

> An unlikely instrument called the cathode ray oscilloscope has become a new art medium. The electronic device from the age of Buck Rogers, in the hands of a sensitive artist like Mary Ellen Bute, has become a tool in an unusual career which has led that former Houstonian to some of the world's most coveted awards, top honors at the Venice and Edinburgh Film Festivals.
>
> Miss Bute worked most often in abstract film patterns, tied in with selected music. If you remember Walt Disney's "Fantasia", you'll know the general field in which she works.[140]

Abstronic is in the collections of Anthology Film Archives, MOMA, the New York Public Library for the Performing Arts, UW-Milwaukee, and the Center for Visual Music, Los Angeles. It is on CVM's DVD *Visual Music 1947–1986*.

That same year, 1952, Radio City Music Hall projected Bute's animated color patterns on a giant curtain as a background for a circus parade.[141] Her school friend from Houston, James Stewart Morcom, was art director there at the time, responsible for the scenery. He no doubt thought of projecting Bute's contemporary images as part of his set.

Mood Contrasts, 1953, 7 min. color, 35mm, part of the Seeing Sound film series, electronically animated short, directed by Mary Ellen Bute. This was a Ted Nemeth Studios production. Ted Nemeth was the cinematographer. Words introduce the short:

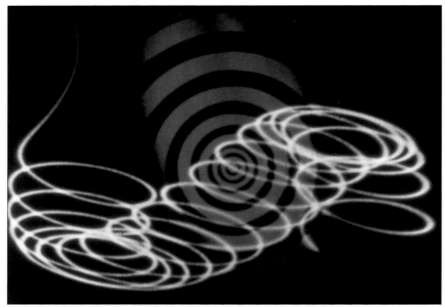

Fig. 15. Film still of *Mood Contrasts*, directed by Mary Ellen Bute.
© Center for Visual Music, Los Angeles.

"Actual Pictures of Sound Captured on a Cathode Ray Oscilloscope … must enter the eye as well as the ear." Opening credits also say: "pioneering electronic animation of Rimsky Korsakov's music, 'Hymn to the Sun,' and 'Dance of the Tumblers,' a 35 mm motion picture sound film in Eastman color."

Oscilloscope images float in the foreground over checkerboards and abstract colored backgrounds. Blues, greens, purples, reds, and yellows blow like smoke behind the vibrating oscilloscope images, reflecting the Abstract Expressionism of Mark Rothko and Robert Motherwell, fashionable in the art world at the time. The tempo speeds up in the middle of the short. Sparklers, swirls, abstract stars, and light beams enrich the patterns and increase the energy of the moving images, more like the action paintings of Jackson Pollock, reflecting his internal moods.

A plaid light screen evolves into reflecting surfaces, recalling Mondrian's grids with colored rectangles. This beautiful film won a prize at the Brussels International Film Festival 1958 for the Best Short Film and showed at Radio City Music Hall with the feature, *The Barretts of Wimpole Street*.

Jesse Zunser in "Kinetic Space" wrote in *Cue Magazine*: "An abstract film which in this fashion provides, in the making as well as the seeing and listening one of the most thrilling experiences the motion picture affords".[142] Bute's film is believed to have been the first electronically animated film shown in a commercial theater.[143] *New York Times* film critic Howard Thompson said:

> A charmingly lyrical interpretation of Rimsky-Korsokov's "Hymn to the Sun" the colors float across the screen forming and transforming with dream-like beauty while capturing the mysterious Oriental mood of the music.[144]

Ted Nemeth Sr. described the technical production:

> For *Mood Contrasts* we used an oscilloscope, high contrast, single role. It was complex. We couldn't remember how we did it. There is no depth to an oscilloscope image. We had to create depth. The image was reproduced on the front of a magazine. At the film festival in Brussels, they ran the film outside the building on a new screen. Mary Ellen went to Brussels, and Cannes, and Venice.[145]

All of Bute's fourteen animated shorts interpreted music with visual images mostly abstract, but sometimes with sculpture, as in the case of *Parabola*, or inanimate objects, such as ping pong balls, stairs or ladders. She created images for the music that you might hear in your head while watching the movement of the forms and colors. Some of these, especially *Color Rhapsodie* and also *Mood Contrasts*, were particularly beautiful as colored forms floated, ran, or bounced through space synchronized to classical music reflecting Bute's positive nature and boundless energy. In an interview, Bute projected the possibilities of abstract, non-narrative film:

> I think we might really get cameras and film that can record and capture things that we can't see with our eyes today, because naturally all of our sense organs, eyes, ears, everything, they're evolving too. As we progress, these sense organs become more and more sensitized.

Asked in 1974 to comment on the direction of animation in the future, Bute said:

> I think it's terrific. It's all across the board. Films by women screened in Los Angeles recently fascinated me because of the great variety. Some of it is very realistic, some completely abstract, a lot surrealistic. There seems to be no one influence. It's all very inventive and very independent.[146]

When asked why more women were working in animation, than when Bute started and was one of the few women experimenting in the medium, she answered:

> I think the reason is that it's a possible field. In animation you can go off in a corner and do your work fairly inexpensively, and then you go and show it. Like a painter would go off into a studio and paint. I think it's fabulous that more women are making films. It really is, there's no question about it.[147]

The most knowledgeable and comprehensive evaluation of Bute's shorts was by William Moritz, Professor and scholar of abstract animation and also a filmmaker. He said:

Oskar Fischinger had almost uncanny synchronization, careful control of color, music and forms, but he was an engineer and could design his own equipment. These opportunities were not there for Mary Ellen Bute … Mary Ellen created out of intense desire to do it. She was enormously successful in getting her films shown at prestigious theaters like Radio City Music Hall…Probably some of the reused images [in some of her films] were dictated by Ted, who was watching the budget … Tarantella … and Pastorale … have soft, nuanced footage, perfect coordination with music – balance between sound, color, music … Images she got were interesting, out of focus, softened … She was a formative influence on Norman McLaren … Her use of titles [educational introductory texts] for audiences who had never seen this before … Her titles were perhaps necessary at the time. McLaren learned about them from her … .

She's important as a pioneer filmmaker making up what she was doing, not copying, who showed her films in front of large, public audiences in the 1930s and 40s. She has a strong sense of being in an abstract tradition. Some of her flaws may be due to Ted's compromises, not with Mary Ellen's aesthetic vision, with tight budgets and deadlines.

Such a lovely person. So respectful of other filmmakers. She considered Oskar Fischinger a master. She was a special person. There was a sweetness in her personality that was in the best of her films.[148]

Bute loved working in abstract animation. She had almost complete control over her compositions, within her limited finances. She accomplished what she set out to do, creating moving drawings with light on film. For whatever reason, just as she had seemingly reached her goal, she started all over with live action film, although she continued to incorporate animation techniques in these, linking her two bodies of work. Larry Kardish, Curator of Film at the Museum of Modern Art, called attention to this connection:

We had always admired her work and wanted to relate her shorts to *Finnegans Wake*, both are abstract films, pure abstract and narrative abstract.[149]

Bute talked about her move from abstract animated films with electronic images to live action:

I did several electronically animated films which were much easier than the frame-by-frame drawings. I was going like great guns with those when suddenly I decided to try actors and actresses. Well, that's a woman's prerogative, isn't it?[150]

Mary Ellen Bute would gain more recognition for her experimental treatment of James Joyce's night dream, *Finnegans Wake,* than for her experimental abstract films, but they were very much a part of her feature. She used a vocabulary of animation techniques to create a surrealistic response to Mary Manning's play, *Passages from James Joyce's Finnegans Wake*.

References

1. Cecile Starr, "Programming Early Avant-Garde Films", *Sightlines* (New York: Educational Film Library Association, Winter 79/80) 19–20, Kit Smyth Basquin Collection of Mary Ellen Bute, Yale Collection of American Literature, Beinecke Rare Book and Manuscript Library.

2. Mary Ellen Bute, transcript of interview with Ramona Javitz, Picture Curator at New York Public Library, 5/4/1976, KSB Collection of MEB, YCAL.

3. William Moritz, *Optical Poetry: The Life and Works of Oskar Fischinger*,(John Libbey Publishing, 2004), 70.

4. William Moritz, *Optical Poetry: The Life and Works of Oskar Fischinger*, (John Libbey Publishing, 2004), 3.

5. "Expanding Cinema's Synchromy # 2", Letters and Art Column, *Literary Digest*, August 8, 1936, www.centerforvisualmusic.org/ButeBiblio.htm.

6. William Moritz, transcript of telephone interview with author 6/8/1987, KSB Collection of MEB, YCAL.

7. Lewis Jacobs, filmmaker, author, and critic, transcript of telephone interview with author 5/28/1987, KSB Collection of MEB, YCAL.

8. Lewis Jacobs, transcript of telephone interview with author 5/28/1987, KSB Collection of MEB, YCAL.

9. Albert Glinsky, *Theremin: Ether Music and Espionage* (Urbana: University of Illinois Press, 2000), 131.

10. Albert Glinsky, *Theremin: Ether Music and Espionage* (Urbana: University of Illinois Press, 2000) 139.

11. Mary Ellen Bute, Art Institute of Chicago, May 9, 1976, transcript of public interview with film critic Stanley Kauffmann, KSB Collection of MEB, YCAL.

12. Theodore J. Nemeth, Sr., transcript of telephone interview with author 5/25/1984, KSB Collection of MEB, YCAL.

13. Lillian Shiff, independent writer with special interest in film, interview with Mary Ellen Bute July, 1983, *Film Library Quarterly* 17, nos. 2–4 (1984), 53–61, KSB Collection of MEB, YCAL.

14. Mary Ellen Bute, typescript of Leon Theremin's report to the New York Musicological Society, January 31, 1932, KSB Collection of MEB, YCAL.

15. Albert Glinsky, *Theremin: Ether Music and Espionage* (Urbana: University of Illinois Press, 2000), 138.

16. Mary Ellen Bute, transcript of interview with Kaye Sullivan, KSB Collection of MEB, YCAL.

17. Mary Ellen Bute, "Light as an Art Material and Its Possible Synchronization with Sound", Typescript of paper read before The New York Musicological Society, January 31, 1932, KSB Collection of MEB, YCAL.

18. Mary Ellen Bute, typescript of talk to the Pittsburgh Filmmakers 6/30/1982, KSB Collection of MEB, YCAL.

19. Mary Ellen Bute, typescript of Guggenheim Grant application, 1932, KSB Collection of MEB, YCAL.

20. Albert Glinsky, *Theremin: Ether Music and Espionage* (Urbana and Chicago: University of Illinois Press, 2000) 131.

21. Mary Ellen Bute, typescript of Guggenheim Grant application, 1932, KSB Collection of MEB, YCAL.

22. Theodore J. Nemeth Jr., transcript of tape answering author's questions 11/8/1988, KSB Collection of MEB, YCAL.

23. Lewis Jacobs, transcript of telephone interview with author 5/28/1987, KSB Collection of MEB, YCAL.

24. Lewis Jacobs, transcript of telephone interview with author 5/28/1987, KSB, Collection of MEB, YCAL.

25. Lewis Jacobs transcript of telephone interview with author 5/28/1987, KSB Collection of MEB, YCAL.

26. Mary Ellen Bute, transcript of interview with Ramona Javitz, Picture Curator at New York Public Library, 5/4/1976, KSB Collection of MEB, YCAL.

27. Marilyn Ripp, friend of Mary Ellen Bute from Parkside Salvation Army Residence in the 1970s, transcript of telephone interview with author 6/26/1984, KSB Collection of MEB, YCAL.

28. James Steward Morcom, Texas school friend of Mary Ellen Bute, transcript of telephone interview with author, 9/20/84, KSB Collection of MEB, YCAL.

29. Albert Glinsky, *Theremin: Ether Music and Espionage* (Urbana: University of Illinois Press, 2000), 143.

30. Albert Glinsky, *Theremin: Ether Music and Espionage* (Urbana: University of Illinois Press, 2000), 309.

31. Louis Jacobs, transcript of telephone interview with author 5/28/1987, KSB Collection of MEB, YCAL.

32. Albert Glinsky, *Theremin: Ether Music and Espionage* (Urbana: University of Illinois Press, 2000), 174–175, 190.

33. Mary Ellen Bute, transcript of interview with Ramona Javitz 5/4/1976, KSB Collection of MEB, YCAL.

34. Mary Ellen Bute, transcript of interview with Ramona Javitz 5/4/1976, KSB Collection of MEB, YCAL.

35. Mary Ellen Bute, typescript of talk to the Pittsburgh Filmmakers 6/30/1982, KSB Collection of MEB, YCAL.

36. Theodore J. Nemeth Sr., transcript of interview in New York with author, 5/30/84, KSB Collection of MEB, YCAL.

37. Louis Jacobs, transcript of telephone interview with author 5/28/1987, KSB Collection of MEB, YCAL.

38. Virginia Gibbs Smyth, mother of author and life-long friend of Mary Ellen, transcript of telephone interview with author 12/26/1985, KSB Collection of MEB, YCAL.

39. Theodore J. Nemeth Sr., transcript of interview in New York with author, 5/30/1984, KSB Collection of MEB, YCAL.

40. Theodore J. Nemeth Sr., transcript of interview in New York with author, 5/30/1984, KSB Collection of MEB, YCAL.

41. Theodore J. Nemeth Sr., transcript of interview with author in Milwaukee 11/22/1984, KSB Collection of MEB, YCAL.

42. Theodore J. Nemeth, Sr., transcript of interview with author in New York 5/30/1984, KSB Collection of MEB, YCAL.

43. Theodore J. Nemeth Sr., transcript of interview with author in New York 5/30/1984, KSB Collection of MEB, YCAL.

44. Theordore J. Nemeth Sr., transcript of interview with author in New York 5/30/1984, KSB Collection of MEB, YCAL.

45. Cecile Starr, aged almost ninety-three, film historian, critic, teacher and Mary Ellen's film distributor after *Finnegans Wake*, transcript of telephone interview with author August 1, 2014, personal collection of Kit Smyth Basquin.

46. Thelma Schoonmaker, later film editor for Martin Scorsese's films, who worked on Mary Ellen Bute's "Passages from Finnegans Wake", transcript of video interview with author ca. 1995 for Larry Mollott's film on Mary Ellen Bute, never completed, audio tape in personal collection of the author.

47. William Moritz, film scholar, professor, author, and filmmaker, transcript of video interview with Larry Mollot, ca. 1995, for film on Mary Ellen Bute never produced, audio tape in personal collection of the author.

48. Mary Ellen Bute, interview for American Film Institute, summer 1974, KSB Collection of MEB, YCAL.

49. Lillian Schiff, interview with Mary Ellen Bute July, 1983, *Film Library Quarterly* 17, nos. 2–4 (1984), 53–61, KSB Collection of MEB, YCAL.

50. Mary Ellen Bute, transcript of talk with Stanley Kauffmann at the Art Institute of Chicago, 5/9/1976, KSB Collection of MEB, YCAL.

51. Theodore J. Nemeth Sr., transcript of interview with author in New York 5/30/1984, KSB Collection of MEB, YCAL.

52. William Moritz, videotaped interview with Larry Mollot for film on Mary Ellen Bute never produced ca. 1995, audio tape in the personal collection of Kit Smyth Basquin.

53. Lillian Schiff, interview with Mary Ellen Bute, *Film Library Quarterly* 17, nos. 2–4 (1984), pp. 53–61, KSB Collection of MEB, YCAL.

54. Mary Ellen Bute, interview for American Film Institute, summer, 1974, KSB Collection of MEB, YCAL.

55. Theodore J. Nemeth Sr., transcript of interview with author in New York 5/30/1984, KSB Collection of MEB, YCAL.

56. Mary Ellen Bute transcript of interview with Peter Wintonick, Montreal, Canada, in November, 1982, for Cinergy Films, Inc., KSB Collection of MEB, YCAL.

57. Theodore J. Nemeth Sr., transcript of interview with author in New York, 5/30/1984, MEB, YCAL

58. Theodore J. Nemeth Sr., transcript of interview with author in New York, 5/30/1984, MEB, YCAL.

59. Theodore J. Nemeth Sr., transcript of interview with author in New York, 5/30/1984, KSB Collection of MEB, YCAL.

60. Mary Ellen Bute, "Expanding Cinema's Synchromy 2", *Literary Digest* (August 8, 1936), KSB Collection of MEB, YCAL.

61. Mary Ellen Bute, "Expanding Cinema's Synchromy 2", *Literary Digest* (August 8, 1936), KSB Collection of MEB, YCAL.

62. Theodore J. Nemeth, Sr., transcript of interview with author in New York, 5/30/1984, KSB Collection of MEB, YCAL.

63. Mary Ellen Bute, "Expanding Cinema's Synchromy 2", *Literary Digest* (August 8, 1936), KSB Collection of MEB, YCAL.

64. Mary Ellen Bute, "Expanding Cinema's Synchromy 2", *Literary Digest* (August 8, 1936), KSB Collection of MEB, YCAL.

65. Mary Ellen Bute, "Expanding Cinema's Synchromy 2", *Literary Digest* (August 8, 1936), KSB Collection of MEB, YCAL.

66. Mary Ellen Bute, quoted by Jesse Zunser, art critic, *Cue*, ca 1936, in publicity compiled by Mary Ellen Bute, KSB Collection of MEB, YCAL.

67. Jesse Zunser, film critic for *Cue* Magazine, ca. 1936, quoted in notes on program for showing at Collective for Living Cinema, November 20, 1981 by Cecile Starr, KSB Collection of MEB, YCAL.

68. Theodore J. Nemeth, Sr., transcript of interview with author in Milwaukee 11/22/1984, KSB Collection of MEB, YCAL.

69. William Moritz, transcript of telephone interview with author 6/8/1987, KSB Collection of MEB, YCAL.

70. William Moritz, transcript of telephone interview with author 6/8/1987, KSB Collection of MEB, YCAL.

71. Mary Ellen Bute, interview for American Film Institute, Summer, 1974, KSB Collection of MEB, YCAL.

72. Mary Ellen Bute, testimonial in William Moritz, *Optical Poetry: The Life and Work of Oskar Fischinger*, (Eastleigh, UK, John Libbey Publishing, 2004), 163.

73. Lillian Schiff, interview with Mary Ellen Bute July 1983, *Film Library Quarterly* 17, nos. 2–4 (1984), 53–61, KSB Collection of MEB, YCAL.

74. Theodore J. Nemeth, Sr., transcript of interview with author in Milwaukee 11/22/1984, KSB Collection of MEB, YCAL.

75. Cecile Starr, undated film notes ca. 1995, KSB Collection of MEB, YCAL.

76. Theodore J. Nemeth Sr., transcript of interview with author in New York, 5/30/1984, KSB Collection of MEB, YCAL.

77. Mary Ellen Bute, typescript of talk to the Pittsburgh Filmmakers 6/30/1982, KSB Collection of MEB, YCAL.

78. Mary Ellen Bute, typescript of talk to the Pittsburgh Filmmakers 6/30/1982, KSB Collection of MEB, YCAL.

79. Theodore J. Nemeth, Sr., transcript of interview with author in New York, 5/30/1984, KSB Collection of MEB, YCAL.

80. Theodore J. Nemeth, Sr., transcript of interview in New York with author, 5/30/1984, KSB Collection of MEB, YCAL.

81. Norman McLaren, Scottish animation filmmaker working in Canada, quoted in film notes by Cecile Starr for program for Collective for Living Cinema, November 20, 1981, KSB Collection of MEB, YCAL.

82. Lillian Schiff, interview with Mary Ellen Bute July, 1983, *Film Library Quarterly* 17, nos. 2–4 (1984), 53–61, KSB Collection of MEB, YCAL.

83. Jesse Zunser, clipping from *Cue*, ca. 1937, KSB Collection of MEB, YCAL.

84. Theodore J. Nemeth, Sr., transcript of interview with author in Milwaukee 11/22/1984, KSB Collection of MEB, YCAL.

85. Mary Ellen Bute, letter to Baroness Hilla Von Rebay, February 14, 1941, KSB Collection of MEB, YCAL.

86. Theodore J. Nemeth, Sr., transcript of interview with author in Milwaukee 11/22/84, KSB Collection of MEB, YCAL.

87. Mary Ellen Bute, "Composition in Color and Light", undated typescript, ca 1940, KSB Collection of MEB, YCAL.

88. Mary Ellen Bute, typescript of talk to the Pittsburgh Filmmakers 6/30/1982, KSB Collection of MEB, YCAL.

89. Theodore J. Nemeth, Sr., transcript of interview with author in Milwaukee 11/22/1984, KSB Collection of MEB, YCAL.

90. Mary Ellen Bute transcript of interview with Peter Wintonick, Canadian filmmaker, November 1982, Montreal, Canada, KSB Collection of MEB, YCAL.

91. "Benjamin Hineses Are Dinner Hosts", *The New York Times*, Friday, November 1, 1940, KSB Collection of MEB, YCAL.

92. Margo Lion, ex-daughter-in-law of Bute, transcript of telephone interview with author, 11/3/1984, KSB Collection of MEB, YCAL.

93. Lois Bute Porter, youngest sister of Mary Ellen Bute, transcript of telephone interview with author June, 1984, KSB Collection of MEB, YCAL.

94. Marilyn Ripp, transcript of telephone interview with author 6/26/1984, KSB Collection of MEB, YCAL.

95. John Bute, youngest brother of Mary Ellen Bute, transcript of interview with author at his home in Houston, 6/20/1984, KSB Collection of MEB, YCAL.

96. Theodore J. Nemeth, Sr. transcript of interview with author in Milwaukee, 11/22/1984, KSB Collection of MEB, YCAL.

97. Mary Ellen Bute, "Composition in Color and Sound", undated typescript ca. 1940, KSB Collection of MEB, YCAL.

98. Mary Ellen Bute, "Composition in Color and Sound", undated typescript ca. 1940, KSB Collection of MEB, YCAL.

99. Mary Ellen Bute, "Composition in Color and Sound", undated typescript ca. 1940, KSB Collection of MEB, YCAL.

100. Mary Ellen Bute, "Composition in Color and Sound", undated typescript ca. 1940, KSB Collection of MEB, YCAL.

101. Mary Ellen Bute, "Composition in Color and Sound", undated typescript ca, 1940, KSB Collection of MEB, YCAL.

102. Lewis Jacobs, *The Rise of the American Film: A Critical History*, 1939 (New York: Teachers College Press, Teachers College, Columbia University, 1969) 561–562.

103. Lewis Jacobs, *The Rise of the American Film: A Critical History*, 1939 (New York: Teachers College Press, Teachers College, Columbia University, 1969) 562.

104. Mary Ellen Bute "Abstronics: An Experimental Filmmaker Photographs The Esthetics of the Oscillograph", *Films in Review*, 5, no. 6 (June–July 1954) , 263–266, KSB Collection of MEB, YCAL.

105. Mary Ellen Bute, interview for American Film Institute, summer, 1974, KSB Collection of MEB, YCAL.

106. Virginia Gibbs Smyth, transcript of interview with author at Mrs. Smyth home in New York 8/11/1984, KSB Collection of MEB, YCAL.

107. Ethel Mae Gullette, long-time friend of Mary Ellen, letter to author 9/6/1984, KSB Collection of MEB, YCAL.

108. Mary Ellen Bute, "Film Music: New Film Music for New films", Untitled Magazine, vol. XII, no IV, ca. 1950, KSB Collection of MEB, YCAL.

109. Cecile Starr, transcript of telephone interview with author 8/1/2014, in personal collection of author.

110. Mary Ellen Bute, typescript of talk to the Pittsburgh Filmmakers 6/30/1982, KSB Collection of MEB, YCAL.

111. Mary Batten, "Actuality and Abstraction: Notes and Comments from an Interview with Mary Ellen Bute", *Vision: A Journal of Film Comment*, June 1962, KSB Collection of MEB, YCAL.

112. Mary Ellen Bute, interview for American Film Institute, 1974, KSB Collection of MEB, YCAL.

113. Theodore J. Nemeth, Sr., transcript of interview with author in Milwaukee 11/22/1984, KSB Collection of MEB, YCAL.

114. Gilbert Seldes, film critic, *Saturday Review*, quoted by Cecile Starr in program at Collective for Living Cinema, November 20, 1981, KSB Collection of MEB, YCAL.

115. Howard Thompson, film critic "Random News on Pictures and People", *The New York Times*, Sunday, April 13, 1952, KSB Collection of MEB, YCAL.

116. Jonas Mekas, filmmaker and film critic, *Soho.Weekly News*, 9/23/1976, quoted by Cecile Starr, in program at Collective for Living Cinema, November 20, 1981, KSB Collection of MEB, YCAL.

117. Theodore J. Nemeth Sr., transcript of interview with author in Milwaukee, 11/22/1984, KSB Collection of MEB, YCAL.

118. Ann Holmes, Fine Arts editor, *Houston Chronicle*, undated clipping ca 1952, KSB Collection of MEB, YCAL.

119. Howard Thompson, "Random News on Pictures and People", *The New York Times*, Sunday, April 13, 1952, KSB Collection of MEB, YCAL.

120. Mary Ellen Bute in Howard Thompson, "Random News on Pictures and People", *The New York Times*, Sunday, April 13, 1952, KSB Collection of MEB, YCAL.

121. Virginia Gibbs Smyth, transcript of telephone conversation with author, 8/11/1984, KSB Collection of MEB, YCAL.

122. Marilyn Ripp, transcript of telephone interview with author 6/26/1984, KSB Collection of MEB, YCAL. Note: This incident was also reported by Virginia Gibbs Smyth at various times including a telephone interview with author 12/26/1985.

123. Marilyn Ripp, transcript of telephone interview with author 6/26/1984, KSB Collection of MEB, YCAL.

124. James House Bute Nemeth, younger son of Mary Ellen Bute, transcript of interview at his home 8/9/1984 in Hampton Bays, L. I., NT, KSB Collection of MEB, YCAL.

125. Theodore J. Nemeth Sr., transcript of interview with author in Milwaukee 11/22/1984, KSB Collection of MEB, YCAL.

126. Hilary Harris, filmmaker, taped interview with filmmaker Larry Mollot for film about Mary Ellen Bute, never completed, ca.1995, audio tape in private collection of author.

127. Theodore J. Nemeth Sr., transcript of interview with author in Milwaukee, 11/22/1984, KSB Collection of MEB, YCAL.

128. Theodore J. Nemeth Sr., transcript of interview with author in Milwaukee, 11/22/1984, KSB Collection of MEB, YCAL.

129. Cecile Starr, undated film notes ca. 1995 for Mary Ellen Bute's films, KSB Collection of MEB, YCAL.

130. Theodore J. Nemeth Sr., transcript of interview with author in Milwaukee, 11/23/1984, KSB Collection of MEB, YCAL.

131. Joan M. Lukach, *Hilla Rebay: In Search of the Spiritual in Art*, (New York: George Braziller, 1983) xiv.

132. Mary Ellen Bute, interview for American Film Institute, summer, 1974, KSB Collection of MEB, YCAL.

133. Cecile Starr, "Ideas on Film", *Saturday Review* 35 no. 50 (December 13, 1952).

134. Mary Ellen Bute, "Abstronics: An Experimental Filmmaker Photographs the Aesthetics of the Oscillograph", *Films in Review*, 5, no. 6 (June–July 1954) 263–266, KSB Collection of MEB, YCAL.

135. Mary Ellen Bute, "Abstronics: An Experimental Filmmaker Photographs the Aesthetics of the Oscillograph", *Films in Review*, 5, no. 6 (June–July 1954) 263–266, KSB Collection of MEB, YCAL.

136. Mary Ellen Bute, "Abstronics: An Experimental Filmmaker Photographs the Aesthetics of the Oscillograph,' *Films in Review*, 5, no. 6 (June–July 1954) 263–266, KSB Collection of MEB, YCAL.

137. Mary Ellen Bute, "Abstronics: An Experimental Filmmaker Photographs The Esthetics of the Oscillograph, "*Film in Review* 5, no. 6 (June–July 1954), 266, KSB Collection of MEB, YCAL.

138. *New York Herald Tribune*, 1955, quoted by Cecil Starr in program at Collective for Living Cinema, November 20, 1981, KSB Collection of MEB, YCAL.

139. Lillian Schiff, interview with Mary Ellen Bute July, 1983, *Film Library Quarterly* 17, nos. 2–4 (1984), 53–61, KSB Collection of MEB, YCAL.

140. Mary Ellen Bute, interviewed by art critic Ann Holmes, *Houston Chronicle*, ca. 1952, undated clipping, KSB Collection of MEB, YCAL.

141. Cecil Starr, undated film notes ca. 1995, KSB Collection of MEB, YCAL.

142. Jesse Zunser, "Kinetic Space", *Cue*, ca. 1953, KSB Collection of MEB, YCAL.

143. Cecile Starr undated film notes, KSB Collection of MEB, YCAL.

144. Howard Thompson, *The New York Times*, Sunday, April 13, 1952, quoted by Cecile Starr in program at Collective for Living Cinema, November 20, 1981, KSB Collection of MEB, YCAL.

145. Theodore J. Nemeth, Sr., transcript of interview with author in Milwaukee 11/22/1984, KSB Collection of MEB, YCAL.

146. Mary Ellen Bute, interview for American Film Institute, summer, 1974, KSB Collection of MEB, YCAL.

147. Mary Ellen Bute, interview for American Film Institute, summer, 1974, KSB Collection of MEB, YCAL.

148. William Moritz, videotaped interview with Larry Mollot, ca. 1995, for film on Mary Ellen Bute never produced, audio tape in personal collection of the author.

149. Larry Kardish, Curator of Film, Museum of Modern Art, New York, demo tape for Bute bio by Larry Mollot ca 1995, personal collection of author.

150. Mary Ellen Bute, interview for American Film Institute, summer 1974, KSB Collection of MEB, YCAL.

Chapter 4

The Boy Who Saw Through

Mary Ellen Bute synchronized light, form, color, sound, and movement on film. A critic suggested that she would be good at live action films. Perhaps she wanted a new challenge. Asked how she moved into live action films after having made fourteen animated shorts, Bute said:

> A critic, Marie Hamilton, looked at all of my work on the Moviola and she said, 'I think you have a great dramatic flair. Have you ever tried live people?' I was horrified at the thought, but her idea evidently took root and I found myself in love with a story to do with live actors. It was a short feature called *The Boy Who Saw Through*, about a boy just entering adolescence who starts seeing through walls because of his curiosity about life …

> Dealing with a live cast and a camera crew and locations and all of that it's, well, two percent creative and 98 per cent hard work. Whereas with animation, especially if you're not dancing to anyone else's tune, you have your little stand off in some odd inexpensive corner and just shoot away.[1]

Like Bute's creative decisions, her professional choices were often spontaneous. Although she took courses in directing at Columbia's film

Fig. 1. Film still of Christopher Walken at age fourteen in *The Boy Who Saw Through*.

school, she had little understanding of the team work involved in live productions.[2] She was accustomed to complete control, especially over artistic decisions. The huge expenses of filming a cast required artistic concessions she was not prepared to make to raise money. She started with a narrative film, thirty minutes, interpreting a story by British author John Pudney, whose writing had been published in many magazines and journals, including *Harper's Bazaar*, where Bute read it.[3]

All of her live action films were based on literature or on literary figures. This enabled her to use the words of the authors as dialogue. She incorporated literary quotes much like musical ones, hearing the sound of the words as one element in her visual compositions of movement.

> Ted Nemeth Sr. said: "*The Boy Who Saw Through*, 1958, gave M. E. experience working with people … George Stoney was nice. He wanted a filmmaker. [He became the director of *The Boy Who Saw Through*] He went to a Port Washington Screening. We had met him in the 1930s."[4]

No surprise that the story appealed to Bute. It essentially reflected her experience as a person who could see through hypocrisy to the truth but learned, for the sake of gracious manners, to keep silent about what she understood. The doctor in the film hired to treat the boy says to him, "You see the truth … the truth is incompatible with your present surroundings … never mention seeing through walls … a lie in defense of truth".

Bute produced the black and white, twenty-five-minute film in 1958 with Ted Nemeth, who was associate producer and director of photography, George Stoney directed the film, and Guy Glover, the poet/ producer partner of filmmaker Norman McLaren, wrote the screenplay, based on John Pudney's story. The art director Eleanor Fast supervised still photography and assisted Mary Ellen Bute. Albert Tompkins was the production manager and assistant producer. Vladimir Ussachevsky, who taught at Columbia University, specializing in electronic music, and had a PhD from the Eastman School of Music, composed and performed the music. Murray Sherman designed the sets. Special effects included opening up visions through walls, transforming an image of a full dessert into an empty plate, and quick cutting to indicate parallel action.

The star was Ronnie Walken, who with his expressive face and convincing body language, conveyed the feelings of a misunderstood teenager. He changed his name to "Christopher" in 1964 at the suggestion of a friend. He became a much sought-after character actor for film, TV, and Broadway with parts ranging from gangsters to a love interest. He won an Academy Award in 1978 for Best supporting Actor in *The Deer Hunter* portraying a steelworker emotionally destroyed by the Vietnam War. In

2000 he was the lead in James Joyce's *The Dead*, a play on Broadway with music. In 2010 he received a Tony award nomination for Best Performance by a Leading Actor in a play, a black comedy, *A Behanding in Spokane*. He also starred in music videos. In 2014 he sang and danced the part of Captain Hook in NBC's *Peter Pan Live*.

Casting Christopher Walken as the star of *The Boy Who Saw Through* testified to Bute's special ability for choosing the best people for the acting job and helping them attain the characterization they wanted. She was impressed enough with Christopher Walken to test him later for early takes of *Passages from James Joyce's Finnegans Wake*, but did not select him for the final footage, perhaps more a function of how he fitted in with the mostly Irish cast, rather than of how he acted or sang. Bute's casting skill would be essential for her feature film, *Passages from James Joyce's Finnegans Wake*.

Other members of the cast of *The Boy Who Saw Through* were Vivian Dorsett, theater and TV actress, as the mother and Thomas Barbour, a film and TV actor, as the father. There were also ten other small parts. One of the scenes was filmed in the Dutch Reform Church at Old Brookville, L. I. The Victorian home was courtesy of Mr. and Mrs. H. Learmonth.

The plot synopsis outlined in promotional material said:

> Earnest Tarch, a young teen-age boy, has the phenomenal ability of being capable of seeing through walls. This physical power of "Ernie" causes his mother and father much embarrassment and consternation. It is finally decided to take Ernie to see a Doctor Roople, who has a long talk with the boy, and gets Ernie to promise never to mention his seeing powers to anyone. The story ends happily with the parents thinking Ernie's is "cured" and Ernest realizing he must keep his secret made with Dr. Roople to himself.[5]

George Stoney, the director, later said in an interview that although he and Mary Ellen Bute had agreed on Ronnie Walken for the young boy, because of his ability to project subtle emotion, after trying out half a dozen boys, they both realized later that he should have appeared younger on camera.[6] Fourteen at the start of the filming, he was already an experienced actor and a student at the Children's Professional School in New York, and had worked in several theatrical productions, sometimes as a tap dancer.

George Stoney, also Southern, said that he and Bute were comfortable with each other's accents! He added:

> In the 1950s and 60s, there were few women producers in fiction films. Some were in documentaries. Mary Ellen had her own studio ... She took real delight in costumes. Knew what she wanted. She got the costumes from a costume house.[7]

George Stoney commented that Bute, who was always a lady, and Ted worked well together and trusted each other to do their own jobs. Stoney was especially pleased with the sound quality on location, which sometimes could be a problem. Describing the shooting, he said it took one day in the studio for casting and finding the location, which Bute had picked out in advance, and two days on location, where they rehearsed just before the takes. He commented "It was an efficient production. Ted had it wonderfully worked out … It was great fun to work with professional actors on a set script."[8]

The Boy Who Saw Through gave Bute a chance to interact with live actors, an experience needed for her feature film, the more complex *Passages from James Joyce's Finnegans Wake*. Coordinating the performances of actors was a big jump from controlling the elements of abstract animation in a room by herself. Live-action film, much more expensive to make than animation, required business skills which neither Bute nor Nemeth had. Fundraising would be a continuous problem, sapping Bute of much needed strength for creativity, as her health deteriorated. Unfortunately, society in the 1950s, was not able to deal with themes of social hypocrisy. The length of *The Boy Who Saw Through* was awkward, neither a short nor full-length feature. Bute confided in director George Stoney, that though the operation was a success, the patient had died![9] The film was never booked. It won a Brussels Film Festival Prize in 1958. It is in the collection of the University of Wisconsin-Milwaukee.

While Mary Ellen Bute prepared for her next live-action film and only full- length feature, *Passages from James Joyce's Finnegans Wake*, Ted Nemeth was cinematographer for two shorts which were nominated for Academy Awards, *Cliff Dwellers*, and *Time Piece*.

One Plus One, later called *Cliff Dwellers*, 1962, 35mm color film. Ted Nemeth was the cinematographer, Hayward Anderson the director of this story of city dwellers, and Jim Nemeth the assistant cameraman. It was nominated for an Academy Award. Ted said:

> It was a simple film made by a group of young men. One was my assistant. He got the money, rented a garage in Westchester. Shot the film there. After it was nominated for an Academy award, changed the name to "Cliff Dwellers", because there was another film by the same name.[10]

Time Piece, 1965, 8 min, color, directed, written by and starring Jim Henson, produced by The Muppets, Inc. Ted Nemeth was the cinematographer. This short film was nominated for an Academy Award. The live action of a doctor listening to a patient's beating heart with a stethoscope explodes into an abstract animated sequence of squares and rectangles moving in syncopated rhythm, suggesting the passage of time.

Centering around the tick of a clock, a metaphor for a beating heart, the main character runs through life, back to primitive time and forward again to death. Joy and stress speed by repeatedly, ending all too fast.

Ted described watching the Academy Awards ceremony on TV with Mary Ellen: "Mary Ellen didn't say much and fell asleep while we were watching the TV … She was more supportive [of me] in the 1950s and 1960s … We never argued, only over artistic things in film and I always gave in to her, because she was always right."[11]

References

1. Mary Ellen Bute, interview for American Film Institute, summer, 1974, Kit Smyth Basquin Collection of Mary Ellen Bute, Yale Collection of American Literature, Beinecke Rare Book and Manuscript Library.

2. Theodore J. Nemeth, Sr., transcript of interview with author in Milwaukee 11/22/1984, KSB Collection of MEB, YCAL.

3. John Pudney, "The Boy Who Saw Through", *Harper's Bazaar*, undated ca. 1956, KSB Collection of MEB, YCAL.

4. Theodore J. Nemeth, Sr., transcript of interview with author in Milwaukee 11/22/1984, KSB Collection of MEB, YCAL.

5. Guy Glover, plot synopsis, *The Boy Who Saw Through*, in undated promotional material, KSB Collection of MEB, YCAL.

6. George Stoney, interview with Larry Mollot for video bio of Mary Ellen Bute never finished, 1995, sound tape in personal collection of Kit Smyth Basquin.

7. George Stoney, interview with Larry Mollot for video bio of Mary Ellen Bute never finished, 1995, sound tape in personal collection of Kit Smyth Basquin.

8. George Stoney, interview with Larry Mollot for video bio of Mary Ellen Bute never finished, 1995, sound tape in personal collection of Kit Smyth Basquin.

9. George Stoney, interview with Larry Mollot for video bio of Mary Ellen Bute never finished, 1995, sound tape in personal collection of Kit Smyth Basquin.

10. Theodore J. Nemeth Sr., transcript of interview with author in Milwaukee, 11/22/1984, KSB Collection of MEB, YCAL.

11. Theodore J. Nemeth Sr., transcript of interview with author in Milwaukee, 11/23/1984, KSB Collection of MEB, YCAL.

Chapter 5

Passages from James Joyce's Finnegans Wake, 1965 Directed by Mary Ellen Bute: The Inner Essential Picture

Reasons for Selecting *Finnegans Wake*

Mary Ellen Bute answered in various ways the question frequently asked her by critics, "Why did you film *Finnegans Wake*, perhaps the most difficult book in the English language to read". She won a Cannes Film Festival Prize for it in 1965, for her direction of a first feature film. She was the first person to film any work by James Joyce.

Bute said at one time:

> My interest was peculiar to myself. I was searching for something which apparently I've not found but I've tried damn hard! ... I challenged myself when I left the abstract field and decided to use people ... I asked myself why ... perhaps I have no answer.[1]

Bute reflected that she first learned about Joyce's *Finnegans Wake* at her father's ranch in Texas.[2] She may have seen excerpts from *Finnegans Wake* serialized in the *Transatlantic Review* in 1924, but it is unlikely that she had access to that scholarly journal. It is more probable that she read in the newspapers about the obscenity controversy over the publication of *Finnegans Wake* and was fascinated by the drama. Sexual descriptions and innuendoes, often hilarious, run throughout the book. The text, with made up words, a non-linear time frame, stream of conscious passages, and experimental form, challenged critics who tended to be negative about what they could not understand. The fantasy of a night dream would have intrigued the imaginative Bute. Her awareness of avant-garde literature and art, such as Duchamp's *Nude Descending a Staircase*, excited her about the "greater world". When she first arrived in New York, she was disappointed to learn that few others were reading Joyce and viewing avant-garde art.[3] Even in New York she was ahead of her time. Joyce scholar Zack Bowen said about Bute's attraction to *Finnegans Wake*:

When Mary Ellen switched to live action...she extended her creative perception of the inanimate, which seemed to have life-like properties, to the study of people in a grand scheme of unity. She had a big synthesizing imagination, which I am certain constituted her major attraction to Joyce. She synthesized, as did Joyce, in artistic media, out of a conviction that everything was a part of the same artistic impulse, an impulse that went beyond art, that could be found in science and technology, in motion pictures and in all things."[4]

As Zack Bowen observed, Bute's artistic, synthesizing nature allowed her to connect diverse, and sometimes unexpected visual elements into a creative whole. She expanded on her reasons for tackling Joyce in two other slightly different ways, the first was informally and emotionally in an interview with Ramona Javitz, Curator of Pictures at the New York Public Library, who was a good friend, May 4, 1976. This interview brings out Bute's determined struggle to make *Finnegans Wake* and her vulnerability as an artist:

I couldn't have found a bigger challenge than James Joyce, which was untouchable. So I took Joyce and spent my sleeping and waking hours trying to understand what the hell he was saying. And I got sunk into all sorts of Irish. I was sunk among a flock of scholars no two of which interpreted any of Joyce's language the same way. He is one of the greatest sources of humor and visual imagery and I decided to be bold, not being a scholar, and not being afraid of what was being said. I just took it upon myself to run around with an alms pocket and beg for money to make an attempt at putting a piece of Joyce's most obscure writing into a film … This thing is satire, it's sex, it's pornography, it's poetry, it's indecent, it's pure, and it flows. It's a river and it flows and I was determined even with my borrowed and begged and stolen money with which to make it to see what I could do. I just had to, because first of all the thing flowed in itself. [Secondly], I would have excellent camera work done, top camera work, and I would work with a script that had as much humor as we could possibly put into it – and I've jumped from the abstract things into this and I've asked myself why? … I am not a storyteller. My interests have been in seeking. I have been sort of a laboratory bug … interest in the material and media, it's not been a literary thing … it's been more the painter … it was sort of an inner essential picture. I had a personal, experimental urge, a laboratory urge … and I wanted the sound and image and the tempo coordinated.[5]

A few days later, Bute described more formally in a public program her reasons for wanting to film Joyce's experimental novel, in an interview with film critic Stanley Kauffmann at the Art Institute of Chicago, May 9, 1976:

I think that by filming, it helped me to get some more of Joyce, and Joyce's … method of writing where he unfolds the multiple development of events simultaneously with the particular way they pass through the consciousness and the feelings, the associations, and the emotions – why that's thematic material of the first order! … All the dream dramas are filmmakers delights … Both the title and the initial selection was done in Mary Manning's very brilliant play, *Passages from Finnegans Wake*. I saw it for the first time at Barnard and it was a great production. Broadway actors and the girls carried [it] ... So that got me off the ground. I had wanted to do a film on *Finnegans Wake* long before that. There're so many exciting, wonderful passages I couldn't set on one, but Mary did, so I just got the rights to Mary's play.[6]

Bute kept the unwieldy title *Passages from James Joyce's Finnegans Wake* because she could obtain film rights from Mary Manning to base a film on her play. She could not get the film rights to Joyce's book from the often-difficult Society of Authors, trustees of Joyce's estate, although she tried three years. Bute, in her creative flair, did not stick to either the book or the play but updated both to include television, a rocket launch, and other events. She improvised scenes like a cosmetics commercial on TV and a romp through the futuristic TWA Pavilion at JFK Airport. Joyce would have approved. His book was about all people throughout time.

Fortunately, Bute only learned later of some of the famous filmmakers who had been discouraged from making a film out of *Finnegans Wake*:

> It wasn't until after the film was completed that I learned that great and famous filmmakers all over the world – including the fabulous Sergei Eisenstein – shared my dream but were unable to make it a reality. My ignorance surely protected me when I was making the film. Such company might have shaken my confidence, but not very much. I loved the material and reveled in Joyce's "dazzling verbal maneuvers" and quite enjoyed the effort of trying to keep up with all the threads of events that were happening simultaneously in "this noonday diary, this allnights newsyreel ... " I read somewhere: "Joyce split the word and from it flowed the pure music of *Finnegans Wake*". I took this as a clue and hurried over to the Joyce Society where I listened to members discuss the book. Seeing the passages in my mind's eye as they read them aloud I realized that here is one of the greatest sources of visual imagery and humor to be found anywhere. Gradually I was drawn into doing the film. Joyce's ... "special kind of reality" is irresistible. "It is not a form of knowledge but a form of being ... "[7]

The Plot

Robert Benayoun, critic at the Cannes Film Festival May 3–16, 1965, a devotee of Surrealism, succinctly summarized the plot as Mary Ellen Bute structured it after James Joyce's novel and Mary Manning's play:

> *Finnegans Wake* is a linguistic free-for-all – an almost undecipherable piece of analogical, phonetic, and semantic word play, offering in the form of puns and words having many significances, a total reconstruction of the universe and the intellectual testament of a master of language and thought. ... Bute's film gives us a carefully thought out interpretation of *Finnegans Wake*. The film places it in the actual location of its visionary delirium, Dublin transfigured. It gives life to the characters and their relationships which, from complex and obscure, become luminous and exert a direct charm. First of all the merit of the director and her victory on the creative level is the opening of a door to Joyce's work, permitting its playful, lyrical legendary exploration, underlining its

contemporary (and nuclear) aspect, in brief, rendering it indispensable. By means of audacious and insolent cutting, by the utilization of every conceivable prop (Mary Ellen Bute, who made *Spook Sport* and *Color Rhapsodie* is a virtuoso of animation), by the casting and directing of archetypal actors in transforming roles, by bringing the material up to date which includes television, the H-bomb, the twist, interplanetary rockets, publicity, alongside moth-eaten accessories (stuffed seagulls, velvet backdrops) or the sublime Irish landscape, the film makes the adventures of Finnegan, or H. C. Earwicker, or Here Comes Everybody, accessible to everyone.

Everything is resolved in a night of chaotic and healing sleep. The unconscious of the sleeper, in struggle with its essential components, goes through a cycle of shock and disintegrations which take it back to the sources of history, sexuality, myth and symbolism, in order to prepare the final outcome which is a glorious awakening, a true apotheosis of resurrection.

Finnegan, in the arms of his wife and anima, Anna Livia Plurabella, who is also River Liffey, divides himself into his two sons, Shem and Shaun, the poet and the politician, perpetual adversaries. He sees again the wake of Finn McCool whom friends awaken in his coffin with whisky, his fatal fall which is also that of the egg, Humpty Dumpty. He sees his offense of indecency committed in Phoenix Park which torpedoes his electoral campaign. He turns into King Mark, Oedipus Rex, a tavern – keeper, and a commentator and apostropher of himself … . Dawn comes and with it the white vision of a pillow fight in a nursery where the eternal and completely inner plot resumes. Finnegan, all in white, transforms his wake into a silvery wedding. The sun is resplendent over an awakening Dublin. Reunited with his "self", he sublimates himself in action.[8]

Preparation for the Film

First, Bute saw Mary Manning's play, *Passages from Finnegans Wake by James Joyce* produced at Barnard College, Columbia University, in 1958. Manning had selected incidents from Joyce's text, with dialogue quoted from the book, arranged with a focus on the resurrection theme. Bute improvised a visual riff on the play. She kept her focus on the resurrection theme and incorporated all of Manning's scenes except the washerwomen gossiping at the River Liffey, which was identified with the earth mother ALP. Ted Nemeth, Sr., cinematographer for the film, said that Bute did shoot some takes of the washerwomen, but eventually eliminated them from the final production. Bute's reasons could have included lack of time, lack of money, sexual innuendoes unacceptable to the filmmaker, or unsatisfactory shots.

In preparation for the film, Bute took a course on *Finnegans Wake* with Professor William York Tindall, Joyce scholar at Columbia University. Creative Art Television, Camera Three, in 1965, filmed a joint televised interview conducted by Jim McCander with Mary Ellen Bute and Professor Tindall. Professor Tindall said that Joyce's language appealed to the ear rather than the eye. In contrast, Bute commented that she thought

Fig. 1. Frances Steloff, owner of Gotham Book Mart, Padraic Colum, head of the James Joyce Society, and Mary Ellen Bute at the Gotham Book Mart, New York, ca. 1965, courtesy Kit Smyth Basquin Collection of Mary Ellen Bute, Yale American Literature Collection, Beinecke Rare Book and Manuscript Library.

Joyce's descriptions were so visual. Professor Tindall added that Mary Ellen Bute had to select, condense, and transform the book. He felt that the round elevator scene, which was not really in the book, was a great metaphor for the circularity of the book.[9] Joyce scholar Zack Bowen also singled out the elevator scene, but he saw it as a sign of Finnegans' aggrandisement, of going up in the world. The film, like the book is open to endless interpretations. Bute said that none of the actors had been under camera before. "We rehearsed it like a play and then broke it down into shots."[10] Professor Tindall called attention to the many cinematic words in the book. Bute mentioned Joyce's enormous wit. Professor Tindall said the book was "a fun for all, not a funeral".[11]

Ted Nemeth Sr. described the technical challenges of making *Passages from James Joyce's Finnegans Wake*. He said that Bute took a course in TV production at a film school in preparation, and tested parts of the film with practice runs in the class. Ted added, "Mary Ellen was determined and could get people to let her do anything".[12]

Bute researched, studied, and wrote the film script for her film on *Finnegans Wake* over seven years. She not only took Professor Tindall's class on *Finnegans Wake* at Columbia University, she also attended James Joyce Society meetings at the Gotham Book Mart, where she met the owner of the bookshop, Frances Steloff. Padraic Colum, an Irish poet, was an advisor.

Zack Bowen, an authority on the music in Joyce, with a beautiful singing voice himself, became a musical advisor on the film, along with a leading authority in the field, Mabel Wentworth. They identified music mentioned in Joyce's text, including Irish folk, pop tunes of Joyce's period, nursery tunes like Humpty Dumpty, songs from many countries, operas, including Wagner's Tristan and Isolde, and classical concert works, such as the Rossini's William Tell Overture. Bute's network of Joyce scholars gave her a needed support system and advice that she lacked later when she was filming *Out of the Cradle Endlessly Rocking* on Walt Whitman.

Bute's *Finnegans Wake* reflected her positive attitude and buoyant sense of humor. She said in an interview with Gretchen Weinberg while still working on the film: "He [Joyce] was an enormous, healthy, robust affirmation of life".[13]

Shooting the Film

Passages from James Joyce's Finnegans Wake is 97 minutes, shot in 35mm and 16mm, black and white, 1965. The actual shooting time for the film was thirty-two days.[14] Mary Ellen Bute, T. J. Nemeth, Jr., and Romana Javits, Curator of Pictures at the New York Public Library, created the shooting script, incorporating James Joyce's words. Grove Press distributed the film first and then film critic and historian Cecile Starr took over distribution.

Film editors were M. E. Bute, Yoshio Kishi, Paul Ronder, Thelma Schoonmaker, and Catherine Pichonnier. Later, Yoshio Kishi worked as associate editor with editor Thelma Schoonmaker on Martin Scorsese's *Raging Bull*, 1980. Thelma Schoonmaker, who said that none of her editing remains in *Passges from James Joyce's Finnegans Wake*, won an Academy award for her editing of *Raging Bull*, and other Scorsese films. James Nemeth shot still photography for *Passages from James Joyce's Finnegans Wake*. The film was dedicated to Frances Steloff, owner of the Gotham Book Mart in New York. She was a devoted friend of Mary Ellen. Miss Steloff appeared in the film in a crowd scene in Dublin.

The cast were mostly pulled from Irish actors in New York performing in Brendan Behan's *The Hostage* in English. They included:

Finnegan (H. C. Earwicker)	Martin J. Kelly
Anna Livia Plurabelle (ALP)	Jane Reilly
Shem	Peter Haskell
Shaun	Page Johnson, from West Virginia
Commentator	John V. Kelleher, head of Irish Studies at Harvard U.
And others.	The accordion player was Luke J O'Malley

Passages from James Joyce's Finnegans Wake benefits from being read out loud so that the sound of Joyce's many compounded and made-up words helps communicate their meaning. The words have a musical lilt to them. Joyce himself was a professional singer in his early years, a tenor. Bute, who had spent decades visualizing music on film, mentally connected Joyce's words to music, and his graphic descriptions to images. She opened *Passages from James Joyce's Finnegans Wake* with silent, instructive words, a technique used in her short films, describing *Finnegans Wake* as a night dream in which HCE (Here comes Everybody), married to ALP (Anna Livia Plurabelle), goes to sleep and separates into psychological parts, twin sons Shem and Shaun. After refreshing sleep, he unites and reawakens whole to a new day. Joyce's famous opening words, which also open Mary Manning's play, are read in voice over by Harvard's Joyce scholar, John V. Kelleher:

> Riverrun, past Eve and Adam's, from swerve of shore to bend of bay, brings us by a commodious vicus of recirculation back to Howth Castle and Environs.

These words set the structure of the text and the film, which are both circular, like film reels. Joyce loved film and started a movie theater in Dublin. He referred to film in his novel with words such as "movietone" (*FW* p. 62, line 9), "film folk (*FW* p. 221, line 21), and "roll away the reel world" (*FW* p. 64, lines 25–26).

The opening words of the novel, play, and film also call attention to the musical quality of Joyce's language. Bute's treatment of the text was a response to Joyce's novel and Mary Manning's play, not a cinematic translation of the text.

Bute updated the play and text. Bute visually enriched the humor in the play and added a complex musical score, as well as additional dialogue from Joyce's text. For example, Manning depicted ALP with a mirror in a dream scene. Bute included a mirror dream scene with the leads costumed as Tristan and Iseult in Central Park. In another scene she showed ALP in a bubble-bath acting in a commercial for a skin product. ALP and Iseult were interchangeable characters, as they might be in a dream, played by the same actress. Manning depicted cave men, a link with prehistory described in Joyce's text. Bute in contrast, costumed the twins as aborigines on TV, associated with Shem and Shaun, also linked to the contemporary comedy Mutt and Jeff, a creative leap.

Art consultants were Ronnie Solbert, Eleanor Fast, and John Duane Kelly. Members of the James Joyce Society were literary consultants. The location manager in Dublin was John Manning. The crew was only in Dublin for about one month. Most of the shooting was done on location in the New York area and in the Ted Nemeth Studios.

Fig. 2. Shem (Peter Haskell) and Anna Livia Plurabelle, ALP (Jane Reilly), film stil from *Passages from James Joyce's Finnegans Wake*, ca. 1964, courtesy KSB Collection of MEB, YCAL.

Elliot Kaplan created original music for the film and incorporated some songs and music referenced in Joyce's text. He also conducted the nineteen piece orchestra in one five hour marathon session. His textual music consultants were: Mabel P. Worthington, Zack Bowen, and Leslie Wendell. Mr. Kaplan was a graduate of Yale undergraduate and graduate schools, where he studied harmony and composition with Quincy Porter and Paul Hindemith. He won a Fulbright Scholarship and continued his musical studies with Nadia Boulanger at Fountainbleau, France. He also earned a degree from the Paris Conservatory in conducting. He composed scores for the Joffrey Ballet, among others.[15] He wrote:

> Scoring *Finnegans Wake* was more complex than that of scoring other films. The film itself is more diffuse and multileveled in narrative terms than other films and the depth of significance in the serious episodes and the humor of the "punny" parts is profound. The abrupt transitions between these extremes also

called for a greater than usual emphasis on the structural clarifying function of the music.

In addition, there is the uniquely Joycean sub-language of musical allusion. At given points in the book there are actual quotations, strangely parodied quotations in which, often, there is only the rhythm remaining to identify the selection, mentions of titles, of songs. The songs are of all conceivable kinds: Irish folk, popular tunes of Joyce's period, nursery tunes, songs from many other countries, operas and concert works.

I consulted with noted Joyce scholar, Dr. Mabel P. Worthington, whose book, *Songs in the Works of James Joyce*, lists some 800 separate musical allusions in *Finnegans Wake* alone. We reduced the list for our purposes to an essential 80, from which 26 are in the film. In the Tristan and Iseult sequence, for example, it was almost mandatory that I use Wagner's material, even at the possible risk of raised eyebrows on the part of those familiar with Tristan but new to *Finnegan*.

The principal theme composed by me for the picture is the one associated with the person of Finnegan himself. And in keeping with the tremendous trajectory of the largest aspect of the book's (and the film's) form – the long gradual emergence to resurrection in reality – it is not revealed in its true guise until the end, where it assumes identity as a broad, virile, striding, sunlit, festive march.

Among the other music used in the allusions are: Humpty-Dumpty, His Hair Was Black, Peg O' My Heart, Mendelsohn's Wedding March, Little Brown Jug, A Nation Once Again (the I.R.A. song), Sweet Rosie O'Grady, and William Tell Overture.[16]

Zack Bowen advised Bute on *Passages from James Joyce's Finnegans Wake* when he was a recent graduate student teaching at Harper College, State University of New York at Binghamton in 1964. He commented on her film when it came out in 1965 in an article he called "Lots of Fun with *Finnegans Wake*". He explained how Bute connected with him and the James Joyce Society:

> Armed with her innovative imagination and a lack of awareness that she was attempting the impossible, Miss Bute toyed with the idea of doing a movie of *Finnegans Wake*, but she was held up by the difficulty of formulating a script … She decided to use Mary Manning's play as a basis for her shooting script of the movie...Miss Bute concentrated on the death-rejuvenation theme of the novel, particularly as it involves HCE-Finn and his family …
>
> When the actual filming was completed, Miss Bute began to concentrate on the sound track. About that time I was invited by the James Joyce Society to give a lecture on the music in *Ulysses*. Miss Bute cornered me after the meeting and we walked over to her studio about midnight to see the rushes of the film. I was so impressed that I enthusiastically pledged to help in any way I could. I enlisted the aid of Mabel Worthington, whose book, *Song in the Works of James Joyce*, is the definitive book on the musical allusions in *Finnegans Wake* … The problem was predominantly one of selection once the musical references were identified. Miss Worthington and I were able to supply the music and lyrics to which Joyce referred. Elliot Kaplan actually fit the music into the sound track and composed

the enormous amount of additional original background music. Mr. Kaplan conducted the orchestra in one continuous marathon recording session. [17]

Leslie Wendell, who met Bute in an NYU television workshop in 1959, also assisted with the lyrics for *Passages from James Joyce's Finnegans Wake*, as well as office work. She said about Ted Nemeth's camera work, "Ted would say, 'Couldn't be done.' Mary Ellen would have ideas. Somehow he did it."[18]

Bute described shooting *Passages from James Joyce's Finnegans Wake*:

> It was made in Dublin and at the Ted Nemeth Studios ... The actors were all experienced theater people. They really took to the material like ducks to water. We rehearsed the shooting script from spot to finish, as Joyce would say, before putting it under the cameras. I got that down thoroughly, all the rhyme of the languages. We worked for about three weeks and then pulled it apart and set up the shots."[19]

Ted Nemeth, Sr. said that locations in New York included Staten Island, the elevator at the police precinct [actually night court], and the Sherry Netherlands Hotel for the scene with mirrors and children.[20] The bedroom scene was shot at the Morris-Jumel Mansion.

The actor who played Shaun, Page Johnson, said that Bute ran into the Morris-Jumel Mansion with cameras, set up the equipment, said "educational film", and filmed the actors in the antique bed before the house museum staff could do anything.[21] Ted Jr. reported to his wife Margo Lion that his mother always said, "If you want to climb over a fence, don't ask first, just do it".[22]

At the Art Institute of Chicago, Mary Ellen Bute discussed the subtitles, first suggested by Gene Moskowitz of *Variety* in Paris, with film critic Stanley Kauffmann, May 9, 1976. Bute said in response to a question about sub-titles:

> You know language plays a great part in anything Irish and I had had the idea because the words themselves are so remarkable when you read them. There are so many meanings to each one. At one of the early screenings there was one of the young exhibitors here in town who had heard about the Joyce screening. He came out and he loved it, but I heard his wife say to him in a stage whisper, "But I didn't get the words". And he said, "Oh, dear, they're Joyce words. You've got to read the book." So I thought that if the words were there like subtitles as you heard them, you could be sure that ... you got all the puns.[23]

Kauffmann commented:

> You didn't use the cinematic devices that one would immediately associate with this material: melting images, dissolves, double exposures, movement from one scene to another is sometimes rapid and abrupt, but the actual pictures are quite clear."[24]

Bute replied:

I know exactly what you mean. The treatment that I finally arrived at came through Joyce's text and really a few things that Joyce himself had said about his masterwork *Finnegans Wake*. One of the things he said was that *Finnegans Wake* is as realistic as Flaubert's *Mme. Bovary* only it's a night realism. So I thought that by observing one's own dreams and going to his text, you come up – it's not a superimposition. There's nothing arty or contrived about Joyce. It flows like any stream from the subconscious and it also is so timeless and yet he collapses time throughout.

Joyce was a great comic genius. He loved American slapstick films. He loved the film medium. He liked comic strips. His Mutt and Jutte are not only the prehistoric Juttes that lived long, long ago, but they are also Mutt and Jeff and then in that sequence ... you get feelings of evolution. Night realism, flowing and melting, dissolution and resolution.[25]

Next Kauffmann asked about the reaction of the young actors to the dialogue. Bute answered:

The first day was something of a shambles, but after that it progressed. And they progressed so rapidly that inside a week they were ordering coffee in Joycean![26]

Bute went on to discuss the elevator scene, which isn't described by Joyce in *Finnegans Wake*:

I had a feeling of osmosis with the material. [When we had] a calamity of a flood, and had to give up a location, it made me look ... I found the elevator, which isn't mentioned in *Finnegans Wake* but which some Joyceans feel is the epitome of *Finnegans Wake*. This circular elevator going up and down – they feel it captures the spirit. Joyce felt that what he needed came to him when he needed it, and I certainly feel it came true on this first film on Joyce's masterwork.[27]

Kauffmann asked: "The words – they have such an effect. They come to life in the film. What's your feeling about them?[28] Bute replied:

I think too the humor. If you don't see at first when Finn starts to embrace his "legally entitled" – That's so delightful. He's reminded here that they're married. If you don't see it written out – and all the way through the puns come through so at the celebration it's very funny.[29]

Next Kauffmann questioned: "Do you feel that words as words, visual symbols on the screen, fight the idea of film as film?" Bute replied, "I don't at all".[30]

Robert Benayoun in a Critics Section Publication at the Cannes Festival in 1965, where the film was screened before the sub-titles were added, although complementary, expressed the need for sub-titles:

Practically untranslatable, *Finnegans Wake* was presented at Cannes without subtitles, but the artistry of Mary Ellen Bute even overcame this handicap, elucidating the work by imagery and rhythm. One can Truly speak of a tour de force.[31]

Ted Nemeth Sr. talked about some of the obstacles Bute had to overcome to complete her feature film *Passages from James Joyce's Finnegans Wake*.

Money was a major problem. They relied on Bute's ability to hire young people who wanted experience and would work at a low rate.[32] Nemeth said that Bute interviewed twenty-five or thirty people for the parts and videotaped them to facilitate her decision.[33] At first they rented a Ukrainian Club dance hall to shoot scenes for the film. They used the tables for banquettes and built scenery for the wake room. Unfortunately a flood above the studio space ruined the set. Bute quickly had to find a substitute space. She stumbled on an elevator in a police precinct that also had a courtroom, between 53rd and 54th Streets and between 8th and 9th Avenues. They shot sequences there.

Editing *Passages from James Joyce's Finnegans Wake*

Thelma Schoonmaker was recruited by Bute right out of college to edit *Passages from James Joyce's Finnegans Wake*. She was taking a six weeks film course at NYU, where she met Martin Scorsese. The college suggested her when Bute called for a film assistant and editor. She left this work after seven months, feeling exploited by Mary Ellen, who gave no consideration to illness or exhaustion, for herself or anyone else. Ms. Schoonmaker did everything in the office and on locations, as well as editing. There were no crews. "There was Ted on camera and one of his sons helping with clothing … Ted was a good cameraman. The shots on the Staten Island beach show it … The bedroom scene was shot in the Morris-Jumel Mansion. Mary Ellen put people into the antique bed. She had no compunction. She had no permission."[34]

Ms. Schoonmaker also commented that Bute did not dress in a business-like manner: "Mary Ellen was incredibly feminine. She wore amazing high heels, no backs, clear plastic see-through stiletto heels. She splashed Joy perfume. She had curly red hair and feminine dresses … " Thelma added: "Now Mary Ellen would be considered 'a breath of fresh air.'"[35]

The film editor who took over at the end was Yoshio Kishi. Later he would edit for Hollywood films, including *Fame* and *Raging Bull*. His collection of Asian-American memorabelia in diverse media is at New York University Fales Library & Special Collections. He said about Bute:

> She had much talent. There were not many women filmmakers around … she cared. She was sympathetic, talented, hampered by lack of financial support. She had to compromise for budget problems … She was honest, authentic, straight forward. She could be devious to get something accomplished. She would use people terribly to get what she wanted. She would work people very hard … she worked herself too … complete exhaustion. She didn't eat lunch or dinner. 16–24 hour days … I had seven weeks to edit. There were money problems. I was fast. It usually takes six months to a year to edit a feature … She rarely talked about aesthetics … She encouraged us to reach what we were trying to reach."[36]

Ted Nemeth, Sr. added that there was a lot of extra footage for the film and that the editing job was difficult.[37] Yoshio Kishi commented on the editing challenge, but felt that the extensive footage was an asset, as he said:"*Finnegans Wake* is well edited. Changes were able to be made because material was there. Editing just made it neater."[38] Yoshio Kishi was brought in at the last minute to complete the editing of *Finnegans Wake* in time for the scheduled premiere in 1965. The first preview was for the James Joyce Society, a screening at the Museum of Modern Art in January, 1965. Yoshio Kishi was a professional who had been out of college a couple of years and was a friend of Leslie Wendel, who was a secretary for Bute. Kishi described working with Bute on the film:

> I was known as a film doctor. In post-production she [Mary Ellen] called me. She hired me out of desperation … the others were young and wanted to work on the film. They were paid very little. They were exhausted … She said she was up to her neck in work with a deadline for the premiere coming up. Would I help her? I did it out of friendship and speculation. I was the only professional. All the others were in their 20s. She left people alone … She could see things she wanted to accomplish. She had taste and persistence. She got the best out of people. Got performances that no one would get as well – they were inexperienced people. She did good work. She was skilled technically … She was happy with what I did. She did not map it out. I read some of *Finnegans Wake*. I knew Joyce … The film is developed out of the novel rather than the play. [His opinion differs from most others on this point. Bute annotated a copy of Manning's play.] In the film, there is no talking in the beginning, like the novel. The film is like poetry.
>
> There is a concern with images and ideas … not dialogue, scenery … She was nice. A mad woman. Intent on what she was doing. She could be charming when she wanted something … There was no shooting script ... no camera notes, no camera report … The sequences weren't there. I developed them … She needed money and six more months … She rarely talked about the aesthetics of what she was doing … never talked about casting … she never talked about interpretation … She didn't try to persuade them to do it a different way but to make them reach what they were trying to reach … She found it horrendous that people had to eat and sleep … at 3 am I found her in the cutting room, laughing to herself. I was 27–28. She was 60 … .[39]

Bute's son Theodore J. Nemeth Jr., who worked on *Finnegans* Wake, agreed with Yoshio Kishi's comments on Bute's casting ability, her lack of interest in aesthetic explanations and interpretations, and her focus on images:

> I think you can see right off the bat … [her strength] her choice of cast. Many of the people that she chose for the several versions of several parts of the movie, you don't by any means see in the final cut … many of those people were at the early stages of very interesting careers … I think she made very good use of her instincts. Her social instincts. Her feeling for people …

[Actors] wanted … sort of intellectualization of the part, their character, the sort of academic background that she [Mary Ellen] didn't at all feel happy at imparting and didn't impart very confidently or very consistently. However, there were some very interesting performances in these films and this was due to the fact that the actors, quite unhappy about it, were thrown back on themselves, on their own abilities, and she had picked them well. On the other hand, by having the actors go their own way, you did get the feeling, if you watched *Finnegans Wake*, that several of the actors are in different movies. The bottom line is that through a combination of strengths and weaknesses, she got performances that were rather interesting.[40]

Discussing Bute's editing, her son Ted Nemeth, Jr. added:

I think one of her strongest talents was editing … the juxtaposition, the cutting in the wake scenes and in scenes by the ocean, and yet this real strength of hers … was undercut by a weakness – a disinterest almost in telling a story. In putting the whole film together in a series of steps that would lead you in a clear, exciting interesting way … her interest was in the particular, in the specific image. The result was you had some dullish sections, punctuated by some striking imagery – and also I think the emotional impact of the film again went into the particular cuts and editing, rather than into a kind of building of emotional impact as a whole … it is very much a film that looks as though it were directed by a painter.[41]

In an interview with Gretchen Weinberg of *Film Culture*, Bute stressed that her film was not a translation of Joyce's novel but her personal reaction to the book. She was taken with Joyce's breadth of vision, dedication and absorption. She focused on the theme of awakening, not just from sleep but into consciousness.[42] Clearly she had to be selective to encompass the vast amount of material. Awareness or consciousness were characteristics of Mary Ellen Bute herself. She could in a sense see through people's superficialities, like the character in "The Boy Who Saw Through".

Financing the Film

Ted Nemeth, Sr. said that the University of Minnesota supplied the final sums to finish the film. They were given the money by an alumnus who was a filmmaker in New York who had seen test shots of Bute's film. In return, the University got rights to the 16mm film as well as many outtakes and other related materials, but they returned the rights to Expanding Cinema, Bute's production company, which Ted Nemeth, Sr. thought was very good of them.[43] Nemeth added "Eric Barnouw [later director of a short, *Fail Safe*, using Nemeth as a cinematographer] taught at Columbia when M. E. went there. He helped with Minnesota money. Jerry O'Connor worked on getting press for FW."[44]

Bute also had a contact at the University of Minnesota through Ethel Mae Gullette, Bill Gulette's wife, who had attended the University. Ethel Mae and Bill Gullette were old friends of Bute. Bill Gullette ran a screening studio, Preview Theatre, Inc. in New York with theaters for rent, used especially by filmmakers in the process of making films.[45]

Critical Response to Film

Mary Ellen Bute won the prize for a first feature by a director for *Passages from James Joyce's Finnegans Wake* at the 1965 Cannes Film Festival. The judges for feature films that year were: actress Olivia de Haviland, the first woman to be president of the jury; actor Rex Harrison; director Alain Robbe-Grillet; writer Andre Maurois; producer Goffredo Lombardo; writer Max Aub; journalist Michel Aubriant; director Francois Reichenbach; author Constantin Mikhailovitch Simonov; producer Edmond Tenoudji; and director Jerzy Toeplitz.

Many critics praised Bute's film, including Joyce scholar William York Tindall who wrote *A Reader's Guide to James Joyce*. He lauded Mary Ellen's ability to condense and simplify the text and turn sound images into visual ones.[46] Zack Bowen, author of *Musical Allusions in the Works of James Joyce* felt that Mary Ellen, introduced Joyce's *Finnegans Wake* to many who might go on to actually open Joyce's book and experience his unique language for themselves, less fearful of the challenges of the text after experiencing Bute's film.

Zack Bowen also commented on the scale of the film and on its success:

> Watching the *Finnegans Wake* movie is not like looking at *Gilligan's Island* [a TV show]. The *Wake* takes a certain love for the sound of words, and an awareness of nuances of meaning. A ninety-seven minute film cannot hope to comprehend all of a book that is about all of everything. The movie is limited in scope in that it is thematically integrated to the awakening of HCE-Finn and concerns itself primarily with the family. That an attempt was made to make any sort of a picture on *Finnegans Wake* is astounding; that the picture is a genuinely successful work of art is, though perhaps unbelievable, wholly true. [47]

One of Bute's most creative accomplishments was to fabricate time, not chronologically but cinematically. Using montage editing, she juxtaposed different time frames into an integral pattern. Sergei Eisenstein is credited with developing montage editing in which two different images placed in sequence create a third meaning not in either of the distinct images. For example, in *The Battleship Potemkin*, in the famous scene on the steps, the cinematographer showed the menacing boots of the soldiers descending the steps and then the frightened peasants on the steps below. The viewer sees the scene as if the soldiers were actually threatening the peasants, although they never touch. In Bute's film, she incorporated the distant past into the present by having mourners watch cave men on television. Similarly, the mourners studied old photographs of HCE's family, bringing the past into the present.

Another creative technique Bute employed, which helped her visualize changing points of view, and also aided her tight budget, was to cast the same actor in multiple parts but in different costumes. In Joyce's text, HCE's daughter Issy becomes the lover in the stage performance of Tristan and Isolde. The same actress is also cast as HCE's wife, ALP, thus suggesting the fractured personalities and incest alluded to in Joyce's text.

At a preview screening of *Passages from James Joyce's Finnegans Wake* at the University of Minnesota, attended by over 4000 people, including the Mayor of Minneapolis, despite the –28 degree temperatures outside, Mary Ellen's friend Bill Gullette commented "Mary Ellen spoke. Wonderful. Animated. Enthusiastic. Miss Steloff was there too."[48] He wrote Mary Ellen, February 23, 1965:

> I want to thank you for the memorable experience in seeing your Finnegans Wake. Although I've been connected with this industry for over 30 years, I believe you know it has been my fetish to remain a layman in attitude when it comes to viewing pictures of my choice – in a regular audience and usually with my wife.

> A most important factor in the enjoyment of your picture was bringing to life the spirit and meanings of Joyce in a most palatable manner. The "thought and impression" world of this great writer were so beautifully and effectively revealed by the manner in which you used the medium. It was as though a new world of wonderment and pleasure had been opened to me as it would not have been in any other way.

> The technical factor of sound and picture were superb. The production values are of first rank.

> In this picture as in each of your productions, you have demonstrated again your mastery in the use of expressive and appropriate music to enhance and interpret pictoral (sic) values which in turn creates unusual sensory response.
> Very truly yours, Bill Gullette, William B. Gullette[49]

Mary Ellen Bute, obviously pleased with this letter from an old friend in the film business, quoted from this letter in some of her press materials.

Thomas Quinn Curtiss, film critic to *The New York Times*, who was at the Cannes Film Festival in 1965 where Mary Ellen Bute won a prize wrote:

> The vast canvas of Joyce's novel can only be caught in part in a 90-minute movie, but the scenes selected have been expertly managed ... *Finnegans Wake* is a striking cinematic accomplishment, as interesting a film as the festival has revealed.[50]

Mary Manning said in an interview that, like many strict Joyceans, she disliked Bute's creative departure from the text.[51] However, she added, "She was a remarkable woman. Borrowed directly. Didn't wander far."[52]

For example, Bute updated Finn's fall through time with a rocket launch. Joyce scholar, Patrick McCarthy said in a paper delivered at the Modern Language Association in Chicago in 1977:

> Amazing there is a film on a tough book with no plot and difficult language ... Brave, funny, remarkably successful ... a cinematic impression of a literary work.[53]

Zack Bowen commented in his eulogy at Bute's memorial service in 1983 in New York: "She came closer than an army of critics in the last forty years to the essence of his [James Joyce's] spirit".[54]

New York art critic Emily Genauer, very positive about the subtitles, wrote about the film in 1967:

> Produced and directed with extraordinary imagination and invention ... exceptionally beautiful camera work ... like a long drink from a bottle without bottom.

> Miss Bute employs surrealist techniques – juxtapositions, flashbacks, illusions – which have long been familiar through surrealist paintings, and, indeed, through Picasso's own efforts in this area in his earlier days ... Seeing in occasional flashes on film, the actual look of the fragmented, reconstituted comic words, and especially the puns so subtle they elude hearing, suddenly all seems wildly yet marvelously logical.[55]

Emily Genauer's critique juxtaposes Mary Ellen Bute's film alongside Picasso and the Surrealists, exactly where the filmmaker would want to be. Clearly Bute succeeded in her goal to transform film into an art form.

Some Joyceans, however, felt like Jonas Mekas, filmmaker, Artistic Director and Founder of Anthology Film Archives, that *Finnegans Wake* was the *Bible* and shouldn't be altered in any way.[56] Joyce purists were disturbed that some of the lines attributed to the two brothers Shem and Shaun got exchanged and that scenes such as the "Washer Women" were omitted. As with any sensitive artist, particularly one who had spent seven years producing her film, Bute was upset by the negative reviews. But Mary Ellen never claimed that the film was a translation of *Finnegans Wake*, just a response to it. She said "It represents my point of view".[57] The critique that upset Mary Ellen the most, however, was written by film critic Brendan Gill in 1967 for *The New Yorker*:

> "Passages from James Joyce's Finnegans Wake" is a misbegotten oddity of a movie compiled by a lady named Mary Ellen Bute. One hears Joyce in Heaven groaning "*Et tu, Brute?*", for if ever there was a work that defied having its intricate verbiage translated into pictures, it is Shem's purposely featureless inferno of the sleeping mind. As a measure of the vulgarity of the images that have been chosen to illustrate the text, I may mention that when Miss Bute wishes to evoke for us Joyce's haunted "Passage ... passing,' she shows us a train darting in and out of a suburban railway station. Even the Liffey is turned into a laughingstock by being depicted as a tamely prettified park streamlet, while

poor Earwicker proves to be a plump, toothy dandy with soft white breasts and a look so invincibly roguish that it would turn the four stomachs of the staunchest cow in Connaught. In what may have been intended as a big cultural breakthrough, the movie translates the English dialogue by means of English subtitles; the ludicrousness of this procedure reaches its climax when the last uttered word in the movie which is "A" (and is a misquotation from the book), is translated by a subtitle reading (correctly) "The".[58]

This is the same critic, who in an article dated December 11, 1965 in *The New Yorker*, in his "Current Cinema" column, referred to Walt Disney as "The Rembrandt of American marzipan". Clearly Mr. Gill enjoyed playing with words and making extreme statements. I doubt that Disney cared, but unfortunately, Mary Ellen Bute, who spent seven years creating an experimental film in an uphill battle to raise funds, was devastated. Thornton Wilder saw the review in *The New Yorker* and realized how much it would upset the filmmaker. In a note to her while he was visiting France in 1967, he wrote:

Dear Mary Ellen,

Friday I happened to read the spiteful review of your movie in "The New Yorker". I've received those "spite squirts" all my life. I don't get downcast or ruffled by <u>bad</u> reviews, but I get furious at these distillations of venom and malice – because they're so bad for everybody else – for the reader, for the writer, for the cultural atmosphere. I hate injustice … .[59]

In support of Brendan Gill, Mary Manning said, "You can't argue with point of view".[60] True but some crticis are more sensitive to the impact of their power on artists and would have tempered their remarks with an appreciation for what Bute did accomplish.

Bute's son Ted Nemeth, Jr. felt that the negative responses to *Finnegans Wake* surprised Mary Ellen and eroded her confidence:

She worked for a long time on *Finnegans Wake* and expected a kind of strong response from the world, from critics, and when that didn't come, there was a noticeable lessening of her confidence. If there is any point at which you want to talk about a pose or a mask, this is where that may begin to be true. As you know, the charming thing about charm, the appealing thing, is that is so often reflects a kind of inner confidence, a kind of inner warmth and response that is kind of hard to resist. And when the inner part gets a bit eroded, the outer comes across in a much more hollow way, and it just doesn't work as well, and then one pushes harder with it and it works less well even and this is what I think happened with Mary Ellen on this movie. I saw her making social gaffs and mistakes that I would never have thought she was capable of making in her life … I think … that that optimism, that transferable confidence which she had almost all of her life – I really don't think the last few years she did – but through most of it she was very strong and it brought out the best in you and me and many people. – so as a mother I would say she was only so so, except for people like myself who have unusual taste. As a filmmaker, pretty good, but really still learning. As a person … she was right there at the top…She had a lot of confidence and she spread it around like a giddy sixteen-year-old girl. I don't think I've ever met anyone who, to such an extent, gave back more than she got.[61]

Thornton Wilder attended the film showing of *Passages from James Joyce's Finnegans Wake* in Cannes in 1965. Wilder was so impressed with Bute's film, that he gave Bute the film rights to his play, *Skin or Our Teeth*. Wilder's archetypical figures and the telescoping of time from the ice age to the present referenced *Finnegans Wake*.

One of the most fanciful scenes in *Passages from James Joyce's Finnegans Wake* is the finale, HCE, clad in a white suit, marching to theme music identified with him, into the sunrise, waking to a new day. He steps into the brilliant, sparkling light, over and over, a resurrection. Part of Bute's creative intelligence was to juxtapose diverse elements, particularly varied light sources, like the sparkling glow of sunrise, almost turning it into a light show. Special effects like that link *Finnegans Wake* to her earlier experimental abstract films by technique and concept. Another example in the film of an animation technique is Finnegan's fall through time, a paper doll cascading from the cave dwellers through history. Other sections of the film convey an abstract beauty, such as the close ups of glittering water, the River Liffey, also a symbol for Anna Livia Plurabelle. Larry Kardish, Film Curator at the Museum of Modern Art, focused on this uniting of forms when he screened some of Bute's shorts with her feature in 1983:

> We had always admired her work and screened it many times. We wanted to relate her shorts to *Finnegans Wake* … both are films in a different manner … We wanted the audience to see the interpretation of abstraction from pure abstraction to narrative abstraction".[62]

The most comprehensive analysis of Mary Ellen Bute's *Passages from James Joyce's Finnegans Wake* was written by Stanley Kauffmann in his book *Figures of Light: Film Criticism and Comment*, a reprint from his article for *New American Review* in 1968 comparing Mary Ellen's film to Joseph Strick's film on Joyce's *Ulysses* which debuted two years after hers in 1967, several years before Mr. Kauffmann was asked to talk with Mary Ellen Bute in public at the Art Institute of Chicago in 1976. He wrote:

> In contrast to Strick's effort, Mary Ellen Bute's film is called *Passages from James Joyce's Finnegans Wake*, and with this modest title, is succeeds surprisingly well. Miss Bute had to deal with less story than there is in *Ulysses*, but she also had to decide on all settings and in many cases to select the speakers. She based her film script on Mary Manning's dramatization, in regard to which Dennis Johnson wrote: 'Joyce … presents us with a play where, as in the Song of Solomon, we are expected to work out for ourselves who it is that is reporting or being reported in every line.' Even more stringently than the stage adapter, the film maker is pressed against the thorns of this problem every split second

of the time. In the main Miss Bute has coped with this sympathetically and impressively. The proof is not in any checking than can be done – one opinion is as good an another – but that, by and large, the film achieves the inner-most effect of the great dream novel.

It is a bit too long: ten minutes less (it runs 97 minutes) would be twenty minutes better. Some of it is as cornily lighted as Strick's *Ulysses*. The music is often sheer movie music. Some of the pictorial compositions have the whiff of home movies; others have a whiff of the film school. But what keeps the film from slipping into amateurism, what redeems it far past its faults, is the very strong sense of Miss Bute's vision: Her loving perception of the novel and her response to it in cinematic imagination. She has imposed a stern dream logic on her material. She extracts a sequence, almost arbitrarily, from the novel; just when it shows signs of disintegrating, she cuts to a new sequence, which not only starts well but has the effect of reaffirming the sequence we have just left, because the rigor of the change reaffirms Miss Bute's grip of the work. This is doubly so because, dramatically and pictorially, Miss Bute had virtually to invent every sequence.

Subtitles are used. Nearly every word that the actors speak is flashed on the screen. Ordinarily this would be deplorable (except with foreign-language films, where it is still the best method devised for making them available to us.) But *Finnegans Wake* is not an ordinary case, and here the practice is excellent. First the composite words are impossible to understand through the ear alone.

Second, these Joycean words are wonderful visual *objects*, enriching the picture *visually*, like objects in surrealistic art.

The cast, mostly Irish, speak the composite language with such conviction that the reality of a million compressed dreams makes our heads appropriately swim. Martin J. Kelley as Finnegan etcetera and Jane Reilly as Anna Livia etcetera are always effective. It is impossible to say that they play their roles well because there are no roles, but what they have to do, they do interestingly.

The film's central achievement is that it touches myth, touches our old friend the collective unconscious. I heard someone say after seeing Strick's *Ulysses* that it would make a good introduction to the novel. The remark made my blood run cold because it seems both inevitable and dreadful: the film is a facile and ludicrous reduction. But Miss Bute's film, modest and flawed as it is, is in tune with the work it is about, and can even be seen as a small introductory suite to the teeming Joycean opera.[63]

Mary Ellen Bute enjoyed a lot of recognition for her live action feature film, *Passages from James Joyce's Finnegans Wake*, but she felt that this prize winning film overshadowed her earlier experimental work. Her experimental abstract films, though in collections at The Museum of Modern Art, the Whitney Museum of American Art, Anthology Film Archives in New York, the Golda Maier Library at the University of Wisconsin-Milwaukee, the Film Study Center at Yale in New Haven, and the Center for Visual Music, Los Angeles, among other places, are difficult to see and little known today. As film historian and critic Cecile Starr pointed out in many of her articles for *Saturday Review* and for *The New York Times*,

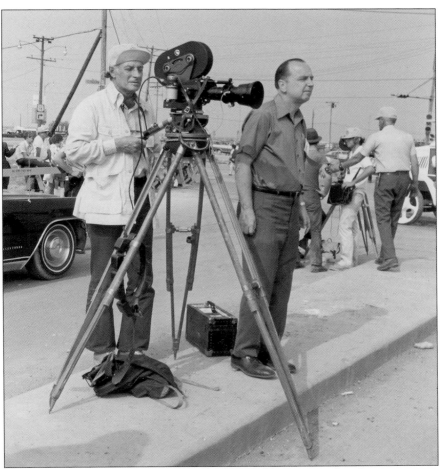

Fig. 3. Ted Nemeth with a representative of Barkin-Herman & Associates in Milwaukee, July 4, 1965, filming Circus Parade, courtesy KSB Collection of MEB, YCAL.

women filmmakers as a whole were less well known than men and less recognized for their talents. This was especially sad for an innovative, experimental film pioneer like Mary Ellen Bute.

Bute said that her *Passages from James Joyce's Finnegans Wake* was not about a narrative or about literature, but about the "inner essential picture". She edited her film for visual effect, like a painter. She succeeded, on a skimpy budget, in orchestrating James Joyce's words, a cast of American and Irish actors, a surrealistic narrative, music as diverse as Humpty Dumpty and the William Tell Overture, locations in the New York area and in Dublin, and special cinematic effects, into a creative piece about death and rebirth, sleep and awakening. Bute's "inner essential picture", the vision of an insightful artist, was about life, joy, and moving energy. This film is in the collections of The Museum of Modern Art, New York, the New York Public Library for the Performing Arts, University of Wisconsin-Milwaukee, and Yale Film Study Center, which preserved it.

Ted Nemeth, Sr.

The summer after completing *Passagesw from James Joyce's Finnegans Wake*, Ted Nemeth Sr. shot an elaborate commercial job in Milwaukee, WI. Mary Ellen Bute accompanied him, as did their son Jim.

40 Horse Hitch, 1973 (filmed 1965), color, 9 min. Ted Nemeth was cinematographer and director. Jim Nemeth was assistant cameraman. Schlitz Brewing Company produced the short. Ernest Borgnine narrated the Schlitz Circus Parade as it traveled through the streets of downtown Milwaukee July 4, 1965. Coleman Barkin of Barkin-Herman & Associates, a Milwaukee public relations firm wrote the script. The film was produced for TV. It Screened at Radio City Music Hall under the title "Fabulous Forty Horse Hitch". Ted Nemeth and Mary Ellen Bute appear briefly in the crowd, smiling and wearing suits and hats, unlike most of the casually dressed spectators. The focus was a team of forty horses, four abreast and ten deep, pulling a circus wagon. The horses were trained for a year before the event by Dick Sparrow. The spectacle was pure showmanship.

See Colour Plate 11
40 Horse Hitch, Milwaukee Schlitz Circus Parade, ca 1965,
courtesy KSB Collection of MEB, YCAL.

A local Milwaukee newspaper described the filming of the circus parade as follows:

> A husband and wife team that has made several award winning films is here [Milwaukee] with a crew of eight to photograph the Schlitz circus parade Monday.

> Mr. and Mrs. Ted Nemeth (professionally she is Mary Ellen Bute) of New York City will record the parade in color and sound for possible distribution to network television and theaters.

> ### Special Equipment

> The filming has been commissioned by Schlitz, with Barkin-Herman & Associates, the brewery's public relations firm, in charge of distribution through a New York firm [Universal Pictures Corp.]

> The Nemeth crew has a specially equipped airplane, walkie-talkies, golf carts and photograph equipment, including seven cameras.

> Directing the parade photography via walkie-talkie will be Nemeth, who also will operate a 250 millimeter zoom camera that enables him to take close-ups across a street. Other crew members will use golf carts for mobility and still

others will be above street level, riding truck mounted booms called "cherry pickers", which will give them a bird's eye view of the parade.

The Nemeths have won film awards at Brussels and Venice and have been nominated for Academy Awards for "Time-Piece and "One Plus One". They also earned critical plaudits for their film "Finnegans Wake, at the film festival in Cannes, France, in May. "We hope to be able to use some avant garde techniques in the parade film, too", said Mrs. Nemeth

Seek Realism

To tell the story of the circus parade, the Nemeths started at the Circus World Museum in Baraboo.

"We'll probably shoot about 60,000 feet of 16millimeter film", Nemeth said, "and from that will come the 1,100 feet we'll need to produce the 26 minute picture. We especially want to get the real sound of the parade spectators. This should add a lot to the movie's realism."

Nemeth, who began his photographic career as a teen age assistant at Bachrach Studios of New York City, met his wife when she was producing her first film in Philadelphia [actually New York] and needed a cameraman. They have two sons, Ted Jr., 24, a writer in London who helped with the "Finnegans Wake" script, and James, 19, who is studying photography in London and is in the crew filming the circus parade.[64]

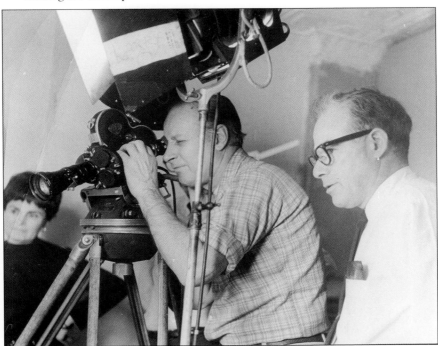

Fig. 4. Ted Nemeth (1911– 1986) and Larry Mollot (1919–2010) ca. 1960, photo by Ted Nemeth Studios.

Ted Nemeth, Sr. obtained this lucrative film production job through his friend Charles Hacker, whom he had known at Radio City Music Hall, where Hacker was Executive Vice-President.[65] About 1966, Nemeth's commercial business failed. His son Jim Nemeth said that when Nemeth's business manager asked for a raise, Ted Nemeth fired him. Nemeth thought he could save money. But as Jim Nemeth added, "Ted was not a businessman".[66] Mary Ellen compounded their financial problems by selling her Bute Paint Company stock to her brother John and putting all her money into Ted Nemeth Studios, so that she no longer had a private income, except for her social security checks. Ted Nemeth,Sr. did not have the money to send Jim Nemeth to an Ivy League College like his brother Ted Nemeth, Jr. who graduated from Cornell, so Jim Nemeth studied film in London, which he enjoyed. Later he completed a degree at New York University. Ted Nemeth, Sr. borrowed the money to send him there. Jim Nemeth worked at night at Lenox Hill Hospital to help pay his expenses. He met his future first wife, Johanna, a nurse, there. After experiencing the highs and lows of the film business, Jim Nemeth wanted a steady life with a reliable income. He became a chemistry teacher and then later made training films for industry.[67]

Ted Nemeth Sr. was a brilliant cameraman who translated into film the creative ideas of directors including Mary Ellen Bute, Jim Henson, Hayward Anderson, and later, Erik Barnouw. Also directing him on camera at times was filmmaker/writer Larry Mollot, who later shot footage for an unfinished biography of Bute, co-produced by Mollot, Cecile Starr, and Kit Smyth Basquin.

References

1. Mary Ellen Bute, transcript of interview with Ramona Javitz, Picture Curator at the New York Public Library and personal friend of Mary Ellen Bute, May 4, 1976, Kit Smyth Basquin Collection of Mary Ellen Bute, Yale Collection of American Literature, Beinecke Rare Book and Manuscript Library.

2. Mary Ellen Bute and Professor William York Tindall, James Joyce scholar at Columbia University, video-taped interviewed by Jim McCander, for Creative Arts Television, Camera Three, Kent, CT, 1965, in personal collection of Kit Smyth Basquin.

3. Mary Ellen Bute and Professor William York Tindall, video-taped interviewed by Jim McCander, for Creative Arts Television, Camera Three, Kent, CT, 1965, in personal collection of Kit Smyth Basquin.

4. Zack Bowen, Joyce scholar and a musical advisor on *Passages from James Joyce's Finnegans Wake*, typescript of eulogy for Mary Ellen Bute, delivered at her memorial service at the Church of the Transformation ("Little Church around the Corner"), November 19, 1983, KSB Collection of MEB, YCAL.

5. Mary Ellen Bute, transcript of interview with Ramona Javitz, May 4, 1976, KSB Collection of MEB, YCAL.

6. Mary Ellen Bute, transcript of interview with film critic Stanley Kauffmann at the Art Institute of Chicago, May 9, 1976, KSB Collection of MEB, YCAL.

7. Mary Ellen Bute, "Some thoughts from the filmmaker", Cineprobe program, Museum of Modern Art, April 4, 1983, KSB Collection of MEB, YCAL.

8. Robert Benayoun, critic at Cannes Film Festival, May 3–16, 1965, undated clipping, KSB Collection of MEB, YCAL.

9. Mary Ellen Bute and Professor William York Tindall interviewed by Jim McCander for Creative Arts Television, Camera Three, 1965, video cassette in personal collection of Kit Smyth Basquin.

10. Mary Ellen Bute and Professor William York Tindall interviewed by Jim McCander for Creative Arts Television, Camera Three, 1965, video cassette in personal collection of Kit Smyth Basquin.

11. Mary Ellen Bute and Professor William York Tindall interviewed by Jim McCander for Creative Arts Television, Camera Three, 1965, video cassette in personal collection of Kit Smyth Basquin.

12. Theodore J. Nemeth Sr., transcript of interview with author in Milwaukee 11/22/1984, KSB Collection of MEB, YCAL.

13. Mary Ellen Bute, interview with Gretchen Weinberg, *Film Culture* 35 (Winter 1964–1965), 28, KSB Collection of MEB, YCAL.

14. Mary Ellen Bute, video interview by James McCander for Creative Arts Television, Camera Three, Kent, CT, 1965, in personal collection of Kit Smyth Basquin.

15. Elliot Kaplan, obituary, *Los Angeles Times*, May 17, 1992, articles.latimes.com/1992-05-17/news/mn-417_1_elliot-kaplan

16. Elliot Kaplan, composer and conductor of music for *Passages from James Joyce's Finnegans Wake*, undated notes on music for *Finnegans Wake* ca. 1964, KSB Collection of MEB, YCAL.

17. Zack Bowen, "Lots of Fun with *Finnegans Wake*", 1965, typed manuscript, KSB Collection of MEB, YCAL.

18. Leslie Wendell, friend of Mary Ellen who worked on lyrics for *Passages from James Joyce's Finnegans Wake*, transcript of telephone interview with author 5/18/1987, KSB Collection of MEB, YCAL.

19. Mary Ellen Bute, transcript of interview with Stanley Kauffmann at the Art Institute of Chicago, May 9, 1976, KSB Collection of MEB, YCAL.

20. Theodore J. Nemeth, Sr., transcript of interview with author in Milwaukee, 11/22/1984, KSB Collection of MEB, YCAL.

21. Page Johnson, who played Shaun in *Passages from Finnegans Wake*, transcript of interview with author for documentary film on Mary Ellen Bute, never produced, August 9, 1995, KSB Collection of MEB, YCAL.

22. Margo Lion, ex-daughter-in-law of Bute, and a Broadway producer, transcript of telephone interview with author 11/3/1984, KSB Collection of MEB, YCAL.

23. Mary Ellen Bute, transcript of interview with Stanley Kauffmann at the Art Institute of Chicago, May 9, 1976, KSB Collection of MEB, YCAL. Note: Joe Smyth, Kit Smyth Basquin's brother, was a Lieutenant in the US Navy stationed on aircraft carrier USS Saratoga in the Mediterranean at the time of the Cannes Film Festival in 1965. He ran into Mary Ellen on the street and she invited him to a showing of *Passages from James Joyce's Finnegans Wake*. At that time, it had no sub-titles. He also suggested that sub-titles would help the viewer.

24. Stanley Kauffman, transcript of interview with Mary Ellen Bute at The Art Institute of Chicago, May 9, 1976, KSB Collection of MEB, YCAL.

25. Mary Ellen Bute, transcript of interview with Stanley Kauffmann at The Art Institute of Chicago, May 9, 1976, KSB Collection of MEB, YCAL.

26. Mary Ellen Bute, transcript of interview with Stanley Kauffmann at The Art Institute of Chicago, May 9, 1976, KSB Collection of MEB, YCAL.

27. Mary Ellen Bute, transcript of interview with Stanley Kauffmann at The Art Institute of Chicago, May 9, 1976, KSB Collection of MEB, YCAL.

28. Stanley Kauffmann, transcript of interview with Mary Ellen Bute, May 9, 1976, at the Art Institute of Chicago, KSB Collection of MEB, YCAL.

29. Mary Ellen Bute, transcript of interview with Stanley Kauffmann at the Art Institute of Chicago May 9, 1976, KSB Collection of MEB, YCAL.

30. Mary Ellen Bute, transcript of interview with Stanley Kaufman at the Art Institute of Chicago, May 9, 1976, KSB Collection of MEB, YCAL.

31. Robert Benayoun, Critics Section Publication, Cannes Festival, May 3–16, 1965, undated clipping, KSB Collection of MEB, YCAL.

32. Theodore J. Nemeth Sr., transcript of interview with author 5/25/1984, KSB Collection of MEB, YCAL.

33. Theodore J. Nemeth, transcript of interview with author, 5/25/1984, KSB Collection of MEB, YCAL.

34. Thelma Schoonmaker, later Academy Award winning film editor for Martin Scorsese, editor and assistant to Mary Ellen Bute on *Passages from James Joyce's Finnegans Wake*, transcript of undated interview notes ca. 1995, personal files of Kit Smyth Basquin. These notes were taken while Larry Mollot was filming an interview with Thelma Schoonmaker for a possible film on Bute, never produced by him, Cecile Starr, and Kit Basquin.

35. Thelma Schoonmaker, transcript of interview with author ca. 1995, KSB Collection of MEB, YCAL.

36. Yoshio Kishi, one of film editors on *Passages from James Joyce's Finnegans Wake*, transcript of telephone interview with author 2/18/1987, KSB Collection of MEB, YCAL.

37. Theodore J. Nemeth Sr., interview with author 5/25/1984, KSB Collection of MEB, YCAL.

38. Yoshio Kishi, transcript of telephone interview with author 2/18/1987, KSB Collection of MEB, YCAL.

39. Yoshio Kishi, transcript of telephone interview with author 2/18/1987, KSB Collection of MEB, YCAL.

40. Theodore J. Nemeth Jr., transcript of taped responses to author's questions 11/8/1988, KSB Collection of MEB, YCAL.

41. Theodore J. Nemeth Jr., transcript of taped responses to author's questions 11/8/1988, KSB Collection of MEB, YCAL.

42. Gretchen Weinberg interview with Mary Ellen Bute, "An Interview with Mary Ellen Bute on the Filming of "Finnegnas Wake", *Film Culture* 35 (winter 1964–65), KSB Collection of MEB, YCAL.

43. Theodore J. Nemeth Sr., transcript of interview with author, 5/25/1984, KSB Collection of MEB, YCAL.

44. Theodore J. Nemeth Sr., transcript of interview with author in Milwaukee 11/22/1984, KSB Collection of MEB, YCAL.

45. Virginia Gibbs Smyth, life-long friend of Mary Ellen Bute and mother of Kit Smyth Basquin, transcript of interview with author in Mrs. Smyth's New York apartment 8/11/1984, KSB Collection of MEB, YCAL.

46. Mary Ellen Bute and Professor William York Tindall interviewed by Jim McCander for Creative Arts Television, Camera Three, 1965, video cassette in personal collection of Kit Smyth Basquin.

47. Zack Bowen, "Lots of Fun with *Finnegans Wake*", undated typescript ca. 1965, KSB Collection of MEB, YCAL.

48. William Gullette, owner of Preview Theatre, Inc. in New York and old friend of Mary Ellen Bute, transcript of telephone interview with author 9/14/1984, KSB Collection of MEB, YCAL.

49. William Gullette, letter to Mary Ellen February 23, 1965, KSB Collection of MEB, YCAL.

50. Thomas Quinn Curtiss, "Finnegan's Movie Shown at Cannes", *The New York Times*, May 22, 1965.

51. Mary Manning, playwright of "Passages from James Joyce's Finnegans Wake", on which Mary Ellen Bute based her film, and professor of drama at Radcliff College (Harvard University), transcript of telephone interview with author 10/20/1986, KSB Collection of MEB, YCAL.

52. Mary Manning, transcript of telephone interview with author 10/20/1986, KSB Collection of MEB, YCAL.

53. Patrick McCarthy, Joyce scholar, "*Finnegans Wake* and Film", typescript of paper delivered at Modern Language Association meeting in Chicago, December 1977, KSB Collection of MEB, YCAL.

54. Zack Bowen, typescript of eulogy given at Mary Ellen Bute's memorial service November, 19, 1983 at the Church of the Transfiguration (Little Church Around the Corner) in New York, KSB Collection of MEB, YCAL.

55. Emily Genauer, "Pinter, Picasso, and Joyce: A Trio for New York", *Newsday* (Oct. 10, 1967), KSB Collection of MEB, YCAL.

56. Jonas Mekas, filmmaker and Program Director of Anthology Film Archives, interview with Kit Smyth Basquin video-taped by Larry Mollot 9/15/ 1995, audio-tape in personal collection of author.

57. Mary Ellen Bute, interview with Gretchen Weinberg, *Film Culture* 35 (Winter 1964–1965) 28, KSB Collection of MEB, YCAL.

58. Gill, Brendan, "The Current Cinema: Talkies", *The New Yorker*, October 14, 1967, 159, CD-Rom courtesy of the New York Public Library, Stephen A. Schwarzman Building.

59. Thornton Wilder, Xerox of note to Mary Ellen Bute from France, October, 1967, KSB Collection of MEB, YCAL.

60. Mary Manning, transcript of telephone interview with author, 10/20/1986, KSB Collection of MEB, YCAL.

61. Theodore J. Nemeth, Jr., transcript of responses to taped questions of author 11/8/1988, KSB Collection of MEB, YCAL.

62. Larry Kardish, Curator of Film, The Museum of Modern Art, New York, demo videotape by Larry Mollot for Mary Ellen Bute documentary ca. 1995, never completed, personal collection of Kit Smyth Basquin.

63. Stanley Kauffmann, *Figures of Light: Film Criticism and Comment* 1967 (New York: Harper & Row, Publishers, 1971) 26–28.

64. "New Yorkers to Film Parade", undated clipping, *Milwaukee Sentinel*, ca. July 3, 1965, KSB Collection of MEB, YCAL.

65. Charles Hacker, friend of Ted Nemeth from Radio City Music Hall, transcript of telephone interview with author, 9/7/1992, KSB Collection of MEB, YCAL.

66. James House Bute Nemeth, transcript of interview with author at his home in Hampton Bays, LI, NY, 8/9/1984, KSB Collection of MEB, YCAL.

67. James House Bute Nemeth, transcript of interview with author at his home in Hampton Bays, LI, NY, 8/9/1984, KSB Collection of MEB, YCAL.

Chapter 6

Thornton Wilder's *Skin of Our Teeth*

Thornton Wilder's *Skin of Our Teeth* failed to be Mary Ellen Bute's second feature film. Lucille Ball was willing to invest in *Skin of Our Teeth* if Bute would cast her in the role of Sabina, the younger woman. Bute said, "No". She felt that the famous actress was too old for the younger part and should play Mrs. Antrobus, the mother. Cliff Robertson would have invested in Bute's film if she had enlarged the part of the father, Mr. Antrobus, for him. She wouldn't compromise.[1] Thornton Wilder invested in Bute's film but was unwilling to be the sole support, although he renewed her option to create a film interpretation of his Pulitzer Prize winning play many times.

Fig. 1. Engagement party of Kit Smyth 1966 at Carlton House NYC. Front row Mary Ellen Bute and Ethel Mae Gullette. Back row Katherine Rorimer, William Gullette, Sally Carey, and Ted Nemeth, Sr.

In Skin of Our Teeth, Thornton Wilder employs archetypes characters in a compression of time sequences rife with anachronisms, as in James Joyce's *Finnegans Wake*. Also like Joyce's novel, Wilder's play is circular, returning at the end to the maid Sabina repeating actions and dialogue from the beginning of the play. In Joyce's text, the final sentence is completed in the first line of the novel.

The Antropos (Greek for "human") family survive the Ice Age, the Flood, and a war, in a comedy about survival with characters who reference Biblical men and women. The title of the play, also about survival, comes from the Book of Job 19:20 in the Bible, "My bone cleaveth to my skin and to my flesh, and I am escaped with the skin of my teeth". Thornton Wilder's message is that civilizations continue to rebuild after disasters, a positive outlook, and timely as he wrote it during the Second World War. In Joyce's text, the lead character, HCE, Here Comes Everybody, is essentially Everyman. He too survives to wake up to a new day. The experimental structure of both Joyce's book and Wilder's play is another element in common. In both cases, the actions are episodic, rather than building in a straight narrative.

Joseph Campbell and Henry Morton Robinson pointed out similarities of themes, plot, language, and characters between *Finnegans Wake* and *Skin of Our Teeth* in two articles published in *The Saturday Review of Literature* on December 19, 1942 and February 13, 1943. Intimately familiar with Joyce's text, they would publish *A Skeleton Key to Finnegans Wake* the next year. Thornton Wilder wrote a response to the assertions but never published it. His reply survived among his papers. He said that after reading Joyce's novel, the idea came to him "that one aspect of it might be expressed in drama:"

> The method of representing mankind's long history through superimposing different epochs of time simultaneously. I even made sketches employing Joyce's characters and locale, but soon abandoned the project. The slight element of plot in the novel is so dimly glimpsed amid the distortions of nightmare and the polyglot of distortions of language that any possibility of dramatization is out of the question. The notion of a play about mankind and the family viewed through several simultaneous layers of time, however persisted and began to surround itself with many inventions of my own. If one's subject is man and the family considered historically, the element of myth inevitably presents itself. It is not necessary to go to Joyce's novel to find the motive of Adam, Eve, Cain, Abel, Lilith, and Noah.[2]

Bennett Cerf wrote a delightful defense of Wilder in *Saturday Review* in 1943. Cerf was a founder of Random House, who had published the first edition of James Joyce's *Ulysses* in the United States in 1933, after winning a landmark court case against government censorship of obscenity. Cerf

Fig. 2. Bute's older son, Ted Nemeth Jr. on his boat with his sons TJ (age 7) and Anthony (age 5) in summer, 1968, on holiday off Block Islands, at the time Bute was working on *Skin of Our Teeth*. Photo by Margo Lion. Courtesy Kit Smyth Basquin Collection of Mary Ellen Bute, Yale Collection of American Literature, Beinecke Rare Book and Manuscript Library.

quoted the opening sentences of Joyce's *Finnegans Wake*, "riverrun, past Eve and Adam's, from swerve of shore to bend of bay, brings a commodious vicus of recirculation ...".[3] Then he declared "that it was utterly incomprehensible to ninety-nine percent of the literate public, and that anybody who can turn that sort of thing into a smash hit on Broadway is entitled to everything he can get".[4]

The Broadway success of *Skin of Our Teeth* related to the dramatic presence of the famous actress Tallulah Bankhead, who played Sabina. The maid/temptress, a comic part, depended on skilled acting to come alive.

Thornton Wilder encouraged Bute many times in letters: "I shall never waver in my conviction that only you can make that picture [Skin of Our

Fig. 3. Ted Nemeth Jr., Mary Ellen Bute, Bill Gullette, Margo Lion, Ted Nemeth Sr. at reception for Virginia Smyth Low, sister of author, in New York, at the York Club, in 1973, photograph by Kit Smyth Basquin, courtesy KSB Collection of MEB, YCAL.

Teeth], bringing to it the same brilliant cinematic instinct and resourceful imagination that you brought to Joyce's work".[5]

Bute tried to raise money for *Skin of Our Teeth* with showings of her *Passages from James Joyce's Finnegans Wake*, and with appearances at schools, museums, and film groups. She also solicited her friends for investments in the film. Thornton Wilder made many loans or gifts.

Somewhat in desperation, Bute decided to sue Sir Kenneth Clark for his Civilization Series, produced by BBC, which used the title "Skin of Our Teeth" for a segment on Viking art and culture. Thornton Wilder had given permission to Kenneth Clark to use the title in a lecture to the BBC.[6] The network agreed to drop the use of the title in subsequent TV showings. Whatever compensation was awarded did not satisfy Mary Ellen, who needed funding for her film, despite Thornton Wilder's continuous investments in it. After much time was lost and money spent on legal fees, Thornton Wilder wrote Bute:

> "Are you prepared to pay and pay for a long litigation against those vast corporations that may bring you no return whatever … ? I hope your lawyer will proceed to draw up in writing a renunciation of those large threatening claims. Then we can start drawing up the contract and I can start making a series of payments as investor in the work … with continued admiration and affection, Thornton.[7]

Bute dropped the suit but she wrote Thornton Wilder:

> "The film industry has changed. It is in a state of chaos. It seems to me it should be possible now to get a commitment to have a musical production done on Broadway first with a guarantee that I will direct the movie, in that way I will be protecting the rights and our interests in every way."[8]

Bute's penchant for expanding productions unrealistically reflected her lack of business acumen and led to her failure to direct a second feature film.

Bute and Nemeth did shoot experimental footage for *Skin of Our Teeth*. The Yale Film Study Center has screen tests for members of the Antrobus family: the parents, George and Maggie Antrobus; the son, Henry; and the daughter, Gladys; as well as the maid Sabina, who became a beauty queen. The actors in the screen tests are not identified. In the process, Bute tried out different combinations of actors. She shot actresses for Sabina's part in bikini bathing suits, appropriate for the second act when Sabina is a beauty queen on the Atlantic City Boardwalk, prior to the deluge. As in James Joyce's *Finnegans* Wake, time is scrambled in *Skin of Our Teeth* from the Ice Age, through Biblical times, to World War II, with civilization rebuilding after each disaster. History repeats itself, the question is, to what end? The structure of the play is experimental. Actors step out of character and address the audience directly.

Bute wrote a film script for the play and created a production schedule scene by scene, but ultimately gave up the project for lack of funding.[9] Isabel Wilder, devoted and loyal to Bute until the end, expressed her disappointment that Bute couldn't be flexible enough to expand the part of Mr. Antrobus for Cliff Robertson in exchange for funding, feeling that a completed film would be a credit to all involved. Isabel Wilder said in a phone interview in 1986:

> She [Mary Ellen Bute] was difficult to work with … Cliff Robertson had loads of money … he compromised. She wanted still more … Oh my what we went through … Theater is a cooperative art … She had so much to give.. She should have been satisfied … She was a loving, darling person … extraordinary ability, conviction in herself. Turned out to be too stubborn for her own good. She was complex."[10]

In another phone conversation, Isabel Wilder commented further on Bute's complexity:

> Mary Ellen was not always wise … her weakness, and she didn't have the success she should have, was that she wanted to do it all alone. She could not cooperate. Our agent and lawyer worked with her long … worked out with Cliff Robertson. It could have gone ahead. She felt he wanted too big a part. He had a right. He was putting up money. He had more experience. She wanted to do it alone. I give her credit for her strength and wanting to do it by herself, but there is compromise. Partnership. You can't do it alone. Any business needs financial backing. I forgive her. The hurt is to see her not do what she wanted … Thornton admired her … he held out. He [Thornton] had many better offers. She was the only one he gave it to … She didn't really trust anyone. Didn't believe in anyone else … Better to produce it first class – would have been to her benefit … I'm devoted to her … wonderful she has gotten full credit for Joyce. I bought a cassette for Yale. I slipped her $10,000 for Whitman. I thought...it would help.[11]

The Wilder brother and sister, who lived together in Connecticut near Yale, were disappointed that she could never raise the money to produce a film of *Skin of Our Teeth*, but remained staunch supporters of Bute. October 17, 1983, two days after Bute died, Isabel Wilder wrote Ted Nemeth Sr.: "I have a solid chain of understanding, communication, affection, and admiration never broken [for Mary Ellen]. I shall miss her so much."[12]

Isabel Wilder was kind and generous to Bute. She wanted Bute to have recognition for her work and was excited to know that a biography was being written about her. She would have been disappointed that it was still in the works over thirty-five years later. She wrote the author in 1985:

> Dear Kit,
>
> Mary Ellen is fortunate to have such a spirited, intelligent, attractive, and inspired young person, determined young woman, to write her biography – I want to help all I can.[13]

Thornton Wilder died in 1975, at which point Bute abandoned her film based on his play. Test footage for Bute's *Skin of our Teeth* is in the Yale Film Study Center.

While Bute was working on *Skin of Our Teeth*, Ted Nemeth Sr. filmed a couple of shorts. *Rama* (1970), was a 16-minute color video mixing dance, nature, and a voice-over monologue. Sugar Cain wrote and directed it. Nemeth used multiple filters to create a gauzy, artistic look.

The following year, 1971, Nemeth was the cinematographer for *Fable Safe*, a color film, 8 min 49 sec., directed by Erik Barnouw, a Columbia University professor and radio producer who had served on the Board of

Fig. 4. Ted Nemeth, cinematographer, *Fable Safe*,
directed by Erik Barnouw, from MOMA brochure,
courtesy KSB Collection of MEB, YCAL.

Governors of the Academy of Television Arts and Sciences. He won a George Polk award for journalism that year for his history of radio and television, *A Tower in Babel*. Professor Henry Graff served as historical consultant. Sumner Jules Glimcher, also a professor at Columbia, produced it for the Center for Mass Communications of Columbia University. Animated figures convey the absurdity of stockpiling weapons, as both sides keep up with each other, augmenting their stock of weapons. The cartoonist was Robert Osborn. Music was composed and sung by Tom Glazer, a folk singer and composer. The film reflects the cold war of military competition between the USA and the USSR. It premiered in the 1971 New York Film Festival. It was purchased by NBC for prime-time use, but not used. The film, however, was shown at the London, Locarno, Tampere, Melbourne, and other film festivals. In 1972, it won Poland's Cracow Silver Dragon Award, the festival's second prize.[14] It was selected for two telecasts on the series "The Threat of Nuclear War", sponsored by the Union of Concerned Scientists,

Physicians for Social Responsibility, released in 1980 by the Museum of Modern Art.

Thornton Wilder died December 7, 1975. Mary Ellen abandoned *Skin of Our* Teeth and started her last film, *Out of the Cradle Endlessly Rocking* on Walt Whitman.[15] In January, 1983, a TV movie was made of *Skin of Our Teeth* directed by Jack O'Brien for PBS American Playhouse.

References

1. Isabel Wilder, sister of Thornton Wilder, transcript of telephone interview with author 7/6/1987, Kit Smyth Basquin Collection of Mary Ellen Bute, Yale Collection of American Literature, Beinecke Rare Book and Manuscript Library.

2. Thornton Wilder, draft of letter to the editor, *Saturday Review of Literature*, enclosed in Wilder's letter to his sister Isabel, December 17, 1942, Private Collection, reproduced in Penelope Niven, *Thornton Wilder: A Life*, 2012 (New York: Harper Perennial, 2013) 547.

3. James Joyce, *Finnegans Wake*, 1939 (New York: Viking Press/Penguin, 1986) 3.

4. Bennett Cerf, "Trade Winds", *Saturday Review of Literature*, January 9, 1943, 12, reproduced in Penelope Niven, *Thornton Wilder: A Life*, 2012 (New York: Harper Perennial, 2013) 547.

5. Thornton Wilder, author of *Skin of Our* Teeth, letter [Xerox] to Mary Ellen Bute 12/10/1970, KSB Collection of MEB, YCAL.

6. Thornton Wilder, letter [Xerox] to Mary Ellen Bute 8/3/1970, KSB Collection of MEB, YCAL.

7. Thornton Wilder, letter [Xerox] to Mary Ellen Bute 12/27/1970, KSB Collection of MEB, YCAL.

8. Mary Ellen Bute letter to Thornton Wilder (Xerox) January 1971, KSB Collection of MEB, YCAL.

9. Mary Ellen Bute, handwritten undated production schedule for *Skin of Our Teeth*, ca. 1970, KSB Collection of MEB, YCAL.

10. Isabel Wilder, transcript of telephone call to author in Milwaukee 2/16/1986, KSB Collection of MEB, YCAL.

11. Isabel Wilder, transcript of telephone conversation with author 7/28/1984, KSB Collection of MEB, YCAL.

12. Isabel Wilder, letter to Theodore J. Nemeth Sr., 10/19/1983, KSB Collection of MEB, YCAL.

13. Isabel Wilder, undated note to author, summer 1985, KSB Collection of MEB, YCAL.

14. Theodore J. Nemeth Sr., transcript of interview with author in Milwaukee, 11/22/1984, KSB Collection of MEB, YCAL.

15. Penelope Niven, *Thornton Wilder: A Life*, 2012 (New York: Harper Perennial, 2013) 425.

Chapter 7

Out of the Cradle Endlessly Rocking: The Odyssey of Walt Whitman, A Builder of the American Vision and Final Days

ary Ellen Bute started her final film, *Out of the Cradle Endlessly Rocking: The Odyssey of Walt Whitman, A Builder of the American Vision*, shortly after Thornton Wilder's death in 1975. Wilder, a fan of Walt Whitman (1819–1892), sparked Bute's interest in the poet.[1] "Out of the Cradle Endlessly Rocking" is the first line of a poem Whitman called "Sea-Drift", 1859. A sad bird calls for his lost mate, heard by a little boy who interprets the bird song as a call to him, to Whitman, for his own song, his own poetic voice. The "rocking" is a metaphor for the musical shuttling of the mocking-bird, the warble of the bird song, which awakens Whitman. He also hears the word "death" in the bird song, reminding him of time passing, of the inevitable end, of the need to speak now. Clearly Bute, like Whitman, heard the call to create a film now, before her end, which she knew was approaching.

Bute's Whitman film was her lifeline. As long as she was working, she was living. Despite a shortage of support, she extended her film from ten minutes, with a focus on Walt Whitman's publication of *The Leaves of Grass*, to thirty minutes, and then to an hour, feature-length film. It would have included not only *The Leaves of Grass*, but also the Civil War, the other major influence on the writer's life.

By the late 1970s, Bute, out of money and separated from her husband, was living in one small room at the Parkside Residence, a Salvation Army home on Gramercy Park, intended for young girls starting out in New York. Bute's friend Virginia Gibbs Smyth said that the residence made an exception for Mary Ellen Bute.[2]

In 1976 Bute was awarded a grant from The American Film Institute for her Whitman film. Out of 1000 applicants, 43 were chosen, according to a congratulatory letter from U. S. Senator from New York, Jacob K. Javits.[3] The jury of filmmakers selecting Bute's work included: Storm De

119

Hirsch, John Hanhardt, Chuck Jones, Gordon Parks Sr., Ivan Passer, Julia Phillips, Willard Vandyke, Haskell Wexler, and Oscar Williams.[4] In 1977, the Rockefeller Foundation also awarded her a grant.[5] But the cost of her film climbed as she extended it in length from a short to a feature.

Bute's son Jim Nemeth was a stand in for the main actor playing Walt Whitman, John Getz, who would later go on to a long career in television. Jim Nemeth said that Bute conceived beautiful shots interspersed with the reading of Whitman's poetry. He added, "She started to get good. Pretty images, pretty horse farm. Alvin Topping donated his time and ranch [on Long Island]. Poetic images."[6] Jim Nemeth felt that this film expressed the upbeat, encouraging, positive Bute more than any of her others.[7] Bute, like Whitman, suffered criticism and economic hard times but persevered to create. Whitman, now considered the father of American literary modernism, was praised by Ralph Waldo Emerson and by many British writers and intellectuals, including Oscar Wilde, Robert Louis Stevenson, and Alfred Lord Tennyson, among others, but he was not widely accepted in his own country during his lifetime.[8] In 1881, a Boston publisher prepared to print Whitman's expanded version of *Leaves of Grass*, was threatened with obscenity charges. The book was published in Philadelphia.

Also like Whitman, Bute saw through social hypocrisy. Her short film, *The Boy Who Saw Through* expressed her awareness of the reality behind social conventions. However, she did not possess Whitman's fierce independence. She was rooted in Southern refinement. She was more concerned with a pretty surface, accompanied by mellifluous words and music, than by a revelation of inner expression. She had the eye of a painter. To the end, she framed shots like beautiful compositions. She was not a feminist. As her son Ted Nemeth, Jr. said, "She did not have that language".[9] She enjoyed the amenities that accompanied lady-like or flirtatious behavior, although she bemoaned her lack of power and especially her lack of funds. Like Whitman, Bute was driven to create and to experiment with form. But unlike Whitman, who was notorious for explicit sexual content, Bute's refined upbringing prevented her from revealing sex as physical passion. In *Passages from James Joyce's Finnegans Wake*, sex was a tease, like a strip act, not an earthly mingling of bodies. She could not have spoken of Whitman's homosexuality, nor was she planning to do it. It was irrelevant to her picture of his artistry.[10] Like Whitman, she chose contemporary images when dealing with time, such as the rocket launch in *Passages from James Joyce's Finnegans Wake* and the orbit around the moon in *Whitman*. Perhaps her biggest link with Whitman was her optimism and belief in the good of all.

Bute quoted from Walt Whitman's *November Boughs* in her film and in her promotional material:

> The new world needs the poems of realities and science and the democratic average and basic equality … in the center of all, and object of all, stands the human being, toward whose heroic and spiritual evolution poems and everything directly or indirectly tend, old world and new.[11]

Clearly Bute subscribed to the idea of the human being as heroic, with spiritual evolution. Her writing was at its best when she was quoting famous authors, which she did for her live action feature films. Even in her short feature, *The Boy Who Saw Through*, she and her scriptwriter, Guy Glover, used words written by the author of the short story on which her film was based, John Pudney. Joyce's melodious, insightful words were part of her attraction to *Finnegans Wake*, as were the words of Thornton Wilder for *Skin of Our Teeth* and Walt Whitman for *Out of the Cradle Endlessly Rocking*. In some materials for her Whitman film, Bute actually added the words "Passages from" to emphasize her use of his quotes.

At the beginning of Bute's *Whitman* film, she quoted Whitman's poem from *Leaves of Grass*, recited by the late Chet Huntley in his newscast at the time of the Apollo 8 Mission, when Americans orbited the moon, December, 1968:

> Dearest now thou O soul,
> Walk out with me toward the unknown region,
> Where neither ground is for the feet nor any path to follow?
> No map there, nor guide
> Nor voice sounding, nor touch of human hand,
> Nor face with blooming flesh, nor lips, nor eyes, are in that land …

This passage paired with imagery of a rocket firing off showed the relevancy of Whitman for future generations. Bute wrote the following synopsis of her hour-long film, *Out of the Cradle Endlessly Rocking: The Odyssey of Walt Whitman, A Builder of the American Vision*:

> The film dramatically portrays Whitman as a young man who has attained the full realization of the power of his poetic and social "visions" of man as a creature of magnificent beauty, worth, potential.

> Intermixed with the dramatic portrayal of Whitman will be footage of the present, demonstrating the remarkable foresight and prophetic qualities of his writing.

> For example, the initial footage will combine Whitman, NASA film excerpts and voiceover reading from Whitman by the late Chet Huntley taken from his televised reportage of the Apollo 8 Mission.

> Whitman's enormous impact as a "new" American artistic force will be defined dramatically by portrayal of the impact of his work and personality upon Ralph Waldo Emerson.

The use of original documents and still photographs vividly evoke these crucial years in Whitman's and America's development. In addition, the frequent use of live actors and location shooting further dramatize the periods.

The film, produced and directed in color by Mary Ellen Bute, will run approximately 60 minutes. Locations will include Long Island and New England.

The film is suitable for wide and extended showing. Distribution is specifically projected for Public Broadcasting Television, Colleges and High Schools. Foreign distribution is also anticipated especially in Europe where Whitman's popularity is broadly based.[12]

In addition, Bute hand-wrote a progress report dated August 30, 1976 on stationery from the C.W. Post College on Long Island, where she could have been shooting footage for Whitman:

"Walt Whitman" – Prod. No. 60 Progress Report August 30, 1976

Script –   First revision made to fit possible shooting locations
              First revision typing and Xerox
              Daily breakdown scene by scene

Casting – over 40 actors and narrators interviewed
              – recording voice tests …
              Video tape tests –
              Nagra recording equipment rental
              Recording tape purchase

Locations – Survey of possible locations –
              Negotiations for use of locations
              Examined electrical power available at each site
              Travel to and from Princeton NJ
              Location release acquired
              Walt Whitman's home on Long Island
              George Eastman House in Rochester, NY
    Material and props to be used in Rochester NY
              To Eastman House for old photos
              Search for photographic material
              Copies of photo material for filming
              Purchase of photo material
              Preparation of material for animation photography[13]

Bute's report gives some idea of her process, including adapting her script to the locations available, casting from a wide selection of actors, research for shooting locations, securing releases for use of them, checking on the electrical power available at each, the use of old photographs from the George Eastman House, and the addition of animation footage.

Unfortunately, the cost of silver, an element of film stock, tripled during Bute's production. Her request for completion funds October 31, 1980 for a 16mm color sound film running 60 minutes for *Out of the Cradle Endlessly Rocking*, shows how much work she still needed to finish and the huge financial odds she was up against:

Post-Photography and Completion Budget

EDITORIAL facilities and services	$10,000.
OPTICALS special effects and laboratory processing	4,000.
INSERT PHOTOGRAPHY documents, pictures, etc.	3,000.
STOCK SHOTS research, duplication & rights	3,000.
MUSIC & SOUND EFFECTS musicians, recording studio	12,000.
SOUND MIX voice & music, studio facilities	4,000
TITLES & CREDITS art work, photography & processing	3,000
NEGATIVES matching & conforming: equipment & service	4,000
ANSWER PRINT complete with opticals	3,000
Contingencies	4,000
Total completion costs	$50,000.

Bute noted that major photography completed cost $60,000, funded by The American Film Institute, The Rockefeller Foundation, and the Producer.[14] In another memo dated the same day, she added to the roster of supporters, Dry Salvages Foundation, an educational film organization.[15] She also solicited donations from her family and friends.

For Bute's Whitman film, she was more responsible about the use of locations than for the Wake film fifteen years before. No doubt the whole procedure for using locations had changed. For *Passages from James Joyce's Finnegans Wake*, Bute would often just show up at a location, announce "educational film", and start shooting.[16] For *Whitman*, for example she, under the auspices of Expanding Cinema, sent a check to the historic house for filming in the Morris Jummel Mansion for Ralph Waldo Emerson's study, photographed April 13, 1977.[17]

On March 16, 1979, Adam Reilly, Theater Supervisor at The American Film Institute in Washington, D.C. offered Mary Ellen Bute a retrospective at the John F. Kennedy Center, adding that Jonas Mekas of Anthology Film Archives in New York would also like to do a retrospective of Bute's films:

> I would like to pursue the idea of doing a retrospective of your work at the AFI Theater in the Kennedy Center. A good deal of your films have not been seen for a while, and I think this event will help put your contribution to the art of film in its proper perspective.
>
> I've talked to our archive department and they are very much interested in seeing that your work is properly preserved for posterity … The archives program works in collaboration with the Anthology Film Archives which has been working assiduously for years to preserve important experimental/independent filmmakers work and they recommend that you get in touch so that Jonas Mekas can help you … Jonas would like to do a retrospective of your work in New York … .[18]

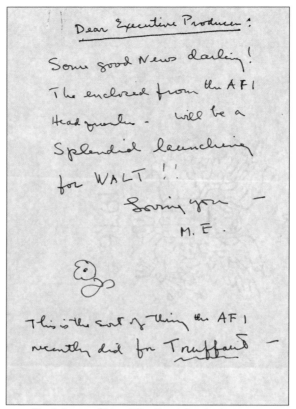

Fig. 1. Image of Mary Ellen Bute's handwritten note
to Virginia Gibbs Smyth in two colors of ink with a
hand drawn flower, Kit Basquin collection of Mary
Ellen Bute, YCAL.

Bute was so excited that she sent a copy of the letter to her good friend
Virginia Gibbs Smyth, who had invested in her Whitman film:

> Dear Executive Producer,
>
> Some good news darling! The enclosed from AFI Head ... Will be a splendid
> launching for WALT! Loving you – M. E. This is the sort of thing the AFI
> recently did for Truffaut – [19]

This handwritten note is in two colors of ink, red and blue, with a hand
drawn flower at the end. Bute probably got the idea to write in multiple
colors of ink from Thornton Wilder, who was known to do it for
emphasis in his correspondence.

Sadly, Bute's husband insisted that the AFI buy Bute's films in order to
show them, short sighted on his part. This may be the reason the
retrospective did not take place. A Bute retrospective would have brought
attention to her films, added credibility to her work, and attracted funds

124

for her Whitman film. Possibly she wanted to conserve her flagging energy for her Whitman film, but that is not the impression she gave in her note to Mrs. Smyth. Bute missed out on related offers for a retrospective in D.C, a retrospective at Anthology Film Archives in New York, and on the opportunity to conserve and preserve her films for future viewers. This was a big loss.

Bute's arthritis, back pain, and heart condition grew worse throughout these last years, but she tried to ignore her health, until she couldn't. In 1980, during a transit strike in New York City, Bute, hearing of my visit from Milwaukee to my mother in New York, walked two miles from her apartment to my mother's to leave me a present. It was small and wrapped, but I don't remember what it was. Bute could not have afforded a taxi. Unfortunately, she did not call to say she was coming. My mother and I were at the theater. The next day Bute was in Cabrini Medical Center, on east 19th Street near her apartment on Grammercy Park . Nearing the end of her life, she was in frail health with a heart condition and severe arthritis. Her hands were gnarled and her back was stooped. She would be in and out of Cabrini many times over the next few years. She was in continuous pain, although she never mentioned it, except once, when she referred to having a "blessed shot of cortisone" in her back.

The Yale Film Study Center has original footage shot by Bute for her Whitman film, without the sound. It can be viewed on a Steenbeck flat-bed viewer. Thanks to a donation from Bute's friend Isabel Wilder, Yale bought films and files from Bute's husband after Bute's death in 1983. Ted Nemeth Sr. was in poor health with Parkinson's disease and needed money.

Bute's film script for Whitman at the Beinecke helps to place these pieces into her narrative.[20] The final shape of the film that Bute conceived is impossible to know. Her son Jim Nemeth said that she had shot about thirty per cent of the film.[21]

In one scene in the film, Whitman compares his poetry from a notebook with the proof sheet coming out of the printing press. In another, he helps set the type. The assistant in the print shop wears an old-fashioned printer's apron. The close-ups of the printing press add authenticity to these early scenes of Walt Whitman, who self-published his first edition of *Leaves of Grass* in 1881. The Eastman color film has faded, but the original was shot in 4-color. Another reel of sound only for the print shop has Whitman reading his "I Speak the Sound".

One shot shows Whitman (John Getz) reading a manuscript next to an artful still-life of fruit. The aesthetic composition reflects Bute's background as a painter.

Fig. 2. John Getz as Whitman, In the Print Shop, *Out of the Cradle Endlessly Rocking* (unfinished film), ca. 1976, film still, Courtesy Kit Smyth Basquin Collection of Mary Ellen Bute, Yale Collection of American Literature, Beinecke Rare Book and Manuscript Library.

Fig. 3. Mary Ellen Bute with actor John Getz during a shooting break for *Out of the Cradle Endlessly Rocking* (unfinished film), ca. 1975. Courtesy KSB Collection of MEB, YCAL.

Another shot of Whitman (John Getz) and a pretty young woman on a picnic "Whitman Having Problems with a Muse" suggests his involvement with women, but distracts the viewer from an awareness of Whitman's homosexuality. This was a conscious choice for Bute and in

Fig. 4. Whitman (John Getz) reading manuscript, film still from *Out of the Cradle Endlessly Rocking* (unfinished) ca. 1976. Courtesy KSB Collection of MEB, YCAL.

keeping with her love of surface refinement. She also constructed a pretty picture, always a plus.

A film clip with a beautiful shot of branches in front of a full moon extends long enough for a poem to be read as a voice over. The film script suggests this view of a moon as a reflection of the calm of night between military battles of the Civil War. In 1867 Whitman published a series of

Fig. 5. Whitman (John Getz) Having a Problem with a Muse on a Picnic (actress unknown), *Out of the Cradle Endlessly Rocking* (unfinished film) ca. 1976, film still. Courtesy KSB Collection of MEB, YCAL.

Fig. 6. Brad Garnett (actor), Mary Ellen Bute, Virginia Gibbs Smyth and Herndon Werth in New York ca. 1978, Cashman Photo, Enterprises Inc. Waldorf Astoria, Courtesy KSB Collection of MEB, YCAL.

poems, *Drum-Taps*, responding to the Civil War, during which he volunteered as a nurse.

Additional Civil War footage illuminates Whitman at night, with a lantern, tending a fallen soldier, who has a gun next to him. In another war scene, Whitman moves in and out of his tent, the drape of which is used as a patterned background behind him. In the tent, Whitman writes and also lies on a cot. Clearly visual space was extended to give time for the reading of some of Whitman's war poems. Bute interprets the Civil War in close-ups, focusing on the actions of Whitman. These scenes were shot "night for day", in the daytime but with filters on the light to make the views look like night.

Six months before Bute died, film historian Cecile Starr, who distributed Bute's films, secured arrangements for a Cineprobe on Mary Ellen Bute at the Museum of Modern Art in New York, part of their series on independent and experimental filmmakers. Cecile Starr and critic Lillian Schiff developed promotional materials under the auspices of the Women's Independent Film Exchange, WIFE as the Exchange was called. Bute was a constant supporter of it. Joyce scholar Zack Bowen delivered an elegant accolade to Bute at MOMA on April 4, 1983. Only his memorial remarks later that year have survived.

Larry Kardish, Curator of Film at The Museum of Modern Art wrote to Cecile Starr afterward:

Fig. 7. Mary Ellen Bute at Cineprobe at The
Museum of Modern Art, New York, April 4, 1983.
Photograph by Cecile Starr, Courtesy KSB
Collection of MEB, YCAL.

> Mary-Ellen is a marvel, and her evening here went very, very well. Her short films, and we must show more of them (if not preserve them) are revelations. Thank you, Cecile, for helping make the Cineprobe with Mary-Ellen possible … .[22]

Writer Lillian Schiff described the filmmaker the year she died:

> It was immediately apparent that the body of work couldn't be separated from the comfortable upbringing, the endless seeking for knowledge, and sharp perception and intelligence, the humor and tenacity. This very small, thin, youthful person with honey-colored hair and a Houston accent, this lady with most considerate manners, was one of the first Americans to make abstract animated films, the first [woman] in the world to use electronically generated images on film, and the first to make a film based on James Joyce's novel.[23]

Bute's friend Virginia Gibbs Smyth depicted Mary Ellen Bute at the end, still working relentlessly on her Whitman film:

> Nobody ever enjoyed her work more than Mary Ellen did. She worked from morning until night and sometimes when she was sick. I remember that last

horrible summer when she was in one hospital twice and another one also. Even when she fell and had a concussion and a bruise – the last time I saw her she had a big bruise on her forehead from the concussion – why she was still trying to work and had work spread out in front of her."[24]

Mrs. Smyth also said that the hospital called Bute's brother John in Houston and told him that she was in critical condition and needed a pace maker. He sent a check for $5,000. Bute tore it up and said, "I'm not an object of charity". She hurt his feelings.[25]

Isabel Wilder had sent Bute $2,000.00 for heart surgery. Mary Ellen spent the money on film.[26] Bute's son Jim Nemeth said that she believed "you could heal yourself with the power of positive thinking", a combination of a Christian Science doctrine and Yoga.[27] She tried to focus on mind over body, but in the end, her body failed. Mary Ellen Bute died at Cabrini Medical Center October 17, 1983, a few weeks before her 77th birthday.

Mrs. Smyth said that she would miss Mary Ellen Bute's "sparkling, bubbling personality and the way she laughed and her sense of humor".[28]

Playwright Mary Manning also expressed loss in response to Virginia Gibbs Smyth's note informing her of Bute's death: "What a dear, loving, and loyal friend she was to me … What many talents she had."[29]

Howard Beckerman of *Backstage* wrote:

> Mary Ellen was a very special person. She was an enthusiastic, creative, original artist as well as a delightful and gracious woman. She lived a long full life, her films were precedent setting and important to the historical flow of animation and film art; they will endure.[30]

Among Bute's papers was a quote attributed to Ralph Waldo Emerson, "Success", although recent scholarship questions that authorship. Whoever wrote it, the quote captures the spirit of Mary Ellen Bute, a warm, enthusiastic, energetic, supportive person who made a difference to the people around her, and through her films, to a wide circle:

> To laugh often and much; to win the respect of intelligent people and the affection of children; to earn the appreciation of honest critics and endure the betrayal of false friends; to appreciate beauty, to find the best in others; to leave the world a bit better, whether by a healthy child, a garden patch or redeemed social condition; to know even one life has breathed easier because you lived. This is to have succeeded.[31]

Jim Nemeth encapsulated his mother: "She was a dynamite lady, lots of energy. Created against all odds".[32]

The most comprehensive description of Bute is in Zack Bowen's eulogy at the Church of the Transfiguration ("Little Church around the Corner") November 19, 1983:

Fig. 8. James Liddy (1934–2008) and Ted Nemeth Sr. (1911–1986) at University of Wisconsin-Milwaukee, 1984.

Mary Ellen can best be summed up by two words – motion and imagination. She was a person constantly in motion, either in the process of making something new or promoting some new project. Her vitality, her energy, her enthusiasm, her good humor, her etiquette were all a part of the process of creativity with which she was so closely identified and which was the essence of her professional life … I have never known anyone who was as unselfish professionally as Mary Ellen – attributing her own creativity and success to others.[33]

Ted Nemeth Sr., suffering from Parkinson's Disease, lived another three years. In 1984, he lectured on experimental animation and on *Passages from James Joyce's Finnegans Wake* at the University of Wisconsin-Milwaukee in the classes of Dick Blau, Head of the Film Department. Kit Smyth Basquin introduced his talk on animation, prior to the screening of several of Bute's shorts. An Irish poet on the faculty at UW-Milwaukee, James Liddy, introduced Nemeth for his commentary prior to the screening of *Passages from James Joyce's Finnegans Wake*.

Thanks to a generous donation to the Beinecke Library at Yale University by Isabel Wilder, Ted Nemeth Sr. sold prints of Bute's films, along with test footage for unfinished films, documents, and photographs to the Beinecke. The film footage was housed by the Yale Film Study Center. Years later, in 2009, Basquin, prior to moving to a new apartment, donated nine boxes of research notes, photographs, and documents on Bute to the Beinecke.

Mary Ellen Bute pioneered abstract animation in the US producing fourteen shorts starting in 1934, assisted by cinematographer Theodore J. Nemeth. She was one of the first filmmakers in the US to use electronic imagery, paving the way for the future. Her live action narrative films included a half hour film, *The Boy Who Saw Through*, starring Christopher Walken as a child actor, and *Passages from James Jouyce's Finnegans Wake*, the first interpretation of Joyce on film, which won a Cannes Film Festival prize for direction. Musician and writer Albert Glinsky, author of a biography of electronics pioneer Leon Theremin, wrote in 2014, "She [Mary Ellen Bute] was a true pioneer, and her important place in history should be established, especially with regard to primacy, as she was there with many techniques ahead of some who are today credited with her discoveries".[34]

She will be remembered for her innovative, creative films and also for her drive, determination, warm personality and support of filmmakers, musicians, friends, and family.

References

1. Penelope Niven, *Thornton Wilder: A Life*, 2012 (New York: Harper Perennial, 2013) 425.

2. Virginia Gibbs Smyth, friend of Mary Ellen Bute, mother of author, transcript of interview with author in Mrs. Smyth's New York apartment 8/11/1984, Kit Smyth Basquin Collection of Mary Ellen Bute, Yale Collection of American Literature, Beinecke Rare Book and Manuscript Library.

3. Jacob K. Javits, U. S. Senator from New York, letter to Mary Ellen Bute 3/30/1977, KSB Collection of MEB, YCAL.

4. Western Union Mailgram to Mary Ellen Bute from George Stevens Jr. of the American Film Institute 2/4/1976, KSB Collection of MEB, YCAL.

5. Mary Ellen Bute, copy of letter to Ms. Jan Hag, Head of the Independent Filmmaker Program, The American Film Institute, 1976, KSB Collection of MEB, YCAL.

6. James House Bute Nemeth, younger son of Mary Ellen Bute and Ted Nemeth, Sr. , transcript of interview with author at his home in Hampton Bays, LI, NY 8/9/1984, KSB Collection of MEB, YCAL.

7. James House Bute Nemeth, transcript of interview with author at his home in Hampton Bays, LI, NY 8/9/1984, KSB Collection of MEB, YCAL.

8. Justin Kaplan, *Leaves of Grass by Walt Whitman* (New York: Bantam Books, 1983) xvii.

9. Theodore J. Nemeth Jr., older son of Mary Ellen Bute, transcript of taped response to author's questions, 11/8/1988, KSB Collection of MEB, YCAL.

10. James House Bute Nemeth, transcript of interview with author at his house in Hampton Bays, LI, NY, 8/9/1984, KSB Collection of MEB, YCAL.

11. Mary Ellen Bute, American Foundation for the Arts Grant, undated, ca. 1978, KSB Collection of MEB, YCAL.

12. Mary Ellen Bute, undated synopsis of *Out of the Cradle Endlessly Rocking* ca. 1976, KSB Collection of MEB, YCAL.

13. Mary Ellen Bute, handwritten progress report on Walt Whitman, 8/30/1976, KSB Collection of MEB, YCAL.

14. Mary Ellen Bute, Request for Completion Funds for *Out of the Cradle Endlessly Rocking*, October 31, 1980, KSB Collection of MEB, YCAL.

15.   Mary Ellen Bute, "Current Status", October 31, 1980, KSB Collection of MEB, YCAL.

16.   Page Johnson, actor playing Shaun in *Passages from Finnegans Wake*, transcript of interview with author, August 9, 1995 for Larry Mollot's unfinished video on Mary Ellen Bute, KSB Collection of MEB, YCAL.

17.   Mary Ellen Bute, letter to Washington Headquarters Assn., Morris-Jumel Mansion, June 6, 1977 and Xerox of check, KSB Collection of MEB, YCAL.

18.   Adam Reilly, AFI Theater Supervisor, letter to Mary Ellen Bute 3/16/1979, KSB Collection of MEB, YCAL.

19.   Penelope Niven, *Thornton Wilder: A Life* 2012 (New York: Harper Perennial, 2013) xv.

20.   Mary Ellen Bute, film script for one-hour feature on poet Walt Whitman, *Out of the Cradle Endlessly Rocking*, KSB Collection of MEB, YCAL.

21.   James House Bute Nemeth, transcript of interview with author at his home in Hampton Bays, L I, NY, 8/9/1984, KSB Collection of MEB, YCAL.

22.   Larry Kardish, Film Curator, Museum of Modern Art, letter to Cecile Starr, April 5, 1983, KSB Collection of MEB, YCAL.

23.   Lillian Schiff, writer, interview with Mary Ellen Bute July, 1983, *Film Library Quarterly* 17, nos. 2–4 (1984), 53–61, KSB Collection of MEB, YCAL.

24.   Virginia Gibbs Smyth, transcript of interview with author at Mrs. Smyth's apartment in New York 8/11/1984, KSB Collection of MEB, YCAL.

25.   Virginia Gibbs Smyth, transcript of telephone conversation with author 10/11/1984, KSB Collection of MEB, YCAL.

26.   Virginia Gibbs Smyth, conversation with author in her New York apartment 12/26/1985, KSB Collection of MEB, YCAL.

27.   James House Bute Nemeth, transcript of interview with author at his home in Hampton Bays, LI, NY 8/9/1984, KSB Collection of MEB, YCAL.

28.   Virginia Gibbs Smyth, transcript of interview with author in Mrs. Smyth's New York apartment 8/11/1984, KSB Collection of MEB, YCAL.

29.   Isabel Wilder, note to Virginia Gibbs Smyth 10/31/1983, KSB Collection of MEB, YCAL.

30.   Howard Beckerman, *Backstage*, Nov. 11, 1983, KSB Collection of MEB, YCAL.

31.   Author unknown, attributed to Ralph Waldo Emerson, typed definition of "success" found among Mary Ellen Bute's papers, KSB Collection of MEB, YCAL.

32.   James House Bute Nemeth, transcript of telephone conversation with author, 7/8/1984, KSB Collection of MEB, YCAL.

33.   Zack Bowen, Eulogy For Mary Ellen Bute, Church of the Transfiguration (Little Church Around the Corner), November 19, 1983, typescript given to author, KSB Collection of MEB, YCAL.

34.   Albert Glinsky, note to author 12/26/2014, in private collection of Kit Smyth Basquin.

Cecile Starr (1921–2014)
ca. 2000, courtesy Suzanne Boyajian.

Chapter 8

Cecile Starr:
Champion of Women Filmmakers

ecile Starr represented and distributed the films of Mary Ellen Bute from 1976 until Starr's death December 9, 2014. Even her last year, Starr arranged for the Whitney Museum of American Art, New York, to purchase three of Bute's films, two of which were screened at the opening of their new facility south of the High Line, on 10th Avenue and about 11th Street. One week after I retired from over thirteen years as Associate Administrator in Drawings and Prints at The Metropolitan Museum of Art, January 10, 2014, Starr called me up and said, "Now you have time to write the biography of Mary Ellen Bute. Let's do it." I had given my nine boxes of files to the Beinecke Library at Yale thinking I would never write the book. Cecile was a film historian. I thought, she would be the perfect co-author. She knew my familiarity with the Bute family from having worked on a video biography of Bute with Larry Mollot and me, which never materialized. We could not raise the money for it. Starr was 92. I needed to work fast. I agreed to write the biography with her. I immediately embarked on fourteen visits to the Beinecke Library in New Haven, where I digitally photographed my files, so I could work on them at home. I sent Starr each chapter as I finished it. She cheered me on, but she was occupied with selling three Bute films to the Whitney Museum and transferring the distribution of Bute films and her film prints to Center for Visual Music.

See Colour Plate 12.
Cecile Starr (1921–2014) ca. 2005, Courtesy Suzanne Boyajian.

Cecile Starr, film historian, teacher at Columbia University, The New School, and Hunter College, and film critic for *Saturday Review*, long supported equality for women and men filmmakers. Her outspoken article for *The New York Times* January 9, 1977, asked "Is the Government Subsidizing Sexism in Film?" With statistics, she pointed out the imbalance of government supported grants and positions of influence for women and men filmmakers. Male filmmakers with power hated her revelations and criticized her at the time. Jonas Mekas, filmmaker and

Artistic Director of Anthology Film Archives, wrote a particularly hurtful comment published in the *Soho Weekly News*, but years later, in 1979, expressed interest in giving Mary Ellen a retrospective, when she was offered one by the American Film Institute in Washington, D. C. Experimental filmmaker and teacher Stan Brakhage vehemently opposed showing Mary Ellen's films at the School of the Art Institute of Chicago, where he had taught, while she was alive, but after a film presentation by Cecile Starr including Mary Ellen's films at a film conference at Harvard years after Mary Ellen's death, he wrote Starr a note February 9, 1996:

> Dear Cecile,
> You made so biographically clear the details of the struggle of Mary Ellen Bute (out of Texas, etc.) that I was enabled to feel the particularity of "flower" her work is – enabled to see it (against all previous prejudice) ... thus to give insight on the particularities which shape my own works (no sense being a cactus in Eden – somesuch) ... (we need every flowering, including ... cactus-sharits, soforth). You were/are lovely. Blessings, Stan[1]

Then professor Brakhage wrote to Starr again June 10, 1999:

> Dear Cecile,
> Well, and so here we both are on the far side of the Dark Tower once again. Congratulations to you: I'm so proud to know you – such a wonderful spirit you have! I'll be doing Claire Parker, Mary Ellen Bute, et al again in the fall. Blessings, Stan[2]

Cecile Starr was born July 14, 1921 in Nashville, TN, where her uncle Milton Starr owned movie theaters for African-Americans. That same year, Starr's parents moved with her and her older brother to New Orleans. As a teenager, Starr went to two or three movies a week. Her brother, six years older, worked in a movie theater downtown.

In college at Louisiana State University, Baton Rouge, Starr saw avant-garde films from a series distributed by the Museum of Modern Art. After graduation, she moved to New York to study French in graduate School at Columbia University, but World War II broke out in 1941 in the USA, and Starr left for a typing job at the Australian News and Information Bureau. She typed radio messages about the war until 1945. Then she took a typing job with The March of Time, a newsreel for movie theaters. In NYC she saw documentaries at MOMA and met filmmakers at film luncheons. In the late 1950s she taught at Columbia Teacher's College. As part of her salary, she was given a scholarship to complete her master's degree. After completing it, she taught graduate students at Columbia University film history, documentary filmmaking, and film criticism, 1955–1960. She also wrote for *Film Forum*, a quarterly publication of Columbia University's Teacher's College. In addition, from 1949–1959 Starr wrote film reviews for *Saturday Review* and for the *Encyclopedia Britannica*. Later she taught at Hunter College and The New School.

In 1957, she married filmmaker/producer/editor, Armenian/American Aram Boyajian (1922–1915). In 1960, they moved with their son Marco to Paris for four years, where Aram edited for NBC. Their daughter Suzanne was born there. In Paris, Starr met filmmakers Alexander Alexeieff and his wife Claire Parker, a graduate of MIT in engineering who patented the pin screen, used in animation.

See Colour Plate 13.
Aram Boyajian and Cecile Starr ca. 2005, courtesy Suzanne Boyajian.

On returning to the USA, Starr became distributor for Alexeieff and Parker's films. In about 1976, Bute asked Starr to distribute her *Passages from James Joyce's Finnegans Wake*, which had won a prize at the Cannes Film festival in 1965. Starr agreed to the distribution if she also could handle Bute's shorts.

Starr, who had written about Bute's films starting in 1952, was a staunch supporter of Mary Ellen Bute's work, which Starr included in her early textbook on the history of film animation with Robert Russett in 1976, *Experimental Animation: An Illustrated Anthology*. In their revised edition, 1988, they changed the title to *Experimental Animation: Origins of a New Art*. Starr was also one of the initial organizers and an early director of the Women's Independent Film Exchange (WIFE). It was founded in 1977 as a result of her article on sexism in film, by Barbara Rochman, a lawyer; Sophie Hohne Reu, a woman at The March of Time, a newsreel for movie theaters; and the Chair of the New York Chapter of NOW [National Organization for Women]. WIFE scheduled monthly meetings to show films by women filmmakers, including Mary Ellen Bute, one of the early members. First these screenings for members were at the studio of filmmaker D. A. Pennebaker. Then the group sought premises for meetings open to the public. The different sites then prepared calendar entries, sent invitations, and paid for the projector and the rent. Showings were scheduled at the Museum of Modern Art, The Metropolitan Museum of Art, The Museum of the City of New York, the Donnell Library, and at the Collective for Women in Film, among other places. The New York State Arts Council made a donation of $150. to W.I.F.E.[3]

A year later Cecile Starr published a follow-up in *Variety*, January 1978, bemoaning the lack of change for women filmmakers. She concluded: "As to those that still resist change or ignore the need for it, we may just have to wait until they find themselves caught with their grants down!"

Through WIFE and as a distributer of Mary Ellen's films, Starr arranged numerous speaking engagements for the filmmaker at colleges across the country and at film showings in film conferences and conventions here and abroad. She also placed Bute's films in museum and archival collections, including the Museum of Modern Art, the Whitney Museum of American Art, Anthology Film Archives in New York, Yale Film Study Center in New Haven, and the Center for Visual Music in Los Angeles. One of Starr's more notable arrangements was a Cineprobe for Mary Ellen Bute at the Museum of Modern Art in April 4, 1983. MOMA screened *Passages from James Joyce's Finnegans Wake* and three of Mary Ellen's shorts, about six months before the filmmaker died.

Starr's personal files on Mary Ellen Bute went to The Beinecke Rare Book and Manuscript Library at Yale University. Starr also arranged for Ted Nemeth, Sr., Bute's husband and a cinematographer, to place his films and files at the Beinecke and the Yale Film Study Center. Isabel Wilder, Thornton Wilder's sister and Mary Ellen's classmate in the Department of Drama at Yale in 1925, donated money to Yale for acquiring this material from Ted Nemeth shortly before he died of Parkinson's disease in 1986.

In 1995, Cecile Starr and Larry Mollot, a writer and film director who had worked with Ted Nemeth, asked me to co-produce with them a biographical film on Bute. Larry was the filmmaker, Cecile the film historian, and I knew the Bute-Nemeth family history. We were never able to raise the money for this film, although Mollot shot promotional footage with the help of his daughter, Jaime Ressler.

See Colour Plate 14.
Larry Mollot, Cecile Starr, and Kit Smyth Basquin, 2000, in Kit's New York apartment. Courtesy Kit Smyth Basquin Collection of Mary Ellen Bute, Yale Collection of American Literature, Beinecke Rare Book and Manuscript Library.

Cecile Starr used her energy to support Mary Ellen Bute's work to the end, selling three of her films, *Escape*, *Spook Sport*, and *Tarantella* to the Whitney Museum of Art in 2014 and asking me to write this biography with her. Sadly, she was too frail and too busy to start on this book. Cecile Starr died at age 93 December 9, 2014. She will long be remembered by her devoted family, by many filmmakers, by women, and especially by me.

References

1. Stan Brakhage, Xerox of postcard to Cecile Starr 2/9/1996 in the personal collection of Kit Smyth Basquin.

2. Stan Brakhage, Xerox of postcard to Cecile Starr 6/10/1999 in the personal collection of Kit Smyth Basquin.

3. Cecile Starr, telephone interview with author, 8/1/2014, Transcript in the personal collections of Kit Smyth Basquin.

Colour Plates

Plate 1 (*left*). Mary Ellen Bute, *One-Eyed Pete*, ca. 1928, oil on canvas, collection of Tom Harrison, photo by Tom Harrison, courtesy Kit Smyth Basquin Collection of Mary Ellen Bute, Yale Collection of American Literature, Beinecke Rare Book and Manuscript Library. [see page 27]

Plate 2 (*below left*). Mary Ellen Bute, *Untitled*, oil on canvas, ca. 1928, Collection of Tom Harrison, photo by Tom Harrison, courtesy KSB Collection of MEB, YCAL. [see page 28]

Plate 3 (*below right*). Marcel Duchamp, *Nude Descending a Staircase, No. 2*, 1912, oil on canvas, Philadelphia Museum of Art, The Louise and Walter Arensberg Collection, 1950 @Artists Rights Society (ARS) New York/Estate of Marcel Duchamp. [see page 28]

Plate 4. Film still from *Escape*, 1937, (also called *Synchromy #4*),
directed by Mary Ellen Bute.
©Center for Visual Music, Los Angeles. [see page 48]

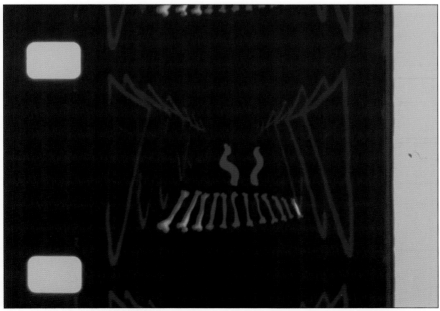

Plate 5. *Spook Sport*, 1939 animation by Norman McLaren,
directed by Mary Ellen Bute, film still
Courtesy Yale Film Study Center. [see page 51]

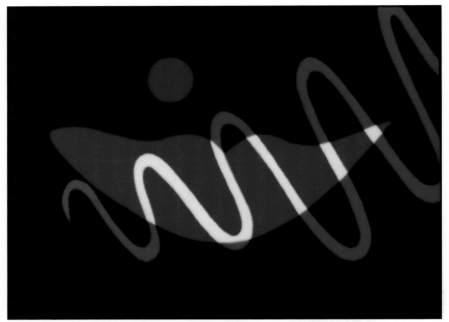

Plate 6. Film Still from *Tarantella* (1940), directed by Mary Ellen Bute,
© Center for Visual Music, Los Angeles. [see page 54]

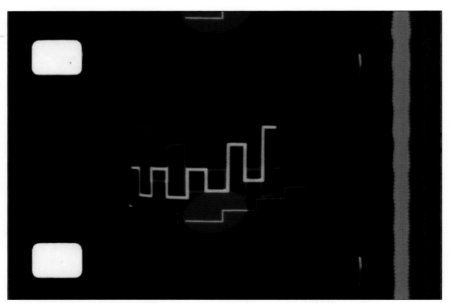

Plate 7. *Polka Graph* (1947), directed by Mary Ellen Bute, film still courtesy of Yale Film Study
Center. [see page 58]

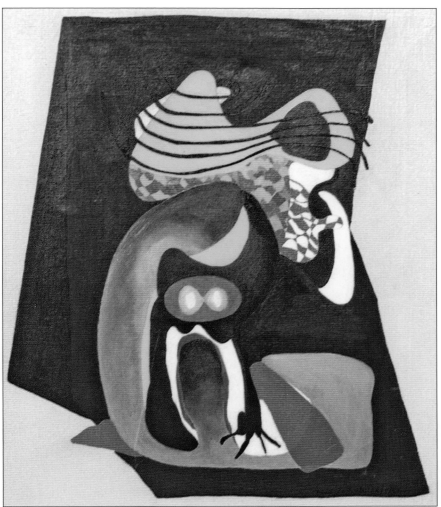

Plate 8. Mary Ellen Bute, *Sketch # 1* for *The Loved Ones* (a film short after Evelyn Waugh, never produced) 1948, oil on canvas, 15 x 12 ¾ in.,
Collection of Matthew Nemeth, photo courtesy Kit Smyth Basquin.
[see page 59]

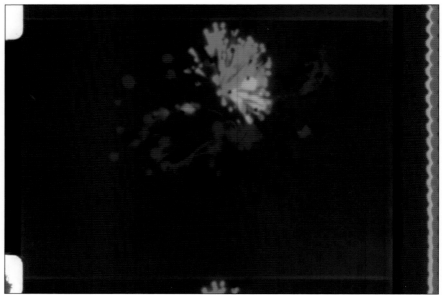

Plate 9. *Color Rhapsodie* (1948) directed by Mary Ellen Bute, courtesy of Yale Film Study Center.
[see page 60]

Plate 10. Leopold Stokowski in Film still of *Pastorale* (ca. 1950) , directed by Mary Ellen
Bute, courtesy Yale film Study Center.
[see page 63]

Colour Plates

Plate 11. *40 Horse Hitch*, Milwaukee
Schlitz Circus Parade, ca 1965,
courtesy KSB Collection of
MEB, YCAL
[see page 104].

Plate 12. Cecile Starr
(1921–2014) ca. 2005,
Courtesy Suzanne Boyajian
[see page 135].

Colour Plate 13. Aram Boyajian and Cecile Starr ca. 2005, courtesy Suzanne Boyajian [see page 137].

Colour Plate 14. Larry Mollot, Cecile Starr, and Kit Smyth Basquin, 2000, in Kit's New York apartment. Courtesy Kit Smyth Basquin Collection of Mary Ellen Bute, Yale Collection of American Literature, Beinecke Rare Book and Manuscript Library [see page 138].

Acknowledgements

Mary Ellen Bute's biography started and stopped several times over thirty-five plus years. The year after she died, 1984, I began research. My mother, Virginia Gibbs Smyth, life-long friend and former Houston neighbor of Bute, provided names of Bute's family, schoolmates, and friends, those in Houston and in New York. I interviewed them on the telephone and made personal visits in Houston. Although my mother was helpful with contacts, she resented my biography. She wanted me to write about her family. Eventually I was able to interview her with a tape recorder, but she talked about her family the first hour. Then she said, "Turn off that thing!" I didn't. Finally she talked about Bute.

I had no experience writing a book. I lived in Milwaukee as a single parent with my three school aged children. I had an MA in art history but needed training in film, playwriting, poetry, James Joyce literature in particular, and in music. I enrolled in a PhD program at the University of Wisconsin-Milwaukee in Modern Studies, but I soon learned that the department considered biography an unacceptable format for a dissertation in the 1980s. I left the school after a couple of years of useful course work. Lenore Rinder taught me a class in animation. Pat Mellencamp challenged me in a film history course. Paul Dickinson and Rob Yeo explained the oscilloscope to me, and Rob Danielson advised me on filmmaking. Janet Dunleavy taught courses on James Joyce's *Ulysses* and on *Finnegans Wake*. I read both novels completely. Irish poet James Liddy encouraged me to lengthen my poems. Tinsley Helton focused on point of view in her Shakespeare course. I appreciate all of this help.

Dick Blau, Professor and co-founder of the Film Department at University of Wisconsin-Milwaukee, encouraged me to donate Mary Ellen Bute's short films and *Passages from James Joyce's Finnegans Wake* to the Golda Maier Library at U.W.-Milwaukee. Cathy Cook was in charge of my donated Bute films at U.W.-Milwaukee. Bute's husband, cinematographer Ted Nemeth, who suffered Parkinson's Disease and had limited funds, appreciated my purchase of the short films and a video of *Finnegans Wake* in 1984. Blau made videos of all the films for me, priceless study tools. He insisted that I read *Finnegans Wake*. Later he read and made invaluable comments on my Bute biography. He has inspired me always.

My brother, Joe Smyth, a Lieutenant in the US Navy stationed on aircraft carrier *USS Saratoga* in the Mediterranean at the time of the Cannes Film Festival in 1965 where Bute was screening *Passages from James Joyce's Finnegans Wake*, saw Bute and her film and made helpful comments then and later to me. At the festival he suggested English sub-titles for the difficult Joycean language, a suggestion made previously by critic Gene Moskowitz at *Variety* in Paris. Bute added sub-titles after Cannes. Joe's wife Janet Smyth assisted in identifying family photographs, as did my first cousin Mary Laura Gibbs. My father Joe Smyth and my sister, Virginia Smyth Low contributed interviews. Bute's family members cooperated extensively, including her husband Ted Nemeth Sr., her sons Ted Nemeth Jr. and Jim Nemeth, Jim's daughter Krisy Nemeth, and Margo Lion, Ted Nemeth Jr.'s ex-wife, who was a Broadway producer. Lion's son Matt Nemeth gave permission for use of family pictures. I greatly appreciate the support of my family and of Mary Ellen Bute's.

Early research in 1984 at the Pennsylvania Academy of Fine Arts was helped by the archivist there, Cheryl Leibold. She Xeroxed articles and class descriptions long before this material was available on the Internet.

In the summer of 1985, I enrolled in a playwriting course at Yale Summer School with Forrest Stone. This class showed me that I preferred writing descriptions and had no ear for recreating distinctive dialogue. Clearly playwriting was not my medium. Isabel Wilder, sister of author Thornton Wilder, who lived near New Haven, enthralled me in an interview and wrote warm, appreciative notes to my mother and to me. Needless to say, I was pleased. Later, Tappan Wilder, Thornton Wilder's nephew, generously approved my use of a Wilder family photograph, quotes from Isabel Wilder, and made helpful comments on the text of my Bute biography.

Also, in 1985 authors at the Bread Loaf Writers' Conference at Middlebury College critiqued a partial draft of my Bute biography. Biographer Ron Powers encouraged me to present Mary Ellen Bute's own voice, to make her come alive as a person. Biographer and poet Paul Mariani recommended including negative as well as the positive material about my subject. I gratefully took their advice.

In 1988, I became Curator of Education at the Haggerty Museum of Art, Marquette University, Milwaukee, under the Direction of Curtis Carter, for six-and-a-half years. I had no time to write. I picked up the Bute book in 1995 while working on a filmed biography of Mary Ellen Bute with filmmaker Larry Mollot, assisted by his daughter Jaime Ressler, and film historian, critic, and teacher Cecile Starr. We never raised the money to complete the film.

Moving back to New York in 1999, I dropped the book again in 2000 to work full time at The Metropolitan Museum of Art in the Print Study Room. I also completed my PhD in Interdisciplinary Studies at Union Institute and University, Cincinnati, in 2009 while working at the Met. I moved to a new apartment and needed to free up space. Thinking I would never write the Bute biography, I donated nine boxes of Bute notes and pictures to the Beinecke Library at Yale.

In New York, I gained musical training in the volunteer choir at St. Bartholomew's church starting in 1999, under the leadership of music director and organist William Trafka, and from associate director of music Paolo Bordignon, who became director of music, and from associate director of music and organist Jason Roberts, who became director of music at Blessed Sacrament. Soprano and composer Martha Sullivan also advised me. Beginning in 2013, I acquired additional training singing in the Collegiate Chorale under the direction of James Bagwell and later under Ted Sperling, assisted by Julie Morgan, for the re-named group, MasterVoices.

January 10, 2014, after thirteen-and-a-half years at the MMA, I retired. Cecile Starr, then ninety-three, called me the next week and asked me to write a biography of Mary Ellen Bute with her. How could I say "No?" Starr had trusted me over the years and directed speaking engagements to me about Bute's films at Anthology Film Archives, Sarah Lawrence College, and others.

Cecile Starr, a film critic and teacher, had the film background, but I knew Bute's family history. I thought Starr and I would be a good team. She credited herself with firing me up! Her supportive husband, Aram Boya-jian, a filmmaker, was also helpful. I knew that time was limited so I digitally photographed my nine boxes of notes, on fourteen visits to New Haven. Nancy Kuhl, Curator of Poetry, Yale Collection of American Literature, at the Beinecke, had accepted my notes, photographs, and tapes in 2009. Michael Rush had picked up the boxes from my New York apartment. The helpful staff at the Beinecke in 2014 were: Sara Azam, Mary Ellen Budney, Dolores Colon, Moira Fitzgerald, Ingrid Lennon-Pressy, Anne Marie Menta, John Monahan, Laurie Klein, Karen Nangle, Matt Rowe, and archivist Michael Rush. Anne Marie Menta was particu-larly helpful in securing high resolution images for me. In addition, June Can and Moira Fitzgerald provided images. I also made appointments in the Yale Film Study Center, under the direction of Michael Kerbel, which had film footage donated by Ted Nemeth Sr. Film archivist Brian

Meacham showed me Bute's reels, assisted by Josh Glick, and made film stills from Bute's films. In September, 2018, I visited the Beinecke again to round up more images for high resolution. The following people helped me: Michael Rush, Moira Fitzgerald, Paul Civitelli, John Monahan, Dolores Colon, Anne Marie Menta, and Jessica Tubis. In addition, in October, 2018, Matthew Rowe, Ingrid Lennon-Pressey, and Yasmin Ramadan helped me in the Beineicke Library.

Also important to my research was the New York Public Library that permitted me to use the Shoichi Noma Research Reading Room under the direction of Jay Barksdale. Anne Coriston, vice-president for public service at the Library, expedited this privilege. The Library at The University Club, New York, under the direction of Andrew Berner was a valuable study space. Library staff including Scott Overall, Laurie Hulse Schwartz, and Maureen Manning always cooperated with enthusiasm. The Watson Library at the Metropolitan Museum of Art also provided useful services. Linda Seckelson, librarian there, was particularly encouraging. The New York Society Library on east 79th Street offered quiet spaces for editing text.

Mary Ellen Bute films screened at Anthology Film Archives, selected by one of the founders, Jonas Mekas, and at The Museum of Modern Art, under film curator Larry Kardish, were important aids to my research. Anthology, MOMA, and the Yale Film Study Center, among others, restored some of Mary Ellen's films. Bruce Posner, film historian and curator with a special interest in film preservation, incorporated seven of Bute's restored animated shorts into the historic DVD series, "Unseen Cinema: Early American Avant-Garde Film 1894–1941", sponsored by Anthology Film Archives, New York, and Deutesches Filmmuseum, Frankfurt am Main, in 2005. Posner included: *Rhythm in Light*, 1934; *Synchromy No. 2*, 1935; *Dada*, 1936; *Parabola*, 1937; *Escape*, 1937; *Spook Sport*, 1939; and *Tarantella, 1940*, with commentary by Cecile Starr and by Bruce Posner. In the second historical DVD collection, *Masterworks of American Avant-Garde Experimental Films 1920–1970*, Posner included Bute's *Tarantella*, 1940, and *Abstronic*, 1952.

David Shepard and Serg Bramberg produced the DVD *Early Women Filmmakers*, 1917, for Blackhawk Films and Flicker Alley, which included Bute's *Parabola* (1937) and *Spook Sport* (1939).

Center for Visual Music, under the direction of Cindy Keefer, produced *Visual Music 1947–1986*, 2018, a DVD which included Bute's *Polka Graph* (1947), *Color Rhapsodie* (1948), and *Abstronic* (1952).

John Mhiripiri, Director, and John Klacsmann, Archivist, at Anthology Film Archives; Ashley Swinnerton, Collections Specialist in the Film

Study Center, MOMA; and Sophia Lorent, Curatorial Assistant at George Eastman House helped locate Bute's films for her filmography. The New York Public Library and Yale list Bute's films in their on-line catalogues.

Cecile Starr, who lived in Vermont, received drafts of all my chapters except the last two on *Skin of Our Teeth* and on Walt Whitman, Mary Ellen's unfinished films. Starr encouraged me but was too frail and too busy to write. In 2014 she sold Mary Ellen's films *Escape*, *Spook Sport*, and *Tarantella* to The Whitney Museum of American Art in New York in time for a continuous showing in the opening exhibition at their new building in lower Manhattan next to the High Line. I interviewed Starr by phone August 1, 2014. Sadly, she died December 9, 2014. Now I had a double reason to complete the book, to honor Mary Ellen Bute and to memorialize Cecile Starr. I hope I have done this.

Martina Kudlácek, filmmaker selected to film the never completed Bute documentary, suggested resources for finding a book agent. She attended the tribute service for Cecile Starr, October 1, 2015, in New York at the New York Public Library for the Performing Arts, Lincoln Center, arranged by Cindy Keefer, Director of the Center for Visual Music, Los Angeles, which distributes Bute's films. Keefer asked me to speak at Starr's tribute. Keefer also reviewed my biography of Bute. I greatly appreciate her helpful suggestions.

Solidelle Fortier Wasser reviewed a draft of my text, made helpful suggestions, contributed research, and continually encouraged me. Other supportive friends were her son and daughter-in-law, Frederick Wasser and Nancy Berke. Frederick, Chair of the Television and Radio Department at Brooklyn College, CUNY, suggested possible publishers for my book. Jeff Rosenheim, Chair of the Photographs Department at the Metropolitan Museum of Art, also suggested a possible publisher. Scholar, Spence School alumna, and friend Susan Teommey Rydell, kept me laughing and provided continuous support. In New York, Gerry Hempel Davis (who visited) Carol Lamberg, Gretchen Royce, Susan Rush, Willa Cox, Gayle Jaeger, Deborah Harding, Jane Randall, Erik Eickhoff, Nadine Orenstein, Perrin Stein, Elizabeth Zanis, Femke Speelberg and Jim Hug cheered my efforts. Filmmaker Yemane Demissie suggested Bute film programs. Furio Rinaldi encouraged me to register my text for a copyright. Jeff Guerrier catalogued my Bute research materials and Marina Nyszczuk organized my home. Also in New York, Larry Madison helped me find a preliminary editor. Susan Dalsimer took on that job. Robert Morales helped with computer issues, particularly moving images. Christopher Serbagi, suggested by Anne Coriston, in

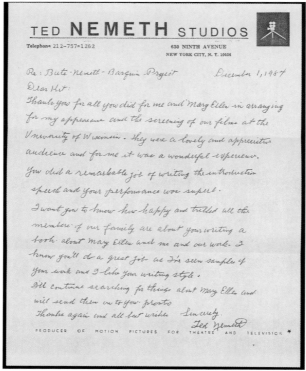

TED **NEMETH** STUDIOS

Telephone 212-757-1262

630 NINTH AVENUE
NEW YORK CITY, N. Y. 10036

Re: Bute-Nemeth-Basquin Project   December 1, 1984

Dear Kit:

Thank you for all you did for me and Mary Ellen in arranging for my appearance and the screening of our films at the University of Wisconsin. They were a lovely and appreciative audience and for me it was a wonderful experience.

You did a remarkable job of writing the introduction speech and your performance was superb.

I want you to know how happy and thrilled all the members of our family are about your writing a book about Mary Ellen and me and our work. I know you'll do a great job as I've seen samples of your work and I like your writing style.

I'll continue searching for things about Mary Ellen and will send them on to you pronto.

Thanks again and all best wishes   Sincerely,
                                    Ted Nemeth

PRODUCER   OF   MOTION   PICTURES   FOR   THEATRE   AND   TELEVISION ✱

Fig. 1. Ted Nemeth Sr., permission letter to Kit Smyth

New York, helped sort out legalities of picture permissions. In New Haven, my friend Anne-Marie Logan, Rubens drawing specialist, augmented my research skills. In Milwaukee, where I had lived, Carol Carpenter, Paula and Allan Goldman, Gerri McNamara, and Tony and Donna Meyer encouraged me. In Frankfort, Indiana, where I also had lived at one time, Gloria Laverty and Bill and Flo Caddell remained on my team.

My sons Bill Basquin and his wife Katherine Agard, Peter Lee Basquin, and William C. Basquin and his wife Bridget Basquin sustained me with love. Bill Basquin, a filmmaker, also provided needed technical information and outreach, read a draft of my book, suggested an editor, and created a video introduction for a symposium of the Center for Visual Music, August, 2018. I so appreciate his interest and aid. My grandchildren Billy Basquin, Madison Basquin, and Jackson Basquin kept me tuned in to the latest technology. I bought an I-Phone! I appreciate the help from the people mentioned and from those I might have omitted inadvertently. Thank you.

Kit Smyth Basquin, New York, 2020

Chronology

November 21, 1906   **Mary Ellen Bute** was born in Houston, Texas, to Clare Robinson Bute (1883–1964) and Dr. James House Bute (1875-1941), a pediatrician and a cousin of Col. Edward M. House, an advisor to President Wilson

1907   brother James born (1907–1967)

1910   brother John (I) born, lived under a year

1911   brother John (I) dies

1911   Theodore Julias Nemeth born in Cambridge, MA, to Hungarian parents

1912   sister Maud Pettit born (1912–1937)

1912   Jim contracted polio. Family moved from Butler Flats, Houston, into grandparents' home at 2316 Fannin Street in downtown Houston. Bute's grandparents were Mary Ellen Pittit Robinson (1857–1936), for whom Bute was named, and C. W. Robinson, president of Markham Rice Milling Company. Virginia Gibbs (Smyth) was a neighbor at 3618 Fannin. Dr. Bute had gone to medical school with Dr. Gibbs at Columbia Physicians and Surgeons in New York

1915   sister Lois Bute (Porter) born (1915–1992). Mary Ellen Bute attended Kincaid School (Private) in third grade

1916   brother John (II) born (1916–2004). Mary Ellen Bute attended Lauderdale-Roach (private) School

1916   Dr. Bute stopped practicing medicine and worked with investments and on his cattle ranch

1917–1920   Mary Ellen Bute attended Allen School (Public) for 5th through 7th grades. Classmates were James Stewart Morcom and Elizabeth Reynolds (Wise). The art teacher was Emma Richardson Cherry.

1920–1921   Mary Ellen Bute attended 8th Grade at South End Junior High School

1921–1923   Mary Ellen Bute attended Central High School for 9th Grade and 10th Grade

1923   spring, she received honorable mention for a painting exhibited in Austin, Texas

1923   Walt Disney opened his film studio, Burbank, CA

1923–1924   Mary Ellen Bute studied at Pennsylvania Academy of Fine Arts, Philadelphia, on a scholarship

1924–1925   she attended Inter-Theater Arts School, 42 Commerce St., New York, in Greenwich Village

1925–1926   She enrolled in the Department of Drama, School of Fine Arts, Yale University to study stage lighting, stage design, and theater production, a classmate was Isabel Wilder, Thornton Wilder's sister

1926–1927	The Floating University, around the world cruise on S. S. Ryndam, hired Mary Ellen Bute to teach dance and drama
1927	November, she had a debutante party in Houston at her grandparents' house and was a debutante for the 1927–1928 season
1927–1928	Little Theater, Houston, hired her as assistant director to paint scenery and supervise lighting
1927	October, *The Jazz Singer* was released by Warner Brothers, first full length talking film
1928	Mickey Mouse debuted in *Steamboat Willie*, one of the first sound cartoons
1928	Bute may have taken a summer course at the Sorbonne, Paris, for foreigners, in English.
1928–1929	Bute was sick with tuberculosis in the hospital in New York and at home in Houston
1929	fall, Bute was Maid-of-Honor for the launching of the USS Houston, Newport News, VA
1929	Bute worked for Thomas Wilfred, inventor of Clavilux color organ
1929	October 24, stock market crash
1930	Bute became Director of Visual Arts, Gerald Warburg Studios, New York
1931	December, Bute met Leon Theremin, electronics pioneer and Russian spy
1932	January 31, Bute studied math with Joseph Schillinger and helped Theremin present his paper to the New York Musicological Society, where she was secretary. She applied but did not receive a Guggenheim Grant in support of the work of Theremin
1932	*Synchromy* (unfinished), an abstract film directed by Joseph Schillinger. Lewis Jacobs was cinematographer. Bute painted rhythmic images for it
1932	December 27, Radio City Music Hall opened
1934	Mary Ellen Bute met Theodore Julias Nemeth at New York Film Service Laboratory, 9th Avenue. Bute lived in one room at Hotel des Artistes, 1 West 67th Street
1934	Bute and Nemeth moved to 422 West 46, "the carriage house", behind a Chinese laundry. 1934 Nemeth resigned from New York Film Service Lab and formed Ted Nemeth Studios, a commercial film production company
1934	Bute directed *Rhythm in Light* (b/w 5 min. film), cinematography by Ted Nemeth
1934	Bute showed *Rhythm in Light* to Leopold Stokowski in Philadelphia
1935	*Rhythm in Light* was screened at Radio City Music Hall
1935	*Synchromy # 2* (b/w 5½ min. film), directed by Bute
1935	Charles Dockum started research on Mobilcolor projection system
1936	*Dada* (b/w 3 min. film), directed by Bute
1936	Oskar Fischinger visited New York and Met Bute and Nemeth
1936	Mary Ellen Pittit Robinson, "Granny", died
1937	*Parabola* 9 min, b/w film, directed by Bute

1937	Maud Pittit Bute, Bute's sister, died
1937	*Escape* (*Synchromy* 4) (4 min. color film), directed by Bute
1939	*Spook Sport* (8 min. color), animated by Norman McLaren
1939	Frances Steloff launched the publication of James Joyce's *Finnegans Wake* in the USA with a party at the Gotham Book Mart, New York
1939	Bute gave a party in Houston to honor the marriage of William Bernreider, at her family home on Fannin Street
1939	Bute and Nemeth rented a professional studio in the United Arts Building, 729 Seventh Avenue at 49th Street
1940	October 15, Mary Ellen Bute and Theodore J. Nemeth married in New York
1940	Nemeth filmed commercials and added English sub-titles to foreign films
1940	*Tarantella* (5 min. color film) directed by Bute and partially filmed by her
1940	November, Walt Disney produced *Fantasia*, with abstract and figurative animation
1941	July 1, Theodore J. Nemeth, Jr. was born in New York
1941	Dr. James House Bute (1875–1941), Bute's father, died
1941	December 7, USA joined WWII after the bombing of Pearl Harbor, Hawaii
Ca. 1945	Mary Ellen Bute and Ted Nemeth, Sr. rented a summer home at Candlewood, NY
1947	January 8, James House Bute Nemeth was born
1947	*Polka Graph* (4½ min color film), directed by Bute
1948	*Imagination* (3 min. color film), directed by Bute
1948	*Color Rhapsodie* (6 min. color film), directed by Bute
1948	Bute painted sketch with black cat for film short *The Loved One* (after Evelyn Waugh), never produced
1950	*Pastorale* (9 min. color film), directed by Bute
1952	Cecile Starr reviewed Bute's films, *Spook Sport* and *Color Rhapsodie*, at Radio City Music Hall, for *Saturday Review*
1952	*Abstronic* (6 min. color film) with electronic imagery, directed by Bute
1952	Ted Nemeth, Sr. was cinematographer for a short film documenting Charles Dockum's performance of his Mobilcolor projector at the Guggenheim Museum
1953	*Mood Contrasts* (7 min. color film) with electronic imagery, directed by Bute, her last abstract short
1957	*The Boy Who Saw Through* (29 min. b/w live action film) with young Christopher Walken, produced by Bute
1958	Bute saw Mary Manning's play, *Passages from Finnegans Wake* at Barnard College, NY
1958	Bute was at the Brussels International Film Festival where *The Boy Who Saw Through* won a Prize
1959	Ted Nemeth Jr. attended Cornell University. He married Janet Eleanor Smith

1960	Mary Ellen Bute and Ted Nemeth, Sr. lived at 130 East 75th Street, NY
1960	Mary Ellen Bute researched *Finnegans Wake* and live action direction
1961–1962	Jim Nemeth attended Choate School, Wallingford, CT
1961	Mary Ellen Bute gave a progress report on her *Finnegans Wake* film to the James Joyce Society at the Gotham Book Mart, New York
1962	Ted Nemeth, Jr. divorced Janet Eleanor Smith
1963–1964	Jim Nemeth attended Riverdale Country School, Bronx, NY
1964	November 4, Zack Bowen reported on music in James Joyce's *Ulysses* at James Joyce Society, Gotham Book Mart, New York
1964	Claire Robinson Bute (1883–1964), Bute's mother, died
1965	February 1, Bute's *Passages from James Joyce's Finnegans Wake* premiered at Northrop Auditorium, University of Minnesota, Minneapolis, to an audience of over 4000 people
1965	Februay 16, 1965 Mary Ellen Bute's *Passages from James Joyce's Finnegans Wake* was screened at the Museum of Modern Art, New York, for the James Joyce Society
1965	*Passages from James Joyce's Finnegans Wake* won a prize for direction of a first feature film at Cannes Film Festival, May 3–16, 1965
1965	Thornton Wilder saw Bute's film and gave her film rights to his play *Skin of Our Teeth*
1965	December 16, Bute's *Finnegans Wake* was booked at Carnegie Hall Cinema, NY
1965–1975	*Skin of Our Teeth*, unfinished live action color film, directed by Bute
1966	Ted Nemeth Jr. was in London
1967	Mary Ellen Bute's younger brother Jim Bute died
1968	Jim Nemeth attended London School of Film Technology
1968	Ted Nemeth, Jr. worked at Expanding Cinema in New York
1968	Ted Nemeth, Sr. suffered financial reverses
1969	Jim Nemeth worked at Lenox Hill Hospital
1970	Jim Nemeth attended NYU
1970	Mary Ellen Bute separated from Ted Nemeth, Sr. and moved to a Salvation Army residence, The Parkside Evangeline Home, room 710, on Gramercy Park, NY
1971	Ted Nemeth Jr. and Margo Lion, who had married, lived in Switzerland
1973	Jim Nemeth married Johanna. They had twins, Ted and Krisy
1975	Matthew Nemeth was born, son of Margo Lion and Ted Nemeth, Jr.
1975	Thornton Wilder (1897–1975) died
1975–1983	*Out of the Cradle Endlessly Rocking*, unfinished live action film on Walt Whitman, directed and filmed by Bute
1976	Cecile Starr and Robert Russett publish *Experimental Animation: An Illustrated Anthology*
1976	Cecile Starr agreed to distribute Mary Ellen Bute's films
1976	Mary Ellen Bute won a grant from the American Film Institute for her Walt Whitman film, along with forty-two others out of the 1000 applicants
1976	Mary Ellen Bute spoke at the Art Institute of Chicago

1976	Ted Nemeth, Jr. and Margo Lion divorced
1977	Bute's brother-in-law Randon Porter died
1979	March 16, American Film Institute offered Mary Ellen Bute a retrospective at the John F. Kennedy Center, Washington, D. C. (never realized)
1980	Four Bute paintings were exhibited at Martin Diamond Fine Art, 1014 Madison Ave.
1981	Friday November 20, Bute screened and discussed four films at the Collective for Living Cinema, 52 White Street, NY: *Rhythm in Light*, *Escape*, *Tarantella*, and *Polka Graph*
1982	Bute was selected for Montreal Film Festival and interviewed by Peter Wintonick. She saw Norman McLaren
1982	January 14, Bute talked in Pittsburgh at the Carnegie Museum of Art
1983	January *Skin of Our Teeth* was produced for PBS TV by Jack O'Brien for American Playhouse
1983	February 10, Bute and Nemeth screened their abstract shorts at the School of Visual Arts, 209 E. 23nd St., NY
1983	April 4, Bute had Cineprobe at Museum of Modern Art, New York
1983	October 17, Mary Ellen Bute died of heart failure at Cabrini Hospital, New York
1983	November, memorial service for Bute at Little Church Around the Corner (Church of the Transfiguration, 1 East 29th Street)
1984	November, Ted Nemeth spoke on Bute-Nemeth films at the University of Wisconsin, Milwaukee. Kit Smyth Basquin donated films by Bute and by Nemeth to the Golda Meir Library at the University of Wisconsin-Milwaukee
1986	December, Ted Nemeth, Sr. died in New York of Parkinson's disease
2011	February, Ted Nemeth Jr. died
2020	January 24, Margo Lion, Broadway producer and ex-daughter-in-law of Mary Ellen Bute, who had been married to Bute's son Ted Nemeth, Jr., died

Mary Ellen Bute and Theodore J. Nemeth, Sr. Filmography

Mary Ellen Bute said about her films, "We need a new kinetic, visual art form – one that unites sound, color, and form. We can take a mathematical formula and develop a whole composition exactly synchronized – the sound and the color following a chromatic scale. Or we can take two themes, visual and aural, and develop them at times in counterpoint."[1]

Mary Ellen Bute's films are in the collections of Center for Visual Music in Los Angeles; Anthology Film Archives; Museum of Modern Art, New York; George Eastman House; Whitney Museum of American Art; Yale Film Study Center; the University of Wisconsin-Milwaukee; and others. Seven of her shorts can be seen on Anthology Film Archives' 2005 DVD set, *Unseen Cinema: Early American Avant-Garde Film 1894–1941*: *Rhythm in Light*, *Synchromy # 2*, *Parabola*, *Dada*, *Escape*, *Spook Sport*, and *Tarantella*. Flicker Alley's 2015 DVD collection, *Masterworks of American Avant-Garde Experimental Films 1920–1970* includes Bute's *Tarantella*. Two are on Flicker Alley's 2017: *Early Women Filmmakers: An International Anthology*, *Parabola* and *Spook Sport*. Three of Bute's shorts are on the Center for Visual Music's 2017 DVD *Visual Music 1947–1986*: *Abstronic*, *Color Rhapsodie*, and *Polka Graph*.

Center for Visual Music, Los Angeles, continues to distribute a Bute Retrospective in 16mm, of all her short abstract films, a program originally assembled by Cecile Starr. Information on this program is at: http://www.centerforvisualmusic.org/Bute.htm. CVM also provides digital exhibition copies of Bute's films to museum exhibitions worldwide.

Synchromy, 1932, an unfinished abstract 8mm film, believed lost. Joseph Schillinger composed the music and Lewis Jacobs filmed the work. Bute created drawings for it illustrating rhythm in motion.

Rhythm in Light, 1934, a 5 minute, black and white, 35mm film, with abstract forms and 3D models. This first Bute film, which moves to the syncopated music of "Anitra's Dance", from Edvard Grieg's *Peer Gynt*

Suite, was directed by Bute, and co-produced by Bute, Theodore J. Nemeth, and Melville Webber. Cinematography was by Ted Nemeth. It premiered at Radio City Music Hall. The introductory text is in a sleek, modern, stylized 1930s font. It is on Anthology Film Archives' DVD set, *Unseen Cinema*, and in the collections of Anthology Film Archives, MOMA, the New York Public Library for the Performing Arts, UW-Milwaukee, and in the Cecile Starr Collection at the Center for Visual Music, Los Angeles.

Synchromy # 2, a 1935, 5 minute, black and white, 35mm film directed by Bute, produced by Bute and Ted Nemeth, with cinematography by Ted Nemeth. This abstract film pairs abstract images, a star, Tannhaüser's flowering rod, and Gothic arches to Wagner's "O Evening Star" from *Tannhaüser*, sung by Reinald Werrenrath. This film premiered at Radio City Music Hall in 1938 with the feature *Mary of Scotland*, starring Katharine Hepburn. It is on Anthology Film Archives' DVD set, *Unseen Cinema*, and in the collections of Anthology Film Archives, UW-Milwaukee, and the Center for Visual Music, Los Angeles.

Dada, 1936, a 3 minute, black and white, 35mm film, created for Universal Newsreel, directed by Bute. Cinematographer was Ted Nemeth. It contains a collage of animated effects from previous Bute films. The film shows rings, bars, ladders, match sticks, mirrors, rectangles, spirals, cubes and other geometric forms moving through space. The music is a waltz. It is on Anthology Film Archives' DVD set, *Unseen Cinema*, and in the collections of Anthology Film Archives, the Yale Film Study Center, UW-Milwaukee, and the Center for Visual Music, Los Angeles.

Parabola, 1937, a 9 minute, black and white, 35mm film, directed by Bute, and produced by Expanding Cinema (Mary Ellen Bute and Ted Nemeth). The cinematography was by Ted Nemeth. William Nemeth, Ted's brother, was technical associate. Music was "La Création du Monde", by the contemporary composer, Darius Milhaud. Film historian Cecile Starr, in undated film notes, wrote that this film was never shown in a major theater, possibly because of conflict with Rutherford Boyd, who created the sculpture in it.[2] It is on Anthology Film Archives' DVD set, *Unseen Cinema*, and in the collections of Yale Film Study Center, the New York Public Library for the Performing Arts, UW-Milwaukee, Anthology Film Archives, and the Center for Visual Music, Los Angeles. It is on Flicker Alley's *Early Women Filmmakers: An International Anthology*, 2017.

Escape, 1937, also called *Synchromy # 4,* a 4 minute color 35mm film, is an abstract narrative film, made from black and white drawings with color filters. An orange triangle, trapped behind horizontal bars, tries to escape to Bach's Toccata and Fugue in D minor, music used later by Walt Disney in *Fantasia*. In the end, the triangle breaks through to freedom, changing from orange to red. Bute directed it. She produced it with Ted Nemeth. Technical associate was William Nemeth, Ted's brother. This is one of Bute's films acquired by the Whitney Museum of American Art and part of its opening exhibition in their new building at the foot of the High Line, in May 2015. It is also in Anthology Film Archives' DVD set, *Unseen Cinema,* and in the collections at MOMA, the Whitney Museum of American Art, at the Yale Film Study Center (in black and white only), the George Eastman House, UW-Milwaukee, and the Center for Visual Music, Los Angeles.

Spook Sport, 1939, an 8 minute, color, 35mm film. Bute conceived and directed this film, featuring a cast of symbolic images, including a spook, a ghost, a bat, a bell, a sun, bones, and a clock which move to Saint-Saens' "Danse Macabre". It was produced by Ted Nemeth Studios. At midnight, spooks and ghosts party in a graveyard. The figures were hand drawn in ink on the film frame by frame by Norman McLaren, a Scottish film-maker hired by Bute, who later developed an animation unit for the National Film Board of Canada and won an Academy Award. The film premiered at Radio City Music Hall. It is in Anthology Film Archives' 2005 DVD set, *Unseen Cinema* and on the Flicker Alley's 2017 DVD, *Early Women Filmmakers: An International Anthology*. It is in the collections of Anthology Film Archives; MOMA; the Whitney Museum of American Art, where it screened at the opening of their new building at the base of the High Line in May, 2015; the Yale Film Study Center; the New York Public Library for the Performing Arts; UW-Milwaukee; and in the Cecile Starr Collection at the Center for Visual Music, Los Angeles. It is also in the collection of the National Film Board of Canada.

Tarantella, 1940, a 5 minute, color, 35mm film, directed by Bute and produced by Bute and Ted Nemeth. The Associate Technician was William Nemeth, Ted's brother. Bute filmed this mostly herself before Ted, Jr. was born July 1, 1941, but Ted Nemeth Sr. was given credit for cinematography.[3] Piano music for *Tarantella* was composed and played by Edwin Gerschefsky (1909–1992), a Yale graduate who had studied with Joseph Schillinger, and later would head music departments at Converse College, the University of New Mexico, and the University of Georgia. It premiered at the Paris Theater in New York and had theatrical bookings in the US and abroad. It was chosen in 2010 for the National Film Registry by the Library of Congress. The National Film Registry show-cases the range and diversity of American film heritage to increase awareness for its preservation. Twenty-five films are selected each year for cultural, historical, or aesthetic significance. *Tarantella* was one of Bute's films acquired by the Whitney Museum and screened in the opening exhibition of their new building in lower Manhattan, spring 2015. It is on Anthology Film Archives' 2005 DVD set, *Unseen Cinema*, on Flicker Alley's 2015 DVD set, *Masterworks of American Avant-Garde Experimental Films 1920–1970*, and in the collections at MOMA, the George Eastman House, UW-Milwaukee, and the Center for Visual Music, Los Angeles.

Polka Graph, 1947, a 4½ minute color, 35mm film, was directed by Bute. Ted Nemeth was the cinematographer. Ted Nemeth Studios produced it. Abstract images polka to the music from the ballet suite "The Age of Gold" by Dmitri Shostakovich. It premiered at the Sutton Theater in New York with the feature film "The Man in the White Suit". Cecile Starr, film historian and critic, suggested to Bute that she send *Polka Graph* to the 1952 Venice Film Festival.[4] Bute went there to do a story for the *New York Times*. *Polka Graph* won a prize. It also won the Festival of Contemporary Art Award, University of Illinois, 1953. It was included in an all-Shostakovich TV program for CBS, February, 1978. This film is in the collections of Anthology Film Archives, MOMA, the New York Public Library for the Performing Arts, the Yale Film Study Center, UW-Milwaukee, and the Center for Visual Music, Los Angeles. It is on CVM's 2017 DVD *Visual Music 1947–1986*.

Imagination, 1948, a 3 minute abstract, color, 35mm film, directed by Bute. Ted Nemeth was the cinematographer. It was seen on NBC television by millions of people on the Steve Allen Show, for which it was created. Characteristic of Bute's other films, abstract and geometric forms move in syncopation to the popular song "Imagination". No credits were given for this short. Animated footage was reused from previous films, including flying forms from *Spook Sport*, and crossed rods and flowering rods from *Parabola*. *Imagination* is in the collections at MOMA, UW-Milwaukee, and the Center for Visual Music, Los Angeles.

Color Rhapsodie, 1948, a 6 minute, color, 35mm film, directed by Bute, a "pioneer film designer", as the titles read at the beginning. Ted Nemeth, who also was the cinematographer, produced it. As in some of Bute's films, she introduced it with lead titles and questions to the viewer about "seeing sound". The music is Hungarian Rhapsody # 2 by Franz Liszt. Beautiful explosions of color in the foreground animate cloud formations and other abstract forms in the background, painted on glass by Bute. The backgrounds suggest Abstract Expressionism, a painting movement emerging in New York at the time. Colored lines spiral toward the viewer and away, creating a sense of three-dimensions. Shaped colors dance over checkerboards. Concentric circles move forward and away. When this film was released, thirty-nine feature film houses across the country were booking Bute's experimental short films.[5] This film premiered at Radio City Music Hall in 1951. It is in the collections of Anthology Film Archives, the Yale Film Study Center, UW-Milwaukee, and the Center for Visual Music, Los Angeles. It is on CVM's 2017 DVD *Visual Music 1947–1986*.

New Sensations in Sound, 1949, a 3 minute, color, 35mm film, produced for RCA TV. It contains a collage of effects from previous Bute films as well as some new images created by an oscilloscope, making Bute a pioneer with electronic imagery in film. The sound track is a catchy jingle. It is in the collections of MOMA, the George Eastman House, and the Center for Visual Music, Los Angeles.

Pastorale, 1950, a 9 minute, color, 35mm film, directed by Bute, filmed by Ted Nemeth, assisted by Hilary Harris, with Leopold Stokowsky conducting his own arrangement on camera of "Sheep May Safely Graze", from Bach's Cantata No. 208, also called the Birthday Cantata, in honor of Duke Christian who commissioned it for his birthday in 1713. The orchestra is Residentie Orchestra, Den Haag, Holland. Sound was recorded by Philips. *Pastorale* premiered at the Paris Theater in New York, with the feature "Seven Deadly Sins". *Pastorale* is in the collections of the Yale Film Study Center, UW-Milwaukee, and the Center for Visual Music, Los Angeles.

Abstronic, 1952, a 6 minute, color, 35mm film, part of the Seeing Sound Series, a Ted Nemeth Studios Production, directed by Bute. In Bute's last abstract films, she incorporated electronic images from a cathode ray oscilloscope, becoming one of the first artists in the US to use the imagery of this instrument on film. The images move to the music of Aaron Copland's "Hoe Down" and to "Ranch House Party" by Don Gillis, recalling Bute's Texas roots. She edited two films together, one for each piece of music. It is in the collections of MOMA, the New York Public Library for the Performing Arts, UW-Milwaukee, and the Center for Visual Music, Los Angeles. It is on CVM's 2017 DVD *Visual Music 1947–1986*.

Mood Contrasts, 1953, a 7 minute, color 35mm film, part of the Seeing Sound film series, with electronic imagery from a cathode ray oscilloscope. This was Bute's last abstract animated film. She directed it, and Ted Nemeth Studios produced it. Ted Nemeth was the cinematographer. Music was Rimsky Korsakov's "Hymn to the Sun" and "Dance of the Tumblers". This film won a prize at the Brussels International Experimental Film Festival in 1958 for the Best Short Film and premiered at Radio City Music Hall with the feature, *The Barretts of Wimpole Street*. *Mood Contrasts* is in the collections of MOMA, George Eastman House, Yale Film Study Center, UW-Milwaukee, and the Center for Visual Music, Los Angeles.

Live Action Films

The Boy Who Saw Through, 1958, a 25 minute, black and white, 35mm film, produced by Bute, directed by George Stoney and filmed by Ted Nemeth, after a short story by John Pudney, with a screenplay by poet/film producer Guy Glover, partner of Norman McLaren. Glover worked for the National Film Board of Canada and later won an Academy award. It starred young Christopher Walken (age 14 at time of shooting, called Ronnie Walken). It won a Brussels Film Festival prize in 1958. *The Boy Who Saw Through* is in the collection at UW-Milwaukee. The Yale Film Study Center also has *The Boy Who Saw Through*, which Yale preserved with a grant from the National Film Preservation Foundation.

Passages from James Joyce's Finnegans Wake, 1965, a 97 minute, black and white, 35mm feature film, after a play of the same name by Mary Manning, based on the experimental novel by James Joyce. Bute produced and directed it. Ted Nemeth was the cinematographer and directed the photography. Elliot Kaplan composed the music. Joyce scholar Zack Bowen was a musical advisor. Filmed in New York and Dublin, it won a Cannes Film Festival Prize for direction of a first feature in 1965. English sub-titles were added after the Cannes showing. This film is in the collections of MOMA, the New York Public Library for the Performing Arts, UW-Milwaukee, and the Yale Film Study Center, which preserved it with a grant from the National Film Preservation Foundation.

The Skin of Our Teeth, an unfinished, 35mm color feature film after Pulitzer Prize winning play by Thornton Wilder, ca. 1966–1975, directed by Mary Ellen Bute. Ted Nemeth was the cinematographer. Some screen tests for this film are in the Yale Film Study Center.

Out of the Cradle Endlessly Rocking: The Odyssey of Walt Whitman, a Builder of the American Vision, an unfinished, color, 35mm feature film, ca. 1976–1983, directed and filmed by Mary Ellen Bute. Some preliminary footage for this is in the Yale Film Study Center.

Ted Nemeth's Films

One Plus One, later called ***Cliff Dwellers***, 1962, a color, 35mm short film. Ted was the Cinematographer. Hayward Anderson directed this story of city dwellers. It was nominated for an Academy Award. Academy Film Archive has a 35mm print of it. https://www.oscars.org/film-archive

40 Horse Hitch, 1973 (filmed in 1965) a 9 minute, color, 35mm film. Cinematography was by Ted Nemeth, assisted by his son Jim Nemeth. Schlitz Brewing Company produced it. Ernest Borgnine narrated the Schlitz Circus Parade in Milwaukee July, 1965. The Script was written by Coleman Barkin for his Milwaukee public relations firm, Barkin-Herman & Assoc. The film was produced for TV. It screened at Radio City Music Hall under the title, "Fabulous Forty Horse Hitch". It is in the collection at UW-Milwaukee.

Time Piece, 1965, 8 minutes, color, 35mm, directed, written and starring Jim Henson. The Muppets, Inc. produced it. Ted Nemeth was the cinematographer. It was nominated for an Academy Award. This is in the collection at UW-Milwaukee and in The Jim Henson Company Archives. The Yale Film Study Center also has a print.

Rama, 1970, was a 16 minute color video mixing dance, nature, and a voice-over monologue. Ted Nemeth was the cinematographer. Sugar Cain wrote and directed it. Nemeth used multiple filters to create a gauzy, artistic look.

Fable Safe, 1971, an 8 minute, 49 second color, 35mm film. Ted Nemeth was the cinematographer for it. Erik Barnouw, a Columbia University professor and radio producer who had served on the Board of Governors of the Academy of Television Arts and Sciences, directed it. Sumner Jules Glimcher, also a professor at Columbia, produced it for the Center for Mass Communications of Columbia University. The cartoonist was Robert Osborn. g30

Music was composed and sung by Tom Glazer, a folk singer and composer. It won Poland's Krakow Silver Dragon Award.[6] Animated figures convey the absurdity of stockpiling weapons, as both sides keep up with each other, augmenting their stock of weapons. The film reflects the cold war of military competition between the USA and the USSR. It is in the collection of the New York Public Library of the Performing Arts and UW-Milwaukee. The Yale Film Study Center also has a print.

References

1. Mary Ellen Bute, "Color, Sound, Light Dance with Harmonious Steps in 'Synchromy,' Art Form Created by Texas Girl", *New York World-Telegram*, July 20, 1936.

2. Cecile Starr, undated film notes ca. 1995, KSB Collection of MEB, Yale Collection of American Literature, Beinecke Rare Book and Manuscript Library.

3. Theodore J. Nemeth, SR., transcript of interview with the author in Milwaukee, 11/22/1984, KSB Collection of MEB, YCAL.

4. Cecile Starr, transcript of telephone interview with author August 1, 2014, private collection of Kit Smyth Basquin.

5. Howard Thompson, "Random News on Pictures and People", *The New York Times*, Sunday, April 13, 1952.

6. Theodore J. Nemeth, Sr., transcript of interview with author in Milwaukee, 11/22/1984, KSB Collection of MEB, YCAL.

Bibliography

Personal interviews and telephone interviews from 1984–1996 by the author with Mary Ellen Bute's family, classmates, and associates, letters, printed materials and type scripts from Bute's files given to the author by Mary Ellen's husband Ted Nemeth, Sr. in 1984, the year after her death, constitute the majority of the research for this biography. These materials in nine boxes were donated to the Beinecke Library at Yale University in 2009 by the author before her move to a new apartment. The files can be accessed as: Kit Basquin Collection of Mary Ellen Bute, Yale Collection of American Literature, Beinecke Rare Book and Manuscript Library.

Other resources include audio tapes of interviews ca. 1995 and a short demo video by filmmaker Larry Mollot for a documentary film on Bute never completed, and the transcript of a telephone interview with Cecile Starr August 1, 2014, in the personal collection of the author. Also referenced was a video tape for Creative Arts Television, Camera Three, 1965 of an interview by Jim McCander with William York Tindall and Mary Ellen Bute in the personal collection of the author. McCander gave the author permission to quote from this video. The New York Public Library, Schwartzman Building, provided a CD-Rom of Brendan Gill's review for the *New Yorker* (October 14, 1967) of *Passages from James Joyce's Finnegans Wake*. These tapes, videos, the CD-Rom and transcript have been footnoted specifically throughout the Bute biography. In addition, the following books and articles were consulted. Copies of most of these articles are in the Kit Basquin Collection of Mary Ellen Bute, Yale Collection of American Literature, Beinecke Rare Book and Manuscript Library.

The Center for Visual Music in Los Angeles, California, distributes a Bute Retrospective of all of her short films, a program in 16mm assembled by Cecile Starr. CVM also provides digital exhibition copies to museum exhibitions word wide.

DVDs of some of Bute's films are available in the following collections, which can be purchased. *Unseen Cinema: Early Avant-Garde Film 1893–1941*, produced by Cineric, Inc. for Anthology Film Archives, 2005, includes *Rhythm in Light* (1934), *Synchromy No. 2* (1935), *Dada* (1936), *Parabola* (1937), *Escape* (1937), *Spook Sport* (1939), and *Tarantella* (1940).

Flicker Alley's 2015 Masterworks of American Avant-Garde Experimental Films 1920–1970 includes Bute's *Tarantella*.

Center for Visual Music, under the direction of Cindy Keefer, produced *Visual Music 1947–1986*, in 2017, and includes *Polka Graph* (1947), *Color Rhapsodie* (1948), and *Abstronic* (1952), that latter which has electronic imagery.

David Shepard and Serg Bramberg produced *Early Women Filmmakers* for Blackhawk Films and Flicker Alley, also in 2017, which includes *Parabola* (1937) and *Spook Sport* (1939).

Basquin, Kit Smyth. "Illustrations for Joyce's *Ulysses*". *Art in Print* 3, No. 4 (November–December 2013) 6–10.

Basquin, Kit. "Mary Ellen Bute: Energy in Motion". *Angles: Women Working in Film & Video* 3, nos. 3–4 (1998).

Basquin, Kit. "Mary Ellen Bute's Film Adaptation of *Finnegans Wake*". *James Joyce's Finnegans Wake: A Casebook*. Edited by John Harty III. New York: Garland Publishing, Inc., 1991: 177–188.

Basquin, Kit. "Mary Ellen Bute's Passages from Finnegans Wake: Introduction to a Screening of the Film at Anthology Film Archives, summer, 2008. www.flashpoint-mag.com/butefilm.htm

Batten, Mary. "Actuality and Abstraction: Notes and Comments from an Interview with Mary Ellen Bute". *Vision: A Journal of Film Comment*, June, 1962.

Beaudet, Louise. *The Art of Animated Films*. Montreal: The Montreal Museum of Fine Art, 1982.

Beckerman, Howard. *Backstage*, November 11, 1983.

"Benjamin Hineses Are Dinner Hosts". *The New York Times*, Friday, November 1, 1940.

Bowen, Zack. *Bloom's Old Sweet Song: Essays on Joyce and Music*. Gainesville, FL: University of Florida Press, 1995.

Bute, Mary Ellen. "Abstronics: An Experimental Filmmaker Photographs the Aesthetics of the Oscilloscope". *Films in Review*, 5, no. 6 (June–July 1954) 263–266.

Bute, Mary Ellen. "New Film Music for New Films". *Film Music* 12 no. 4 (March–April 1953).

Bute, Mary Ellen. "Light. Form. Movement. Sound". *Design* 42, no. 8 (New York, April, 1941): 25.

Campbell, Joseph and Henry Morton Robinson. *A Skeleton Key to Finnegans Wake*. 1944 New York: Penguin Books, 1980.

Curtiss, Thomas Quinn. "'Finnegan' Movie Shown at Cannes". *The New York Times* (May 22, 1965).

"Expanding Cinema's Synchromy #2", Letters and Art Column, *Literary Digest* (August, 1936), www.centerforvisualmusic.org/ButeBiblio.htm

Fargnoli, A. Nicholas and Michael P. Gillespie. *James Joyce A to Z: The Essential Reference to the Life and Work*. New York: Facts On File, Inc., 1995.

Francisco, Charles. *The Radio City Music Hall: An Affectionate History of the World's Greatest Theater*. New York: E. P. Dutton, 1979.

Dewey, John. 1921 *Human Nature and Conduct: An Introduction to Social Psychology*. Editora Griffo, 2015.

Genauer, Emily. "Pinter, Picasso, and Joyce: A Trio for New York". *Newsday*, October 10, 1967.

Gill, Brendan. The Current Cinema: Talkies, *The New Yorker*, October 14, 1967, p. 159.

Glinsky, Albert. *Theremin: Ether Music and Espionage*. Foreword by Robert Moog. Urbana: University of Illinois Press, 2000.

Goldstone, Richard H. *Thornton Wilder: An Intimate Portrait*. New York: Saturday Review Press/E. P. Dutton & Son, Inc., 1975.

Jacobs, Lewis. *The Rise of the American Film: A Critical History*. 1939 New York: Teachers College Press, Columbia University, 1969.

Joyce, James. *Finnegans Wake*. 1939 New York: Viking/Penguin, 1986.

Kaplan, Justin, Introduction. *Leaves of Grass by Walt Whitman*. New York: Banton Books, 1983. xv–xxiii.

Kauffmann, Stanley. *Figures of Light: Film Criticism and Comment*. 1967 New York: Harper & Row, Publishers, 1971.

Keefer, Cindy and Jaap Guldemond, editors. *Oskar Fischinger 1900–1967: Experiments in Cinematic Abstraction*. Eye Filmmuseum, Amsterdam and Center for Visual Music, Los Angeles, 2012.

Lukach, Joan M. *Hilla Rebay: In Search of the Spirit of Art*. New York: George Braziller, 1983.

Manning, Mary. *Passages from Finnegans Wake: A Free Adaptation for the Theater*. 1955, Cambridge: Harvard University Press, 1957.

Mekas, Jonas. *Soho Weekly News*, September 22, 1976.

"Miss Bute Honored at Party". *Houston Post-Dispatch*, November 23, 1927.

Moritz, William "Mary Ellen Bute: Seeing Sound". *Animation World Network*, 1996.

Moritz, William. *Optical Poetry: The Life and Work of Oskar Fischinger*. Eastleigh, UK: John Libbey Publishing, 2004.

Ney, Charles E. *Colonel House: Woodrow Wilson's Silent Partner*. New York: Oxford University Press, 2015.

Niven, Penelope. *Thornton Wilder: A Life*. 2012 New York: Harper Perennial, 2013.

Nordland, Gerald, editor. *Fischinger: A Retrospective of Paintings and Films, 1900–1967*. Denver, CO: Gallery 609, 1980.

Posner, Bruce, editor. *Unseen Cinema: Early American Avant-Garde Film 1893-1941*. New York: Black Thistle Press/Anthology Film Archives, 2005.

Rabinovitz, Lauren, "Mary Ellen Bute", in *Lovers of Cinema: The First American Film Avant-Garde, 1919–1945*, ed. Jan-Christopher Horak, 315–334. Madison, WI: University of Wisconsin Press, 1995.

Rogers, W. G. *Wise Men Fish Here: The Story of Frances Steloff and the Gotham Book Mart*. 1965 Tarrytown, NY: Booksellers House, 1994.

Rosen, Marjorie. "Women, Their Films, and their Festival". *Saturday Review*, August 12, 1972.

Russett, Robert and Cecile Starr. *Experimental Animation: Origins of a New Art*. 1976 New York: Da Capo Press, Inc., 1988.

Schiff, Lilian. "Interview with Mary Ellen Bute, July, 1983". *Film Quarterly* 17, nos. 2–4 (1984) 53–61.

Starr, Cecile. *Discovering the Movies: An Illustrated Introduction to the Motion Picture*. New York: Van Nostrand Reinhold Company, 1972.

Starr, Cecile. *Ideas on Film: A Handbook for the 16mm Film User*. New York: Funk & Wagnalls, 1951.

Starr, Cecile. "Ideas on Film: Eyewitnessing the World of 16 mm Motion Picture, Animation: Abstract & Concrete". *Saturday Review* 35, no. 50 (December 13, 1952).

Starr, Cecile, "Is the Government Subsidizing Sexism in Film?" *The New York Times*, January 9, 1977.

Starr, Cecile. "Programming Early Avant-Garde Films". *Sightlines*. New York: Educational Film Library Association (Winter 79/80) 19–20.

Starr, Cecile. "Restoring Women to Film History". *Women Artist News* 7, no. 2 (1981).

Thompson, Howard. "Random News on Pictures and People". *The New York Times*, Sunday, April 13, 1952.

Tindall, William York. *A Reader's Guide to James Joyce*. 1959 New York: Farrar, Strauss & Giroux, 1981.

Weinberg, Gretchen. "Interview with Mary Ellen Bute on the Filming of *Finnegans Wake*". *Film Culture* 35 (Winter 1964–65).

Whitman, Walt. *Leaves of Grass*. Edited by Sculley Bradley and Harold W. Blodgett. 1965 New York: W.W. Norton & Company, 1973. [First edition, revised later, published in 1855.]

Wilder, Robin G. and Jackson R. Bryer, editors. *The Selected Letters of Thornton Wilder*. 2008 New York: Harper Perennial, 2009.

Wilder, Thornton. *Three Plays: Our Town, Skin of Our Teeth, and Matchmaker*. Foreword by John Guare. 1957 New York: Harper Collins Publishers, 2007.

Women's Viewpoint: Magazine Serving Humanity, Edited and Published by Women. 3, no. 7 (November 25, 1925) 38–39.

Wright, Lucy Runnels, Art Page Editor. "A Woman Extraordinary: Mrs. E. Richardson Cherry", *Texas Outlook Magazine*, May, 1937.

Zunser, Jesse. "Kinetic Space". *Cue: The Weekly Magazine for New York Life*, August 26, 1939.